Teacher Preparation for Linguistically Diverse Classrooms

"... a critically important text that incorporates both concrete examples of practice along with a supporting theoretical and policy foundation."
Michael Vavrus, The Evergreen State College

"The uniqueness of this book is that [it] addresses particular knowledge gaps of educators of mainstream teachers—that is, why and how to address the education of ELLs within mainstream teacher preparatory programs."
Lorrie Stoops Verplaetse, Central Connecticut State University

Teacher educators today need knowledge and practical ideas about how to prepare *all* pre-service and in-service teachers (not just bilingual or ESL specialists) to teach the growing number of students in K-12 classrooms in the United States who speak native languages other than English. This book is at the forefront in focusing exclusively on the preparation of mainstream classroom teachers for this population of students. Part I provides the conceptual and contextual framework for the book, including a comprehensive discussion of relevant demographic trends and an analysis of national and state policies. Part II presents examples of initiatives in different institutional and geographic settings, highlighting three essential elements of teacher preparation: curriculum content, program design, and program coherence.

Meeting a pressing need among teacher educators left to figure out, largely by trial and error, how best to prepare non-specialist classroom teachers to work with ELLs, this book both contributes to the research base and provides practical information to help readers envision possibilities they can apply in their own settings.

Tamara Lucas is Associate Dean of the College of Education and Human Services and Professor of Educational Foundations at Montclair State University.

Teacher Preparation for Linguistically Diverse Classrooms

A Resource for Teacher Educators

Edited by
Tamara Lucas

Routledge
Taylor & Francis Group

NEW YORK AND LONDON

First published 2011
by Routledge
270 Madison Avenue, New York, NY 10016

Simultaneously published in the UK
by Routledge
2 Park Square, Milton Park, Abingdon, Oxon OX14 4RN

Routledge is an imprint of the Taylor & Francis Group, an informa business

© 2011 Taylor & Francis

The right of Tamara Lucas to be identified as the author of the editorial material, and of the authors for their individual chapters, has been asserted by them in accordance with sections 77 and 78 of the Copyright, Designs and Patents Act 1988.

Typeset in Minion by Wearset Ltd, Boldon, Tyne and Wear
Printed and bound in the United States of America on acid-free paper by Walsworth Publishing Company, Marceline, MO

Library of Congress Cataloging in Publication Data
Teacher preparation for linguistically diverse classrooms : a resource for teacher educators / edited by Tamara Lucas.
p. cm.
Includes bibliographical references and index.
1. Teachers–Training of–United States. 2. English language–Study and teaching–United States–Foreign speakers. 3. Linguistic minorities–Education–United States. 4. Bilingual education--United States. I. Lucas, Tamara, 1951–
LB1715.T415 2010
370.71'173–dc22

2010010911

ISBN13: 978-0-415-99791-1 (hbk)
ISBN13: 978-0-415-99792-8 (pbk)
ISBN13: 978-0-203-84323-9 (ebk)

In Memory of My Sister, April Diana Lucas Bolton

Contents

Foreword   x
KEN ZEICHNER

Preface   xiii
Acknowledgments   xix

PART I
Conceptual and Contextual Foundations   1

1. Language, Schooling, and the Preparation of Teachers for
   Linguistic Diversity   3
   TAMARA LUCAS

2. English Language Learners in American Schools:
   Characteristics and Challenges   18
   GUADALUPE VALDÉS AND MARTHA CASTELLÓN

3. Preparing Classroom Teachers for English Language
   Learners: The Policy Context   35
   ANA MARÍA VILLEGAS AND TAMARA LUCAS

PART II
Developing Teacher Expertise for Educating
English Language Learners   **53**

- Curriculum Content

4. A Framework for Preparing Linguistically Responsive
   Teachers   55
   TAMARA LUCAS AND ANA MARÍA VILLEGAS

5. "Accommodating Diversity": Pre-Service Teachers'
   Views on Effective Practices for English Language
   Learners   73
   ESTER J. DE JONG AND CANDACE A. HARPER

6. Systemic Functional Linguistics, Teachers' Professional
   Development, and ELLs' Academic Literacy Practices   91
   MEG GEBHARD, JERRI WILLETT,
   JUAN PABLO JIMÉNEZ CAICEDO, AND AMY PIEDRA

7. "We've Let Them in on the Secret": Using SFL Theory
   to Improve the Teaching of Writing to Bilingual
   Learners   111
   MARÍA ESTELA BRISK AND MARGARITA ZISSELSBERGER

• Program Design

8. Preparing Teachers to Reach English Language Learners:
   Pre-Service and In-Service Initiatives   127
   CONSTANCE L. WALKER AND KARLA STONE

9. Fostering Collaboration Between Mainstream and
   Bilingual Teachers and Teacher Candidates   143
   KAREN SAKASH AND FLORA RODRIGUEZ-BROWN

10. The Growth of Teacher Expertise for Teaching English
    Language Learners: A Socio-Culturally Based
    Professional Development Model   160
    AÍDA WALQUI

11. Toward Culturally and Linguistically Responsive
    Teacher Education: The Impact of a Faculty Learning
    Community on Two Teacher Educators   178
    MILEIDIS GORT, WENDY J. GLENN, AND JOHN SETTLAGE

• Program Coherence

12. Toward Program-Wide Coherence in Preparing
    Teachers to Teach and Advocate for English Language
    Learners   195
    STEVEN Z. ATHANASES AND LUCIANA C. DE OLIVEIRA

- Conclusion

13. Toward the Transformation of Teacher Education to
    Prepare All Teachers for Linguistically Diverse Classrooms   216
    TAMARA LUCAS

    About the Authors   222
    Index   226

Foreword

Despite the growing influence of multicultural education in U.S. teacher education during the last 30 years (e.g., Cochran-Smith, Davis, & Fries, 2003; Hollins & Guzman, 2005; Ladson-Billings, 1995; Sleeter, 2009), most mainstream classroom teachers have not been adequately prepared to teach English language learners (ELLs). In most reviews of literature on multicultural teacher education like the ones noted above, very little attention has been devoted to the central role of language in the educational process and to efforts by teacher educators to prepare prospective teachers to teach the growing numbers of English learners in U.S. schools. When we conducted a review of teacher education research in the U.S. between 2000 and 2005 for the American Educational Research Association, we could find very few peer-reviewed empirical studies focused on preparing mainstream classroom teachers to teach ELLs that met the standards of the panel (Cochran-Smith & Zeichner, 2005).

Over the years, most attention to the preparation of teachers to teach ELLs has been devoted to preparing ESL and bilingual teacher specialists rather than to the preparation of all teachers to teach ELLs. There have never been enough ESL and bilingual certified specialists to support the learning needs of ELLs and, as this book points out, only three states currently require teacher education programs to include content that addresses the teaching of ELLs. In the current political context, special educational programs for ELLs have been de-emphasized, and this change, along with their continually growing numbers, means that more and more ELLs are spending an increased amount of time in mainstream classrooms being taught by teachers who have received very little special preparation to teach them.

It is very clear from this book and from previous work analyzing the knowledge, skills, and dispositions teachers need to teach ELLs successfully (e.g., Lucas & Grinberg, 2008; Valdés, Bunch, Snow, & Lee, 2005) that to teach ELLs well, teachers need special expertise they have not received in most preparation programs across the nation. This situation, like the inequitable distribution of underprepared teachers to teach the children of the poor (Peske & Haycock, 2006), is unacceptable in a democratic society.

This book provides a comprehensive discussion of demographic trends in the growth of immigrant students in the U.S. and the knowledge, commitments, and instructional skills that all teachers need to teach ELLs well. It also provides several examples of how teacher education programs across the country have begun to address this issue and proposes a framework based on existing research that discusses three essential elements in teacher education programs that prepare teachers to successfully teach ELLs—curriculum content, program design, and the degree of program coherence needed to do this work well. One of the most valuable aspects of the book is the extension of the widely influential concept of culturally responsive teaching (Villegas & Lucas, 2002) to include the knowledge, skills, and dispositions needed by teachers to successfully teach ELLs. This framework, like the teacher education models in the book as a whole, are clearly presented, with many examples of what the ideas look like in practice.

The book also includes examples of innovative models of professional development that have enabled in-service teachers in different contexts to acquire the expertise needed to successfully teach ELLs. It discusses the critically important issue of how teacher educators can be prepared through professional development to provide teacher candidates and teachers with the knowledge and skills they need to be linguistically competent teachers. The old model of relying on the one or two ESL or bilingual education faculty members in an institution to assume all of the responsibility for preparing teachers to teach ELLs will not suffice. The preparation of all new teacher educators in the doctoral programs across the nation needs to ensure that the next generations of teacher educators are both culturally and linguistically competent themselves.

Finally, the book analyzes recent policies related to the education of ELLs and offers recommendations to the policy community for strengthening the education of ELLs in U.S. schools. The main policy recommendation set forth, to develop policies that enable reasoned decisions about the extent of mainstream classroom experience that would benefit the education of particular ELLs, makes more sense to me than the extreme positions that have been in conflict with one another for many years.

Tamara Lucas and her colleagues have provided the teacher education community in the U.S. with a valuable resource for helping teacher educators redesign their programs to better prepare teachers to successfully educate all of our students. This book makes a convincing case that pre-service teacher education, continuing teacher professional development, and the preparation and development of teacher educators all need to incorporate greater attention to the education of ELLs, and that the preparation of linguistically competent teachers is an essential element of social justice education.

Ken Zeichner
Seattle, Washington

References

Cochran-Smith, M., & Zeichner, K. (Eds.). (2005). *Studying teacher education.* New York, NY: Routledge.

Cochran-Smith, M., Davis, D., & Fries, K. (2003). Multicultural teacher education: Research, practice, and policy. In J.A. Banks & C.M. Banks (Eds.), *Handbook of research on multicultural education* (2nd ed., pp. 931–975). San Francisco, CA: Jossey-Bass.

Hollins, E., & Guzman, M.T. (2005). Research on preparing teachers for diverse populations. In M. Cochran-Smith & K. Zeichner (Eds.), *Studying teacher education* (pp. 477–548). New York, NY: Routledge.

Ladson-Billings, G. (1995). Multicultural teacher education: Research, policy and practice. In J. Banks & C.M. Banks (Eds.), *Handbook of research on multicultural education* (pp. 747–759). New York, NY: Macmillan.

Lucas, T., & Grinberg, J. (2008). Responding to the linguistic reality of the mainstream classroom: Preparing classroom teachers to teach English language learners. In M. Cochran-Smith, S. Feiman-Nemser, & D.J. McIntyre (Eds.), *Handbook of research on teacher education* (3rd ed., pp. 606–636). New York, NY: Routledge.

Peske, H.G., & Haycock, K. (2006). *Teaching inequality: How poor and minority students are shortchanged on teacher quality.* Washington, D.C.: Education Trust.

Sleeter, C. (2009). Preparing white teachers for diverse students. In M. Cochran-Smith, S. Feiman-Nemser, & D.J. McIntyre (Eds.), *Handbook of research on teacher education* (3rd ed., pp. 559–582). New York, NY: Routledge.

Valdés, G., Bunch, G., Snow, C., & Lee, C. (2005). Enhancing the development of students' languages. In L. Darling-Hammond & J. Bransford (Eds.), *Preparing teachers for a changing world* (pp. 126–168). San Francisco, CA: Jossey-Bass.

Villegas, A.M., & Lucas, T. (2002). *Educating culturally responsive teachers: A coherent approach.* Albany, NY: SUNY Press.

Preface

In 2002, the U.S. Department of Education Office of Bilingual Education and Minority Languages Affairs (OBEMLA) became the Office of English Language Acquisition (OELA). This name change was emblematic of a transformation in U.S. policy regarding the education of English language learners (ELLs) that had been two decades in the making. Beginning in 1968, policies for ELLs were guided by the Bilingual Education Act (BEA) and the subsequent *Lau.* v. *Nichols Supreme Court* ruling (1974), which officially acknowledged the inherent inequity in placing "limited English proficient" students in mainstream classes if no accommodations were made to give them access to the curriculum. The practice that developed after passage of the BEA was to provide programs for K-12 students who were not yet proficient in English where they would be taught by educators with special expertise in ESL and bilingual instructional approaches—teachers prepared to design instruction, taking into account the students' backgrounds and learning needs. While there were never enough specialists to staff all the programs for ELLs, the goal was to provide specially prepared teachers to help them develop proficiency in English and in academic content before they joined their English-proficient peers in mainstream classes.

In the 1980s, education policy-makers turned their attention away from the concern for equity and civil rights that had led to passage of the BEA. While the policies of the G.H.W. Bush, Clinton, and G.W. Bush Administrations varied in the extent and nature of the emphasis on students' socioeconomic and language backgrounds, all three Administrations gave central prominence to accountability, standards, and testing. Under the current policy—the No Child Left Behind Act of 2002 (which terminated the BEA)—federal policies restrict how long the large and growing numbers of ELLs in schools across the country can spend in special programs. ELLs are increasingly placed in mainstream classrooms for most of the school day. They may also spend time in one or more ESL classes, depending on a number of factors (such as the availability of ESL teachers, the number of ELLs in the school, and district resources). Classroom teachers in small towns, rural areas, suburbs, and large urban areas, whether they have had preparation or not, are expected to teach K-12 students who speak languages other than English at home and who are in various stages of English proficiency. Policy and practice are likely to favor inclusion of ELLs in mainstream classrooms for some time to come. All teachers must therefore be prepared to educate this population of students.

About This Book

Teachers cannot simply teach ELLs the way they teach other students; to teach ELLs well, they need special expertise—and this requires special preparation. While many teacher education programs give some attention to preparing teachers for "diverse" student populations, teacher education as a whole is just beginning to embrace its responsibility to prepare all teachers to teach ELLs. This book, by providing insights and models for changing how mainstream teachers are prepared, can serve as a resource for teacher educators and those who prepare teacher educators in meeting this new responsibility. The book is written by and for teacher educators who, like the authors themselves, are working in their own contexts to better prepare mainstream teachers and teacher candidates to educate ELLs. It is relevant for faculty in higher education institutions and those involved in the professional development of teachers in school districts, state agencies, local and state resource centers, and non-profit organizations.

Teacher Preparation for Linguistically Diverse Classrooms: A Resource for Teacher Educators has two primary objectives. Part I situates the preparation of mainstream teachers for teaching ELLs within relevant conceptual, demographic, and policy contexts. Part II provides concrete examples of innovative approaches for preparing teachers to teach ELLs. The chapter authors report on emerging efforts in different institutional contexts, seeking to give all classroom teachers opportunities to build the expertise needed to help ELLs develop the knowledge and skills to achieve in school and beyond.

The three chapters in Part I lay the foundation for the issues addressed and strategies applied in the accounts of particular programs described in Part II. In Chapter 1, Lucas presents an overview of conceptual and practical issues in the preparation of classroom teachers to teach ELLs. She examines the central role of language in school, making the case for special attention to the education of ELLs in teacher preparation. She then examines three fundamental elements of such preparation: curriculum content (what teachers need to know and be able to do to teach ELLs well), program design (program structures and processes for organizing the learning experiences to enact the curriculum content), and coherence across program mission, conceptual framework, curriculum, instruction, and program and institutional structures.

In Chapter 2, Valdés and Castellón lay the demographic foundation for the preparation of all teachers to teach ELLs. They describe the characteristics of the immigrant population in the U.S. overall and in schools, giving special attention to the Hispanic population; examine the complexities involved in determining the number of ELLs in schools; and present data regarding the academic achievement of ELLs and the gap between their achievement and that of non-ELL populations. They conclude with implications of the demographic context for teacher education.

Policy is addressed by Villegas and Lucas in Chapter 3. They first examine relevant aspects of the political climate and the national policy context, showing that these influences have led to a distinct trend toward greater inclusion of ELLs in mainstream classes, and then examine particular national and state policies that directly and indirectly influence the preparation of mainstream teachers for teaching ELLs, concluding with recommendations based on their analysis.

The chapters in Part II report on particular pre-service and in-service initiatives in different institutional and geographic contexts. In addition to presenting findings from research on the initiatives, these chapters include descriptions of the content of the initiatives (what teachers are learning) as well as the processes involved in the initiatives (how the initiatives are organized and carried out). Therefore, the chapters both provide practical information that can help teacher educators envision possibilities they can apply in their own institutional settings and contribute to the research base on the preparation of classroom teachers to teach ELLs. Part II is organized according to three essential elements of teacher preparation that require attention by teacher educators: curriculum content, program design, and program coherence. All of the chapters in Part II give some attention to all three of these elements, but each focuses predominantly on one of them. The chapters have been organized according to their predominant focus.

Chapters 4 through 7 give primary attention to curriculum content. In Chapter 4, Lucas and Villegas present a conception of linguistically responsive teaching that extends their framework for culturally responsive teaching (Villegas & Lucas, 2002a, 2002b, 2007). They argue that seven qualities characterize linguistically responsive teachers. Three are orientations toward language and ELLs: sociolinguistic consciousness, value for linguistic diversity, and the inclination to advocate for ELL students. Four are knowledge and skills: learning about ELL students' language backgrounds, experiences, and proficiencies; identifying the language demands of classroom tasks; applying key principles of second language learning; and scaffolding instruction to promote ELL students' learning.

In Chapter 5, de Jong and Harper report on a study at one institution regarding pre-service teachers' beliefs about what they need to know and be able to do to teach ELLs, how teaching classes with ELLs differs from teaching classes without ELLs, and how confident they are in their ability to teach ELLs. The authors interpret their findings using a framework of knowledge, practices, and dispositions they argue must be included in general teacher preparation to ensure that the inclusion of ELLs does not constitute a return to the submersion ("sink or swim") classrooms of previous generations. They discuss the implications of their findings showing that the teachers in the study emphasized cultural knowledge over linguistic knowledge and viewed teaching ELLs as the application of strategies to make content comprehensible rather than focusing on language development as a goal.

Chapters 6 and 7 present findings from two different professional development initiatives that prepare teachers to apply Halliday's (1985) Systemic Functional Linguistics (SFL) theory to help ELLs develop literacy skills. In Chapter 6, Gebhard, Willett, Jiménez, and Piedra describe the ACCELA Alliance (Access to Critical Content and English Language Acquisition), a district–university partnership, and ways in which Halliday's SFL theory informs its work. They report on an ethnographic case study of the literacy practices enacted by a fourth-grade teacher and one of her students over the course of an academic year illustrating the student's developing skill in writing personal narrative. They show that teacher educators can design programs to engage pre-service and in-service teachers in developing a critical understanding of language in the texts they routinely ask their students to read and write by drawing on SFL scholarship.

Brisk and Zisselsberger, in Chapter 7, describe ways a professional development initiative was adapted to accommodate the needs of the 12 elementary teachers involved, including making explicit connections to the prescribed instructional materials they were using. They present findings from an in-depth examination of the process through which a kindergarten teacher helped a student learn the fictional narrative genre. They conclude with a reflection on the implications of their work for similar professional development initiatives.

The next set of chapters, Chapters 8 through 11, focus primarily on program design. In Chapter 8, Walker and Stone examine two different efforts to prepare teachers of ELLs—one for pre-service teachers and the other for in-service teachers. They describe the structure and content of a one-credit course module designed for different K-12 pre-service content area programs, and a site-based, collaborative two-year professional development initiative designed for elementary school staff. They discuss the key elements of these initiatives and present findings from evaluations regarding participants' experiences.

Sakash and Rodriguez-Brown, in Chapter 9, highlight collaboration between and among mainstream and bilingual teachers and teacher candidates in a variety of initiatives at their institution. They describe structures they have created to infuse attention to teaching ELLs across the pre-service teacher education program, and initiatives involving collaboration between in-service mainstream and bilingual/ESL teachers, illustrated with detailed examinations of two particular programs, and conclude with recommendations based on what they have learned.

In Chapter 10, Walqui describes a multi-year and multi-faceted professional development initiative in the New York City Public Schools created by WestEd to develop the capacity of classroom teachers, instructional support specialists, and administrators to provide quality education for ELLs. The chapter presents the conceptual framework that guided the conceptualization, design, and ongoing refinement of the initiative; provides a detailed examination of the application of that framework in the professional development of ELL Instructional Support Specialists, describing their progression from apprenticeship to the WestEd staff, to their appropriation of the process as they led the professional development of teachers of ELLs; and describes the QTEL professional development for teachers, eventually led by the Instructional Support Specialists.

In Chapter 11, Gort, Glenn, and Settlage focus on the development of knowledge and skills among teacher educators rather than among K-12 teachers. They describe a faculty development initiative and present findings of an autoethnographic study regarding what an English teacher educator and a science teacher educator learned from their participation, showing how they created spaces in their courses to explore both language and culture in teaching and learning. They argue that teacher educators must stop ignoring or minimizing the need to address teaching ELLs in mainstream content area methods courses, and that teacher educators must be willing to become learners themselves.

Chapter 12, the final chapter in Part II, focuses primarily on program coherence. Athanases and de Oliveira discuss the challenges and promise of building coherent programs for learning to teach ELLs. They present a framework that incorporates the content, process, and context of teacher education programs, one that can be used for developing, documenting, and studying program coherence, and they use this framework to examine coherence in one teacher education program that sought to prepare teachers to become advocates for ELLs.

In Chapter 13, Lucas discusses seven salient themes that emerge from the chapters in the book and offers recommendations for practice and research.

As with so many shifts in educational practices, the radical change in direction away from educating English language learners in special programs and classes, and toward wholesale inclusion of ELLs in mainstream classes, is ill-advised. A more thoughtful course would be to ensure that reasoned decisions are made regarding which students can and cannot benefit maximally from spending varying amounts of time in mainstream classes, and what types of instructional scaffolding are needed to give them access to the curriculum. The chapters in this book make the case for such an approach. At the same time, the authors recognize that, even with a more considered approach, mainstream classroom teachers will continue to have growing numbers of ELLs in their classes and they need to be fully prepared to teach them. The conceptual and empirical foundation and the promising examples of practice presented in this book offer support for moving teacher preparation in a direction that will benefit ELLs, their teachers, and those who are responsible for preparing their teachers.

References

Halliday, M.A.K. (1985). *An introduction to functional grammar*. London: Edward Arnold.

Villegas, A.M., & Lucas, T. (2002a). *Educating culturally responsive teachers: A coherent approach*. Albany, NY: SUNY Press.

Villegas, A.M., & Lucas, T. (2002b). Preparing culturally responsive teachers: Rethinking the curriculum. *Journal of Teacher Education, 53*(1), 20–32.

Villegas, A.M., & Lucas, T. (2007). The culturally responsive teacher. *Educational Leadership, 64*(6), 28–33.

Acknowledgments

Editing a book is by definition a collaborative endeavor, and I am grateful to a number of those who made completion of this volume possible. First, I want to express my gratitude to the authors of the chapters. I was honored to work with them in sessions at AACTE, TESOL, and AERA conferences as the idea for the book took shape and then in preparation of the book itself. The quality of their contributions speaks for itself. I also want to thank my editor at Routledge, Naomi Silverman, who provided guidance and support throughout. Special thanks to Sonia Nieto for encouraging me early in the process as I was just beginning to consider the publication of a volume on the issues addressed in this book. Thanks also to colleagues who read and commented on drafts of my own chapters—Maria Brisk and Rosemary Henze—and to my graduate assistants, Mary Kehoe and Jessica Binns, who provided valuable assistance. Finally, I want to acknowledge Ana María Villegas, my partner and colleague, whose inspiration and support are fundamental to everything I do.

Part I

Conceptual and Contextual Foundations

Language, Schooling, and the Preparation of Teachers for Linguistic Diversity

Tamara Lucas

In classrooms across the United States, students like Elena, a 10-year-old whose family recently moved to North Carolina from Mexico, spend hours hearing language that is meaningless to them. Elena enjoyed going to school in Mexico and often did well in her classes, but now she sits at the back of the classroom and rarely interacts with anyone, including the teacher. While she tries her best to concentrate on the flow of speech around her to decipher some of what is being said, she is constantly fearful that the teacher might call on her, or another student might ask her a question she can't understand. She often wishes she were invisible so she could avoid looking stupid. Two other students in her class explain some things to her in Spanish, but she usually finds their explanations confusing. Elena, like many students not yet proficient enough to learn academic content in a mainstream class conducted in English, often feels anxious, frustrated, and embarrassed. As much as she tries to pay attention in class, she simply cannot understand enough of what is said to stay engaged.

Elena's teacher—like many others with English language learners in their classes—is also anxious and frustrated about how to teach Elena. She has developed considerable knowledge and skills through her teacher preparation program and her teaching experience, but she has had little opportunity to build her understanding and instructional repertoire for educating English language learners (ELLs). She has talked to the ESL teacher a few times, but since he is in the school only a few hours, three days a week, he has not been very helpful. The teacher recognizes she is ignoring Elena at times, but she is not sure how to meaningfully engage her in learning.

It has been clear for some time that classroom teachers who are not specialists in the education of ELLs[1] should be prepared to teach them. The demographic trends have been evident for decades (see Valdés & Castellón, this volume), and a number of educational scholars and policy-makers have argued over the years for the necessity of preparing classroom teachers to educate ELLs (e.g., AACTE, 2002; Abramson, Pritchard, & García, 1993; Brisk, 2008; Penfield, 1987; Rhine, 1995; Villegas & Lucas, 2002; Zeichner, 2005). Yet there is still little guidance and no generally accepted approach for preparing teachers to teach students who speak languages other than English at home (Lucas & Grinberg, 2008; Zeichner, 2005). Only three of the 50 states (Arizona, Florida, and New York) require all teachers to have some preparation for working with ELLs. Without such policies in the other 47 states, there is "no uniformity" in the approach taken to ensure that teachers are prepared to teach ELLs, and efforts to do so are "at best spotty" (*Education Week*, 2009, p. 28). This piecemeal approach to preparing teachers to teach ELLs is unacceptable given the increasing likelihood that all teachers in the U.S.—not just those on the coasts and in the Southwest—will have ELLs in their classes (see Frey, 2001; Regional Educational Laboratory—Appalachia, 2008).

In this chapter, I begin to lay a foundation for a more thoughtful, coherent approach to such preparation—a foundation that is reinforced and extended by the other chapters in the book. I examine the central role of language in school to show why all teachers need special preparation for teaching ELLs. I then discuss three fundamental elements of such preparation—curriculum content, program design, and program coherence.

Language, Schooling, and the Education of ELLs

Arguments for preparing all teachers to teach ELLs are commonly made on the basis of demographics: the growing number of ELLs makes it imperative that teachers have the expertise to educate them well. While the logic of this argument may seem transparent, it begs the question: Why do teachers require *special* preparation for teaching ELLs? Why do they need something more than the preparation provided by strong teacher education programs grounded in principles of culturally responsive teaching? The answers come from an examination of the role of language in schooling.

To appropriately modify instruction for ELLs, classroom teachers need to understand the connections between language and schooling and the particular implications of those connections for ELLs. Because most teachers in the U.S. are monolingual English speakers who have never had to use a language other than English in school, they have typically not developed the understandings and insights that come from looking *at* language rather than looking *through* language (de Jong & Harper, 2005). They are not likely to develop the knowledge and perspectives they need to teach ELLs without the conscious effort of teacher educators to incorporate these bodies of knowledge into the curriculum.

For humans, language, thinking, and learning go hand in hand. Without language, we are limited in our ability to think and learn. The influential psychologist Lev Vygotsky (1978) saw language as emerging prior to thought in the process of child development. He argued that language develops because children need to communicate with people in their environment and it only later becomes "internal speech," which organizes thought. Thus, in a sense, language, in the form of speech, becomes thought. The linguist M.A.K.

Halliday, who also placed social interaction at the center of learning language (1977), argued that "language is not a *domain* of human knowledge …; language is the essential condition of knowing, the process by which experience *becomes* knowledge" (1993, p. 94, emphasis in original). Language is the medium through which humans make meaning. In other words, knowing involves the use of language.

This deep interconnectedness of language, learning, and knowing is especially pronounced in the school context. "Schooling is primarily a linguistic process, and language serves as an often unconscious means of evaluating and differentiating students" (Schleppegrell, 2004, p. 2). Almost all the activities of importance in school involve some language use (Trumbull & Farr, 2005). To succeed in schools, students must be able to read academic texts in different subject areas, produce written documents in language appropriate for school (e.g., tests, stories, essays), and interact with their teachers and peers. They must use language to understand and solve problems, and to examine and explain complex ideas. Language is the medium through which students gain access to the curriculum and through which they display—and are assessed for—what they have learned. Therefore, language cannot be separated from what is taught and learned in school.

Not only do students need to have command of the vocabulary, morphology, and syntax of the language of the school, they also need to know how to use particular linguistic elements in particular contexts to accomplish particular goals—goals related to academic tasks such as describing an event or phenomenon, making an argument, and comparing and contrasting, as well as interactional goals such as responding when called on and explaining why they are late to class. People make choices about how they use language to accomplish their goals, but their choices have different results across languages and social contexts (Schleppegrell, 2004). Thus, to succeed in U.S. schools, ELLs must learn not only the structures of English but also how to choose the most appropriate and effective way to use language to accomplish their goals (see Brisk & Zisselsberger, and Gebhard, Willett, Jimenez, & Piedra, this volume). Clearly, this makes their task complex and challenging.

While the connection between language and schooling has implications for all students, it has special significance for ELLs. To be sure, ELLs share many experiences and challenges with other groups of students. They are often marginalized and underestimated like students from other socially subordinated groups, and they too have to learn culturally appropriate ways of "doing" school. Students who speak subordinated varieties of English (e.g., African American English and Appalachian English), like ELLs, face linguistic challenges not faced by peers who come to school speaking "standard" English. But the one aspect of ELLs' experience that sets them apart is the fact that they have grown up immersed in a language other than English. They have not learned English as a home language before entering school, and may not have heard it spoken in their environment. They are learning English as a language while learning the content of the curriculum, so the process of learning English profoundly influences and is influenced by all their other school learning. Depending on their proficiency in English, they may not be able to benefit from instruction in English. Because ELLs are still developing proficiency in English, and because success in school depends on successful use of English, it is not appropriate for teachers to teach ELLs as they would teach students already proficient in English. Teachers must have special knowledge and skills to teach ELLs well (de Jong & Harper, 2008).

Essential Elements in the Preparation of Teachers to Teach ELLs

While the literature on preparing classroom teachers who are not ESL or bilingual specialists to teach ELLs is still in its infancy, growing attention to such preparation is reflected in a number of recent publications examining ways to adapt mainstream teacher education to better prepare all teachers for linguistic diversity (e.g., Brisk, 2008; Lucas & Grinberg, 2008; Valdés, Bunch, Snow, & Lee, 2005). In this section, I examine three essential elements of teacher preparation programs that require attention by teacher educators taking on this important challenge: curriculum content, program structures, and program coherence.

Curriculum Content

The first concern in designing or adapting a teacher education curriculum is the content of the curriculum—that is, what teachers need to know and be able to do to teach ELLs well. While the literature focused explicitly on preparing mainstream teachers to teach ELLs is relatively small, a growing body of literature has given attention to this question over the past 15 years (e.g., August & Hakuta, 1997; de Jong & Harper, 2005, 2008; García, 1993, 1996, 1999; Lucas, Villegas, & Freedson-Gonzalez, 2008; Schleppegrell, 2004; Valdés et al., 2005; Walqui, 2007; Wong-Fillmore & Snow, 2005). Unfortunately, this literature has not made its way into many teacher education programs. One reason may be that some of it is focused on the preparation of specialists (i.e., ESL, bilingual, or sheltered content teachers) rather than mainstream teachers, so generalist teacher educators are simply not aware of it or do not think it is relevant for non-specialist teachers. It is also possible that educators inexperienced in linguistic analysis are put off by the use of linguistic approaches and terminology in many of these publications. Another possibility is that teacher educators persist in assuming that good instruction for ELLs is "just good teaching" (de Jong & Harper, 2005; Harper & de Jong, 2004), so they do not see a reason to modify the curriculum for educating ELLs.

Whatever the reason, the omission of content related to teaching ELLs in many teacher education programs leaves teachers unprepared to teach students who come to their classes not yet fully proficient in English. While classroom teachers need to develop knowledge, skills, and dispositions for teaching all students, including the qualities of culturally responsive teachers (e.g., Gay, 2000; Ladson-Billings, 1990, 1994; Villegas & Lucas, 2002), they must also have opportunities to develop the special expertise required to teach ELLs well.

Despite placing greater or lesser emphasis on different aspects of this expertise, scholars and educators do, in fact, agree to a considerable degree about what it entails (see the work cited in the first paragraph of this section; see also, in this volume, Brisk & Zisselsberger; de Jong & Harper; Gebhard et al.; Lucas & Villegas). A key focus of much of the literature is the need for teachers to have some understanding of the structure of English and of the process of second language learning, and the ability to apply these understandings in their teaching. When teachers understand the forms and mechanics of English, they are better prepared to give useful feedback on ELLs' linguistic output. They can make informed and precise suggestions for improvement instead of relying on a vague notion that a student's speech or writing "doesn't sound right." When teachers understand second language learning, they can anticipate some of their students' learning processes and recognize "errors" that are common in second language learning. Thus, they can make better decisions about when to intervene and when not to intervene in students' learning and production of language, and what types of intervention are likely to be most effective. Knowledge of the linguistic demands of school language in specific disciplines is also increasingly recognized as essential for teachers of ELLs. A number of scholars have advocated for the use of systemic functional linguistics as a tool to teach ELLs how to make good linguistic choices for achieving particular goals in particular contexts (Schleppegrell, 2004; Brisk & Zisselsberger, this volume; Gebhard et al., this volume).

In addition to emphasizing the need to give attention in the preparation of teachers to the linguistically oriented knowledge and skills above, scholars also argue that teachers of ELLs should develop certain types of perspectives, dispositions, and commitments. These include recognition of the sociopolitical dimension of language (Bartolomé, 2000, 2002; Lucas & Grinberg, 2008; Lucas & Villegas, this volume), value for linguistic diversity (Lucas & Grinberg, 2008; Lucas & Villegas, this volume), and commitment to advocating for ELLs (Athanases & de Oliveira, 2007, 2008, this volume). Language is closely tied to its sociopolitical context and can be a powerful political force for inclusion or exclusion of particular groups, often serving as a proxy for other social factors such as race and class. Language policies and practices too often result in inequity for ELLs in school and society. Teacher educators can ensure that future and current teachers engage with these sometimes volatile issues by giving explicit attention to them in the curriculum. Otherwise, they may simply perpetuate the inequalities often associated with linguistic minority status.

Instructional expertise is the other—and most prominent—focus of the literature on what teachers need to know and be able to do to teach ELLs. The many publications that offer suggestions for how to design and adapt instruction for ELLs in mainstream classrooms range widely in breadth, focus, and extent of grounding in theory and research. Some describe very specific, concrete strategies (e.g., Brown, 2007; Carrier, 2006); others examine one broad instructional approach in-depth, such as instructional scaffolding (Gibbons, 2002), promoting classroom interaction (Verplaetse, 2007), teaching writing using the rhetorical approach (Brisk, Horan, & Macdonald, 2007), and using sheltered instruction (Echevarria, Vogt, & Short, 2004; Verplaetse & Migliacci, 2007); others provide context-embedded ethnographic reports of classrooms where individual teachers use various instructional approaches (Hite & Evans, 2006; Yedlin, 2007); and still others present a conceptual framework to guide instructional decision-making (Lucas et al., 2008; Walqui, 2007). Teacher educators can tap this rich body of literature to decide how best to prepare teachers to make sound instructional choices for educating ELLs.

A serious challenge to ensuring that future and current teachers have opportunities to develop all the types of expertise discussed above is that most teacher educators are not familiar with the literature on educating ELLs. As discussed in the next section, in most contexts, teacher educators themselves need professional development to build the knowledge, skills, and dispositions related to teaching ELLs so they can incorporate this content into the curriculum (Lucas & Grinberg, 2008). Thus, the challenge for teacher educators is two-fold: articulating what teachers need to know and be able to do, and ensuring that teacher educators themselves are able to help their students build the necessary knowledge, skills, and dispositions.

Program Structures

Program structures and processes constitute the second focus for redesigning teacher education to prepare all teachers to teach ELLs (Lucas & Grinberg, 2008). With a clear sense of what teachers should know about teaching ELLs, teacher educators still have decisions to make about how to organize the learning experiences to enact the curriculum content (see Athanases & de Oliveira, this volume). Should a special course be added to the curriculum? Should field experiences and student teaching be revised to better incorporate attention to teaching ELLs? Should assignments and activities focused on ELLs be incorporated into existing courses? Could structures be put in place to engage field-based educators with expertise in ELL education in new ways?

In their review of the literature, Lucas and Grinberg (2008, p. 619ff) identified four structural strategies for preparing all teachers to teach ELLs: adding a course to the program, modifying existing courses and field experiences to give attention to ELLs, adding or modifying program pre-requisites, and adding a minor or supplemental certificate program. They identified three process strategies: mentoring and coaching with practicing teachers, collaborating across institutional boundaries, and engaging teacher educators in professional development. Each of these is briefly discussed below.

Teacher educators in higher education institutions who want to incorporate new content related to teaching ELLs into the curriculum are likely to first consider adding a course. While this approach has its drawbacks—e.g., adding to the already packed curriculum and potentially marginalizing ELL education—it also has advantages. It ensures that the material is included in the curriculum rather than depending on many faculty members to incorporate ELL issues in their courses. It also makes faculty expertise related to teaching ELLs more readily available to students in programs where only one or two faculty members have such expertise (which is the case in most teacher education programs). (For descriptions of a special course with different sections for teacher candidates preparing to teach different grades and disciplines, see Walker, Ranney, & Fortune, 2005; Walker & Stone, this volume.) Another approach is to modify existing courses and field experiences to give attention to ELLs—that is, to infuse attention to ELLs across the curriculum. The advantages and disadvantages of this approach are the reverse of those for adding a separate course. It can be undermined by the fact that some faculty may not have sufficient knowledge of ELL education to incorporate it in their courses—which can mean the issues are given minimal or inappropriate attention—and it does not give students the full benefit of faculty who do have ELL expertise. On the other hand, it sends the message that teaching ELLs is part of "regular" teacher preparation and P-12 classrooms, and it does not add additional credits for students. (For examples, see Athanases & de Oliveira, this volume; González & Darling-Hammond, 1997; Hadaway, 1993.)

The second two structural strategies are far less common than the first two. Some educators and scholars have advocated modifying pre-requisites to teacher education—in particular, adding new or more stringent foreign language requirements, or adding a requirement that students take a linguistics course (Valdés et al., 2005; Wong-Fillmore & Snow, 2005). The other structure that can improve the preparation of teachers to teach ELLs is to offer a minor or additional certification that students can (or must) complete along with or after completing a general teacher education program. The original version of the Cross-Cultural, Language, and Academic Development (CLAD) certificate in California functioned as an additional certificate (Carlson & Walton, 1994; Kuhlman & Vidal, 1993). It required all teachers to show that they had developed several types of expertise for teaching ELLs, which they could achieve by taking four college courses focused on those areas of expertise or by taking a test. A number of institutions, including Boston College (Friedman, 2002), Temple University (Névarez-La Torre, Sanford-De Shields, Soundy, Leonard, & Woyshner, 2005), and Northern Arizona University (Delaney-Bermann & Minner, 1995), have developed minors or supplemental certificates.

Some processes for improving the teaching of ELLs do not rely on changes in program structure or organization. One of these is ongoing professional development to help practicing teachers build their expertise for teaching ELLs. Such professional development may or may not be associated with a higher education institution and may or may not result in credits for coursework or formal professional development hours required by a school district. In contrast to the all-too-common practice of having teachers attend individual workshops, meaningful professional development is characterized by ongoing mentoring and coaching relationships solidly grounded in the professional lives of the teachers (see González & Darling-Hammond, 1997; Levy, Shafer, & Dunlap, 2002; see also Brisk & Zisselsberger, Gebhard et al., Walker & Stone, and Walqui, this volume).

Collaboration across institutional boundaries is the second process strategy discussed in the literature for strengthening the preparation and professional development of teachers of ELLs. Such collaboration can involve any of a number of participants—classroom teachers and ELL specialists in schools (Kaufman & Brooks, 1996); pre-service teachers in a general teacher education program and those in bilingual and/or ESL programs (Evans, Arnott-Hopffer, & Jurich, 2005; Gebhard, Austin, Nieto, & Willett, 2002); teacher educators in the general teacher education program and in bilingual/ESL teacher education (Sakash & Rodriguez-Brown, 1995, this volume); and higher education faculty and school-based faculty. When professionals and pre-professionals share their perspectives and expertise in the context of educating ELLs, they build new understandings for themselves and their colleagues to apply in teaching their current and future students. Such collaborations can break down compartmentalization in teachers' preparation and their roles in schools, combining the expertise of educators playing multiple roles in the schooling of ELLs.

Finally, before they can confidently prepare future and current teachers to teach ELLs, many teacher educators need to build their own relevant knowledge, skills, and dispositions. A number of faculty professional development initiatives have been undertaken in recent years, some of which have been reported in the literature (e.g., Costa, McPhail, Smith, & Brisk, 2005). Gort, Glenn, and Settlage (this volume) describe a faculty learning community that led to changes in curriculum and instruction by English and science teacher educators at one institution. Teacher education programs may also need to consider building expertise in ELL education by recruiting new faculty members with that expertise for generalist teacher education positions, or hiring non-tenure-track faculty with expertise to guide efforts to revise the curriculum to incorporate content related to teaching ELLs.

Program Coherence

Program coherence is the third element of concern in ensuring that teachers are prepared to teach ELLs. Enhancing coherence across program mission, conceptual framework, curriculum, instruction, and program and institutional structures has been highlighted by a number of scholars as a way to improve the quality of teacher preparation (Athanases & de Oliveira, this volume; Darling-Hammond, 2006; Grossman, Hammerness, McDonald, & Ronfeldt, 2008; Villegas & Lucas, 2002). They argue that desired outcomes are more likely to be achieved when everyone involved in teacher preparation shares common goals, philosophies, and understandings of teaching and learning, and when program structures are designed to achieve and reflect those goals, philosophies, and understandings. While scholarship to support this assumption is sparse, there is some evidence that coherence in program and professional norms can influence teacher candidates' beliefs about the nature of learning and about teaching diverse students (Tatto, 1996), that particular program elements are associated with perceptions of coherence among students (Grossman et al., 2008), and that some particular efforts can improve coherence in teacher education programs (Hammerness, 2006).

Most of the literature on coherence per se is focused on teacher preparation programs within higher education institutions, but the criticism that programs lack coherence applies to professional development for practicing teachers as well, especially when it is not part of a formal degree program. It is notoriously disjointed and disconnected from teachers' practice, and still too often "delivered" in infrequent workshops with little or no follow-up (Borko, 2004). There are few practices that are so roundly criticized and yet continue to be found in such abundance. (See Gebhard et al., Walker & Stone, and Walqui, this volume, for descriptions of professional development initiatives situated inside and outside higher education institutions that give attention to coherence across program goals, conceptual framework, curriculum, instruction, and program structures.)

Efforts to prepare classroom teachers to teach ELLs tend to be especially fragmented and "spotty," as mentioned previously (*Education Week*, 2009, p. 28). In pre-service and in-service teacher education programs within higher education institutions, often one or two faculty members take it upon themselves to advocate for giving some attention to teaching ELLs in the curriculum. If their advocacy is successful, they may be able to add some ELL-related requirements to the existing teacher education curriculum. For example, a one-credit course may be added, students may be required to spend some time working with ELLs in their fieldwork placements, or an existing course may require an assignment that focuses on teaching ELLs. While not ideal, this is a reasonable initial approach to incorporating some attention to the education of ELLs in teacher preparation given the need for teacher education programs to adhere to state certification requirements and meet professional standards, the pressure to increase the number of courses in the disciplines, and the push to get students through degree programs as quickly as possible. Still, this approach requires special vigilance to ensure some coherence across these learning experiences.

In fact, teacher educators attempting to prepare teachers to teach ELLs need to work toward greater coherence on two levels—overall program coherence and coherence across particular efforts to prepare teachers to teach ELLs. Ideally, shared goals, philosophies, and understandings of teaching and learning would ensure that all teacher candidates are prepared to teach ELLs, and those shared ideas would guide appropriate learning opportunities and institutional supports. Thus, attention to teaching ELLs would be woven throughout the teacher education program. At present, however, few programs can achieve this. More realistically, a few experiences focused on teaching ELLs are built into a larger program. In this case, the teacher educators involved must work toward coherence across these experiences. Rather than attempting to build on the conceptual and structural coherence of the overall teacher education program, they might need to articulate program and professional norms (Tatto, 1996) specific to teaching ELLs and gradually build a base of faculty and students who share those norms, while they design a few learning opportunities grounded in their more focused philosophies and goals for teaching ELLs.

Despite the barriers, coherence is fundamental to the quality of preparation for teaching ELLs and should not be overlooked by teacher educators as they focus on curriculum content and program organization. As Hammerness (2006) cogently argued, coherence is not an outcome, but a process of continuously making adjustments to respond to changes—changes, for example, in K-12 student populations, professional standards, or institutional mission and strategic plans. A program will never fully achieve coherence, but student learning will be enhanced by ongoing efforts to move closer to achieving it. (See Athanases & de Oliveira, this volume, for an examination of how one institution is working toward coherence by using a framework that addresses program content, processes, and context.)

Conclusion

In this chapter, I have argued that the centrality of language in schooling makes it imperative that teachers have special expertise for teaching the growing number of students in U.S. schools who speak home languages other than English. I have highlighted three fundamental elements of teacher education programs that require focused attention in efforts to develop that expertise in pre-service and practicing teachers. These are the starting points for transforming teacher preparation—a process that requires persistence, patience, critique, and creativity. The most productive ways of tackling the transformation vary across teacher education programs depending on many factors, including the geographic location, the demographic and political context, and the availability of university- and school-based professionals with relevant expertise. While this chapter has just scratched the surface in exploring the changes needed, it has laid a foundation upon which the remainder of the book builds. The chapters that follow situate the need for change in teacher education within demographic and policy contexts, and offer inspiring and thought-provoking examples of teacher educators grappling with the exigencies of transforming curriculum content, program structures and processes, and program coherence to ensure that all teachers are prepared to engage English language learners in meaningful learning.

Note

1. The term "English language learner" (ELL) refers to a person whose home language is a language other than English. ELLs have varying degrees of proficiency in English—from none at all to native-like proficiency. The term "limited English proficient" is an official term used by the U.S. Department of Education to refer to students whose English proficiency is not sufficiently developed to allow them to benefit maximally from instruction in English.

References

Abramson, S., Pritchard, R., & Garcia, R. (1993). Teacher education and limited-English-proficient students: Are we meeting the challenge? *Teacher Education Quarterly, 20*(3), 53–65.

American Association of Colleges for Teacher Education, Committee on Multicultural Education. (2002). *Educators' preparation for cultural and linguistic diversity: A call to action*, March. Retrieved from www.aacte.org/Programs/Multicultural/cultural-linguistic.pdf.

Athanases, S.Z., & de Oliveira, L.C. (2007). Conviction, confrontation, and risk in new teachers' advocating for equity. *Teaching Education, 18*(2), 123–136.

Athanases, S.Z., & de Oliveira, L.C. (2008). Advocacy for equity in classrooms and beyond: New teachers' challenges and responses. *Teachers College Record, 110*(1), 64–104.

August, D., & Hakuta, K. (Eds.). (1997). *Improving schooling for language-minority children: A research agenda*. Washington, D.C.: National Academy Press.

Bartolomé, L.I. (2000). Democratizing bilingualism: The role of critical teacher education. In Z.F. Beykont (Ed.), *Lifting every voice: Pedagogy and politics of bilingualism* (pp. 167–186). Cambridge, MA: Harvard Education Publishing Group.

Bartolomé, L.I. (2002). Creating an equal playing field: Teachers as advocates, border crossers, and cultural brokers. In Z.F. Beykont (Ed.), *The Power of culture: Teaching across language difference* (pp. 167–191). Cambridge, MA: Harvard Education Publishing Group.

Borko, H. (2004). Professional development and teacher learning: Mapping the terrain. *Educational Researcher, 33*(8), 3–15.

Brisk, M. (Ed.). (2008). *Language, culture, and community in teacher education*. Mahwah, NJ: Lawrence Erlbaum.

Brisk, M.E., Horan, D.A., & Macdonald, E. (2007). A scaffolded approach to learning to write. In L.S. Verplaetse & N. Migliacci (Eds.), *Inclusive pedagogy for English language learners: A handbook of research-informed practices* (pp. 15–32). New York, NY: Lawrence Erlbaum.

Brown, L.C. (2007). Strategies for making social studies texts more comprehensible for English-language learners. *The Social Studies, 98*(5), 185–188.

Carlson, R., & Walton, P. (1994). *CLAD/BCLAD: California reforms in the preparation and credentialing of teachers for a linguistically and culturally diverse student population.* Paper presented at the Twenty-Third Annual International Bilingual/Multicultural Education Conference, Los Angeles, CA, February.

Carrier, K.A. (2006). Improving comprehension and assessment of English language learners using MMIO. *The Clearinghouse, 79*(3), 131–136.

Costa, J., McPhail, G., Smith, J., & Brisk, M.E. (2005). The challenge of infusing the teacher education curriculum with scholarship on English language learners. *Journal of Teacher Education, 56*(5), 104–118.

Darling-Hammond, L. (2006). Constructing 21st-century teacher education. *Journal of Teacher Education, 57*(3), 300–314.

de Jong, E., & Harper, C. (2005). Preparing mainstream teachers for English language learners: Is being a good teacher good enough? *Teacher Education Quarterly, 32*(2), 101–124.

de Jong, E.J., & Harper, C.A. (2008). ESL is good teaching "plus." In M.E. Brisk (Ed.), *Language, culture, and community in teacher education* (pp. 127–148). New York, NY: Lawrence Erlbaum.

Delany-Bermann, G., & Minner, S. (1995). *Development and implementation of a program of study to prepare teachers for diversity at Northern Arizona University: A preliminary report.* Paper presented at the annual conference of the AERO, Sedona, AZ, November.

Echevarria, J., Vogt, M., & Short, D.J. (2004). *Making content comprehensible for English language learners: The SIOP Model* (2nd ed.). Boston, MA: Allyn & Bacon.

Education Week. (2009). Quality counts 2009. Portrait of a population: How English-language learners are putting schools to the test. *Education Week, 28*(17).

Evans, C., Arnot-Hopffer, E., & Jurich, D. (2005). Making ends meet: Bringing bilingual education and mainstream students together in preservice teacher education. *Equity and Excellence in Education, 38*, 75–88.

Frey, W.H. (2001). *Melting pot suburbs: A Census 2000 study of suburban diversity.* Washington, D.C.: The Brookings Institution.

Friedman, A.A. (2002). What we would have liked to know: Preservice teachers' perspectives on effective teacher preparation. In Z.F. Beykont (Ed.), *The power of culture: Teaching across language difference* (pp. 193–217). Cambridge, MA: Harvard Education Publishing Group.

García, E.E. (1993). Language, culture, and education. In L. Darling-Hammond (Ed.), *Review of research in education, 19* (pp. 51–98). Washington, D.C.: American Educational Research Association.

García, E.E. (1996). Preparing instructional professionals for linguistically and culturally diverse students. In J. Sikula (Ed.), *Handbook of research on teacher education* (2nd ed., pp. 802–813). New York, NY: Macmillan.

García, E.E. (1999). *Student cultural diversity: Understanding and meeting the challenge* (2nd ed.). Boston, MA: Houghton Mifflin.

Gay, G. (2000). *Culturally responsive teaching: Theory, research, and practice.* New York, NY: Teachers College Press.

Gebhard, M., Austin, T., Nieto, S., & Willett J. (2002). "You can't step on someone else's words": Preparing all teachers to teach language minority students. In Z.F. Beykont (Ed.), *The power of culture: Teaching across language difference* (pp. 219–243). Cambridge, MA: Harvard Education Publishing Group.

Gibbons, P. (2002). *Scaffolding language, scaffolding learning: Teaching second language learners in the mainstream classroom.* Portsmouth, NH: Heinemann.

González, J.M., & Darling-Hammond, L. (1997). *New concepts for new challenges: Professional development for teachers of immigrant youth.* Washington, D.C.: Center for Applied Linguistics.

Grossman, P., Hammerness, K.M., McDonald, M., & Ronfeldt, M. (2008). Constructing coherence: Structural predictors of perceptions of coherence in NYC teacher education programs. *Journal of Teacher Education, 59*(4), 273–287.

Hadaway, N. (1993). Encountering linguistic diversity through letters: Preparing preservice teachers for second language learners. *Equity & Excellence in Education, 26*(3), 25–30.

Halliday, M.A.K. (1977). *Learning how to mean: Explorations in the development of language.* New York, NY: Elsevier.

Halliday, M.A.K. (1993). Towards a language-based theory of learning. *Linguistics and Education, 5*(2), 93–116.

Hammerness, K. (2006). From coherence in theory to coherence in practice. *Teachers College Record, 108*(7), 163–171.

Harper, C., & de Jong, E. (2004). Misconceptions about teaching English-language learners. *Journal of Adolescent & Adult Literacy, 48*(2), 152–162.

Hite, C.E., & Evans, L.S. (2006). Mainstream first-grade teachers' understanding of strategies for accommodating the needs of English language learners. *Teacher Education Quarterly, 33*(2), 89–110.

Kaufman, D., & Brooks, J.G. (1996). Interdisciplinary collaboration in teacher education: A constructivist approach. *TESOL Quarterly, 30*(2), 231–251.

Kuhlman, N.A., & Vidal, J. (1993). Meeting the needs of LEP students through new teacher training: The case in California. *The Journal of Educational Issues of Language Minority Students, 12*, 97–113.

Ladson-Billings, G. (1990). Culturally relevant teaching. *The College Board Review, 155*, 20–25.

Ladson-Billings, G. (1994). *The dreamkeepers: Successful teachers of African American children.* New York, NY: John Wiley & Sons.

Levy, J., Shafer, L., & Dunlap, K. (2002). Advancing the professional development of beginning teachers through mentoring and action research. In L. Minaya-Rowe (Ed.), *Teacher training and effective pedagogy in the context of student diversity* (pp. 269–296). Greenwich, CT: Information Age Publishing.

Lucas, T., & Grinberg, J. (2008). Responding to the linguistic reality of mainstream classrooms: Preparing all teachers to teach English language learners. In M. Cochran-Smith, S. Feiman-Nemser, & J. McIntyre (Eds.), *Handbook of research on teacher education: Enduring issues in changing contexts* (3rd ed., pp. 606–636). Mahwah, NJ: Lawrence Erlbaum.

Lucas, T., Villegas, A.M., & Freedson-Gonzalez, M. (2008). Linguistically responsive teacher education: Preparing classroom teachers to teach English language learners. *Journal of Teacher Education, 59*(4), 361–373.

Nevárez-La Torre, A.A., Sanford-De Shields, J.S., Soundy, C., Leonard, J., & Woyshner, C. (2005). *Faculty perspectives on integrating linguistic diversity issues into a teacher education program.* Paper presented at the Annual Meeting of the American Educational Research Association, Montreal, Canada.

Penfield, J. (1987). ESL: The regular classroom teacher's perspective. *TESOL Quarterly, 21*(1), 21–39.

Regional Educational Laboratory—Appalachia. (2008). *Preparing to serve English language learner students: School districts with emerging English language learner communities.* Alexandria, VA: Author.

Rhine, S. (1995). The challenges of effectively preparing teachers of limited-English-proficient students. *Journal of Teacher Education, 46*(5), 381–389.

Sakash, K., & Rodriguez-Brown, F.V. (1995). *Teamworks: Mainstream and bilingual/ESL teacher collaboration.* Washington, D.C.: National Clearinghouse for Bilingual Education.

Schleppegrell, M.J. (2004). *The language of schooling: A functional linguistics perspective.* Mahwah, NJ: Lawrence Erlbaum.

Tatto, M.T. (1996). Examining values and beliefs about teaching diverse students: Understanding the challenges for teacher education. *Educational Evaluation and Policy Analysis, 18*(2), 155–180.

Trumbull, E., & Farr, B. (2005). *Language and learning: What teachers need to know.* Norwood, MA: Christopher-Gordon Publishers.

Valdés, G., Bunch, G., Snow, C., & Lee, C. (2005). Enhancing the development of students' language(s). In L. Darling-Hammond & J. Bransford (Eds.), *Preparing teachers for a changing world: What teachers should learn and be able to do* (pp. 126–168). San Francisco, CA: Jossey Bass.

Verplaetse, L.S. (2007). Developing academic language through an abundance of interaction. In L.S. Verplaetse & N. Migliacci (Eds.), *Inclusive pedagogy for English language learners: A handbook of research-informed practices* (pp. 167–180). New York, NY: Lawrence Erlbaum.

Verplaetse, L.S., & Migliacci, N. (2007). Making mainstream content comprehensible through sheltered instruction. In L.S. Verplaetse & N. Migliacci (Eds.), *Inclusive pedagogy for English language learners: A handbook of research-informed practices* (pp. 127–165). New York, NY: Lawrence Erlbaum.

Villegas, A.M., & Lucas, T. (2002). *Educating culturally responsive teachers: A coherent approach.* Albany, NY: SUNY Press.

Vygotsky, L. (1978). *Mind in society.* Cambridge: Cambridge University Press.

Walker, C.L., Ranney, S., & Fortune, T.W. (2005). Preparing preservice teachers for English language learners: A content-based approach. In D.J. Tedick (Ed.), *Second language teacher education, international perspectives* (pp. 313–333). Mahwah, NJ: Lawrence Erlbaum.

Walqui, A. (2007). The development of teacher expertise to work with adolescent English learners: A model and a few priorities. In L.S. Verplaetse & N. Migliacci (Eds.), *Inclusive pedagogy for English language learners: A handbook of research-informed practices* (pp. 103–125). New York, NY: Lawrence Erlbaum.

Wong-Fillmore, L., & Snow, C. (2005). What teachers need to know about language. In C.T. Adger, C.E. Snow, & D. Christian (Eds.), *What teachers need to know about language* (pp. 7–54). Washington, D.C.: Center for Applied Linguistics.

Yedlin, J. (2007). Pedagogical thinking and teacher talk in a first-grade ELL classroom. In L.S. Verplaetse & N. Migliacci (Eds.), *Inclusive pedagogy for English language learners: A handbook of research-informed practices* (pp. 55–77). New York, NY: Lawrence Erlbaum.

Zeichner, K. (2005). A research agenda for teacher education. In M. Cochran-Smith & K. Zeichner (Eds.), *Studying teacher education: The report of the AERA Panel on Research and Teacher Education* (pp. 737–759). Mahwah, NJ: Lawrence Erlbaum.

Chapter 2

English Language Learners in American Schools

Characteristics and Challenges

Guadalupe Valdés and Martha Castellón

Lizet is nine years old and in the fourth grade. She is a pretty, fair-skinned little girl who, until only a few months ago, enjoyed a full and ordinary life in Mexico. She went to school and played with her friends. Suddenly at the beginning of last summer, her life changed dramatically. Both her parents were killed in a tragic automobile accident; and with no one in Mexico to care for them, she and her sister were sent to live in the United States with her father's two younger brothers. She spends her days in a classroom in which the teacher speaks only English. During the week, she lives with one uncle, and during the weekend she spends time with her other uncle's family and her little sister. Lizet appears lost and unhappy, and struggles to remember that part of herself that was a successful student just a few short months ago. She feels dumb, understands little, and is convinced that she will not learn English.

Teng is five years old and entering kindergarten. Because he was born in this country, he is an American citizen. His family is Hmong (originally from Laos) and, like many other Hmong families, spent a number of years in refugee camps in Cambodia. The family has been in the United States for 10 years, but since they were relocated to areas of the country where other Hmong families were resettled, they have little contact with English-speaking Americans. Teng's parents speak very limited English. The family depends on the two older children in the family to broker their communication outside the community. Teng attends a school where there are other Hmong children and a few teacher aides who are native speakers of Hmong, but all other school personnel speak only English. During the first weeks of school, Teng cried almost all day. Several months into the school year, Teng no longer cries, but he has yet to say a single word.

Alejandro was also born in the United States. Now a tall ninth-grader, he speaks some English but understands very little of what his teachers say. He acquired the English that he knows during kindergarten and first grade when he attended a school in southern California. He returned to El Salvador after his parents divorced and only returned to the United States a few months ago. Unfortunately, the small charter school he attends does not provide special instruction or special support for English language learners. Teachers believe that students will learn best by rapidly being immersed in mainstream classes where their teachers depend on Spanish-speaking classmates to make instruction comprehensible to non-English speakers. Unfortunately, teenagers often tend to be unkind. They make fun of Alejandro and his attempts to speak English. Some of his classmates find great glee in mistranslating assignments and explanations. They find it very amusing to see Alejandro's confusion and the teacher's surprise when she examines his work.

Lizet, Teng, and Alejandro are all "new" American children. Only Lizet could properly be referred to as an immigrant, but all three children are the products of migration. They are here because their family members moved from their original place of residence to this country. All of them, then, are immigrant-origin children. Their place of birth—while important in terms of legal status—is in many ways a geographical accident that does not change the composition of the family, the newness of their experiences as new residents in this country, and the immense challenge of acquiring English.

Worldwide, the number of people who have left their countries of origin is increasing rapidly. Bendixsen and Guchteneire (2004) estimate that from 1990 to 2000, the number of migrants grew by 14% (21 million people). Citing the *International Migration Report of 2002*, these researchers place the total number of migrants at 175 million, or 3% of the world population. They point out that as a result of such dramatic increases, "both host countries and countries of origin must deal with issues such as brain drain, migrants' rights, minority integration, religion, citizenship, xenophobia, human trafficking and national security" (p. 1). Moreover, in the case of most immigrant-origin children, host countries must grapple with the challenges of providing them with a quality education in spite of both linguistic and cultural challenges. These challenges are complex and involve questions about appropriate or effective educational practices that are necessarily embedded in larger issues concerning national identity and the responsibility of governments in educating such children.

In the United States, questions about the appropriate education for children of immigrants have surfaced in numerous debates beginning during the times of increased immigration from southern and eastern Europe at the turn of the twentieth century and continuing today. Because U.S. citizens are concerned about these "new" Americans and about the ways they can be integrated into American society, much attention is given by both the public and educators to this particular group of children. Recently, English itself has taken on greater importance in discussions surrounding the education of immigrant-origin students. These conversations have been deeply influenced by debates about the number of both authorized and unauthorized immigrants, about the security of our borders, and about the challenge of assimilating groups of individuals who appear not to be learning English (Huntington, 2004).

In this chapter, it is our purpose to provide a broad context for the preparation of classroom teachers—many of whom will teach children like Lizet, Teng, and Alejandro—by first providing information about the characteristics of the immigrant-origin population and their children in the United States. Although it is true that not all English language learners are immigrants, the vast majority are either immigrants themselves or the sons and daughters of immigrants. It is important to understand the ways in which this demographic has grown in recent years in order to fully appreciate the ways in which schools have been and will continue to be impacted. Hence, in the first part of this chapter we depict the general characteristics of the immigrant population and then focus on the largest group of foreign-born, the Hispanic or Latino population. In the second section of the chapter, we focus on the school context, presenting the challenges of accurately estimating the number of children who can be classified as English language learners and describing the nature of the ELL student population—including its considerable diversity in different parts of the country. Then, we delve further into the school context by examining the ELL student achievement gap and pointing out the challenges of accurately measuring the academic performance of students who are in the process of acquiring English.

The Immigrant Population of the United States

Characteristics of the General U.S. Immigrant Population

Recent studies of immigrants in the United States, while generally in agreement about numbers and statistics, often emphasize different characteristics of the immigrant population, depending on their particular focus and the interest of their target audiences. Here we draw from the Migration Policy Institute's Data Hub and the work conducted by Terrazas, Batalova, and Fan (2007), as well as from other recent studies on immigration.

Current and Historical Numbers and Shares

- In 2006, there were 37,547,789 foreign-born persons in the United States, representing 12.5% of the total population. Historically, the size of the foreign-born population has varied from 14.8% in 1890 (2.2 million) to 11.6% in 1930 (14.2 million), to a low of 4.7% in 1970 (9.6 million) to 11.1% in 2000 (31.1 million) (Terrazas et al., 2007).
- Of the 37.5 million foreign-born residents in 2006, 44.1% entered the U.S. prior to 1990, 30.5% entered between 1990 and 1999, and 25.3% arrived in 2000 or later (Terrazas et al., 2007).

Geographic Distribution

- In 2006, the top five US states by the number of foreign-born were California, New York, Texas, Florida, and Illinois (Terrazas et al., 2007).

Geographic Origins

- Mexico-born immigrants account for 30.7% of the foreign-born, followed by the Philippines (4.4%), China (excluding Taiwan) (4.1%), and India (4.0%). Immigrants from these four countries, together with Vietnam, El Salvador, Korea, Cuba, Canada, and the United Kingdom, make up 58.4% of the total immigrant population (Terrazas et al., 2007).
- The geographic origins of current immigrants contrast dramatically with the origin of previous groups of immigrants. In 1960, eight of the top 10 source countries of the foreign-born were in Europe (Migration Policy Institute, 2007). By comparison, in 2006, the top-10 source countries of the foreign-born were in Latin America and Asia.

Linguistic Characteristics

- The non-English languages spoken in the United States by the greatest number of people in 2000 were Spanish (28,101,052 speakers), followed by Chinese (2,002,143), French (1,643,838), German (1,382,613), Tagalog (1,224,241), Vietnamese 1,009,627, Italian (1,008,370), Korean (894,063), Russian (706,242), Polish (667,414), and Arabic (614,582) (U.S. Census Bureau, 2000).
- Of the 37.2 million foreign-born persons aged five and older in 2006, 52.4% reported speaking English less than "very well" and were considered limited English proficient (Terrazas et al., 2007).[1]
- In 2000, 55% of the people reporting speaking a non-English language at home (25.6 million) also reported speaking English "very well." When this figure is combined with those who spoke only English at home, 92% of the population aged five and over had no difficulty speaking English. A total of 4.4 million households (11.9 million people) in the entire country, however, were considered to be "linguistically isolated" (Shin and Bruno, 2003).[2]

Characteristics of the Hispanic/Latino Immigrant Population

Because of their numbers, Hispanic/Latino immigrants and their children are necessarily of particular interest to educators in the United States. In this section, we briefly summarize some of the characteristics of this population as a whole.

- In 2006, 47.2% of the foreign-born population reported they were of Hispanic or Latino origin. The Mexico-born population was 30.7% of all foreign-born people residing in the United States (Terrazas et al., 2007).
- According to the Pew Hispanic Center's statistical portrait for 2006, 11,534,972 people of Mexican origin reside in the United States (Pew Hispanic Center, 2008).
- Other sizeable populations include 1.4 million Hispanics of Cuban origin, 1.1 million of Dominican origin, 2.9 million of Central American origin (1.2 million Salvadorians), and 2.2 million of South American origin, including the largest of these groups, 686,000 Columbians (U.S. Census Bureau, 2007).

In terms of language use in the Hispanic population, the analysis by Hakimzadeh and Cohn (2007) of six Pew Hispanic Center surveys of more than 14,000 adults indicated that:

- One in four (23% of Latino immigrants) speaks English "very well."
- A full 88% of their U.S.-born adult children report speaking English very well, as do 94% of later generation Latinos.
- By the third generation, only one in four Latinos reports still speaking Spanish at home.
- Of these third-generation Latinos, 52% consider that they speak English "very well."

Table 2.1 summarizes data on language spoken at home and English speaking ability drawn at a single point in time (2004) from the American Community Survey report on Hispanics (U.S. Census Bureau, 2007). These data suggest that popular perceptions about Hispanic/Latino immigrants "refusing" to learn English are not supported by actual studies of the population. Mexicans and Puerto Ricans are the groups with the largest proportions of people who speak English at home. It is important to note, however, that only 36.4% of the Mexican origin population reports speaking English very well as compared to 47.2% of Puerto Ricans, 45% of South Americans, and 42% of Cubans. According to Hakimzadeh and Cohen (2007), education explains some of these differences. Mexican immigrants, for example, are the least likely of Hispanic groups to have graduated from college. Length of residence and age of arrival are also considered to predict how well immigrants will speak English.

Summary

As noted above, the total percentage of the foreign-born population has increased in the last 30 years to levels characteristic of the turn of the twentieth century. According to Capps et al. (2004), one in five children under the age of 18 in the U.S. is a child of immigrants. Below, we consider how the changing demographics of the U.S. directly impact education for ELLs.

Table 2.1 / Hispanics: Language Spoken at Home and English-Speaking Ability, 2004

	Percent Only English at Home	Percent Non-English at home: English spoken "very well."	Percent Non-English at home: English spoken less than "very well."
Total (100%)	81.3	10.3	8.4
White alone—not Hispanic	94.3	3.9	1.8
Hispanic	22.8	38.5	38.7
Mexican	22.9	36.4	40.7
Puerto Rican	30.9	47.2	22.2
Cuban	14.1	42.7	43.2
Dominican	6.9	41.8	51.3
Central American	7.8	37.0	55.2
South American	12.4	45.1	42.5

Source: The American Community—Hispanics: 2004 (US Census Bureau, 2007).

The Children of Immigrants in American Schools

The Changing Composition of U.S. Public Schools

The presence of new immigrants in the United States and the shifts in the composition of the population in many areas of the country present special challenges to educators. The racial and ethnic composition of American public schools is rapidly and dramatically changing (see Fry, 2007a). In 1993–1994, one-third of all white students attended a school with fewer than 5% non-white students, but by 2005–2006, just one in five white students was attending such schools. At the same time, Black and Hispanic students have become increasingly isolated, as evidenced by the fact that in 2005–2006, 29% of Hispanic students and 31% of Black students attended schools where fewer than 5% of the students were white. The number of all-minority public schools has almost doubled in the same time period. In 2005–2006, 56% of Hispanic students attended schools in which a least half of the students were Hispanic (Fry, 2007a).

ELLs are similarly concentrated in a small number of schools. According to Consentino de Cohen and Clewell (2007), 70% of all limited English proficient (LEP)[3] students enroll in only 10% of elementary schools across the country. In spite of impressions to the contrary, nearly half of elementary schools in the United States do not enroll large numbers of immigrant and ELL students (Consentino de Cohen & Clewell, 2007; KewalRamani, Gilbertson, Fox, & Provasnik, 2007). Thus, the large majority of schools and classrooms have not yet been seriously impacted by the presence of immigrant children who are English language learners. The numbers of English language learners (ELLs) are growing, however, and, absent a coherent immigration policy, it is highly likely that most teachers will at some point in their careers have responsibility for providing English learners with the academic skills and content knowledge that these youngsters will need in order to become productive members of society. Whether schools enroll large numbers of these students or whether there is just one teacher with a student who is acquiring English, teachers need information about such learners and about the best ways of integrating them into their classrooms.

The Identification of Immigrant English Language Learners

For those schools that enroll first-, second-, and even third-generation immigrant-origin students, the first key challenge involves identifying youngsters who are English language learners. While procedures vary, in most districts, when students who are known or suspected to speak a non-English language at home enter school, a Home Language Survey is completed by the family and a test of English-language proficiency is administered to the student to determine if he or she should be classified as an ELL or LEP student and given appropriate support to overcome educational barriers.

Currently, the No Child Left Behind Act of 2001 (NCLB) defines limited English proficient students as those aged 3 through 21 who are enrolled in or are preparing to enroll in an elementary or secondary school and who (1) were not born in the United States or whose native language is a language other than English, and (2) whose difficulties in speaking, reading, writing, or understanding the English language may be sufficient to (a) deny them the ability to achieve academic proficiency on state achievement tests, (b) prevent their success in English-medium classrooms, or (c) limit their opportunities to participate fully in society. Despite this very broad description of LEP students, there is no single operational definition that applies from state to state. This is because each state uses different identification and assessment measures and establishes its own cut-off scores for both entering and exiting programs designed for ELLs (National Clearinghouse for English Language Acquisition, n.d.).

The fact that the criteria for determining a student's ELL status vary across most states makes it difficult to count the total number of ELLs in the country. Other factors that make it difficult to count the total number of ELLs in the U.S. include whether students in Pre-K are counted in each state's total and whether nationwide tallies include or exclude the ELL population in outlying jurisdictions (Puerto Rico, Guam, the Virgin Islands, the Marshall Islands, Micronesia, the Northern Marianas Islands, Palau, and American Samoa). In the absence of uniform criteria, two methodologies for estimating the total number of English language learners are used: (1) counting the number of designated Limited English Proficient (LEP) students in every state and outlying jurisdiction, and (2) using data collected by the U.S. Census Bureau.

Using State-Reported Data to Count English Language Learners in American Schools

State-reported data on English learners, which include the number of LEP students from outlying jurisdictions, provides the following information about this population:

- In academic year 2004–2005, a total of 5,119,561 LEP students in pre-K through Grade 12 enrolled in U.S. schools. This number represents 10.5% of the nation's total public school enrollment (National Clearinghouse for English Language Acquisition, n.d.). (In the 50 states and the District of Columbia, 4,459,603 LEP students enrolled in grades Pre-K through 12 in academic year 2004–2005—9.2% of the total school-aged population.)
- The population of ELL students has grown considerably in recent years, and has by far outpaced the growth of the general school population (National Clearinghouse for English Language Acquisition, n.d.).

- Between the 1989–1990 and 2004–2005 academic years, the LEP population more than doubled, growing approximately 152.0% while the general school population grew by just 20.6% (National Clearinghouse for English Language Acquisition, n.d.).

No other state rivals California in terms of total number of ELLs. In academic year 2004–2005, California reported 1,591,525 LEP students—fully 31% of all ELLs in the country. Texas reported 684,007, followed by Florida (299,346), New York (203,583), Illinois (192,764), and Arizona (155,789). In terms of states with the highest density of ELLs in the public school population, California leads the pack once again. LEP students in that state comprised 25.7% of the school-age population in 2004–2005, compared to 22.4% in New Mexico, 18.1% in Nevada, 15.5% in Texas, and 15.1% in Alaska (National Clearinghouse for English Language Acquisition, n.d.).

Some states with historically low numbers of ELLs are now seeing unprecedented growth among this sector of the population. Between 1994–1995 and 2004–2005, the states that experienced the largest percentage growth in LEP students were South Carolina (714.2%), Kentucky (417.4%), Indiana (407.8%), North Carolina (371.7%), and Tennessee (369.9%) (National Clearinghouse for English Language Acquisition, n.d.). In reality, however, nearly half of the states have seen their LEP populations double between 1994–1995 and 2004–2005. Hence, the growth of ELLs is not just a regional phenomenon as it has been in decades past, but one that is increasingly affecting every corner of the country (Short & Fitzsimmons, 2007).

In 2000–2001, the last year for which we have state-wide data, ELL students spoke more than 460 different languages. The five languages spoken most commonly by English language learners and the proportion of ELLs who spoke each language were: Spanish (79.0%), Vietnamese (2.0%), Hmong (1.6%), Cantonese (1.0%), and Korean (1.0%). Each of the remaining 455 languages was spoken by 1.0% or less of the proportion of ELLs (National Clearinghouse for English Language Acquisition, n.d.).

Using U.S. Census Bureau Data to Count English Language Learners

In contrast to counting the number of students who are designated limited English proficient in each state, the method used by the U.S. Census Bureau for counting the total number of LEP students in the nation relies upon self-report data on English fluency gleaned from the decennial census. All persons who report that they speak English "very well" are considered to be proficient in English. Persons who report that they speak English "well," "not well," or "not at all" are considered to have limited English proficiency.

With respect to the race/ethnicity of students with limited English proficiency, nearly all come from Hispanic/Latino and Asian backgrounds. KewalRamani et al. (2007), using data reported by the Census Bureau's 2005

American Community Survey, note that 10,770,000 elementary and second-ary school students spoke a language other than English at home—20.4% of the school-age population. This number includes those who reported speaking English with and without difficulty. Of those school-age children who reported speaking a language other than English at home, 6,939,000 were of Hispanic/Latino origin compared to 1,323,000 who were of Asian origin.

Given the differences in the methods for arriving at a single number of ELLs in the nation, it is natural that there would be some discrepancy in the numbers of school-age students with limited English proficiency reported by the states and by the U.S. Census. Several sources (e.g., Capps, Murray, Ost, Passel, & Herwantoro, 2005; Short & Fitzsimmons, 2007) have claimed that the U.S. Census consistently underestimates the number of English language learners in the country. Regardless of the method used to count them, English language learners make up a significant percentage of the school-age population.

The Academic Achievement of ELL Students

Historically, the academic performance of English language learners has lagged behind that of other students in the United States (Abedi & Dietel, 2004). By a variety of measures, including scores on standardized tests such as the NAEP[4] and NCLB-mandated statewide reading and math tests, grades, and drop-out rates, ELL academic achievement presents a discouraging picture. Batalova, Fix, and Murray (2007), for example, in a study of 2005 NAEP data and the 2005 results of four statewide reading and math assessments (California, Colorado, Illinois, and North Carolina) determined that:

- On National NAEP, there is a large performance gap between ELL and non-ELL eighth-grade students. ELLs' scores were lower than non-ELL scores by 39 points in reading and 36 points in math on a 500-point scale. More ELL students, on average, scored below "basic" as compared to non-ELLs who scored above.
- On statewide exams, performance varied widely but performance gaps between ELLs and non-ELLs persist across all states.
- The scores of reclassified or former ELLs on NAEP and on the California tests reveal that these students are "roughly equal" to non-ELLs.

Similarly, Fry (2007b) examined the 2005 National NAEP results and 35 state-level NAEP assessments and compared ELLs' performance with that of whites, the vast majority of whom are native English speakers. He concluded that:

- On National NAEP, 46% of all fourth-grade ELL students scored below basic in mathematics and 73% scored below basic in reading. By contrast, the percentages of white students who scored below basic in fourth-grade math and reading were 11% and 25%, respectively.

- The ELL achievement gap widens at the higher grades—a phenomenon that may be a result of the changing composition of the ELL population across grades (redesignated students leave the ELL population and newly arrived students with very limited English are included).

In both of these studies, ELLs included U.S.-born youngsters who had been educated in American schools since the early grades. Interestingly, in most reports (e.g., NAEP), ELL outcomes are not disaggregated by ethnic group. When ethnic achievement is reported, moreover (e.g., KewalRamani et al., 2007), results are reported by broad ethnic categories (e.g, Hispanic, Asian) even though work by a number of scholars has showed that critical differences especially among groups of Asian students are masked by such ethnic aggregations (Kiang, 2006; Lee, 2006; Ngo & Lee, 2007).[5]

With regard to how achievement is measured, many serious questions have been raised about the validity of tests currently used with English language learners (Abedi, 2007; Solano-Flores, 2008; Solórzano, 2008). When academic achievement tests are administered in English to students who are still developing proficiency in the language, scores cannot be seen as true indictors of students' content-area knowledge as it is difficult to isolate what part of their score is due to their knowledge of academic content and what part is due to their limitations in the language. Test scores in cases such as these can be said to be linguistically biased. Other types of test bias that affect ELLs include norming bias, content bias, and cultural bias (August & Hakuta, 1997). While it would be prudent to consider using alternative types of assessments (or test accommodations) in determining students' levels of achievement, there is no consensus in the literature with respect to which types of tests and/or accommodations would yield more valid results for various segments of the English language learner population (Solano-Flores, 2008).

Implications for Teacher Education

All over the country, schools and communities are rapidly changing. Wealthy upper-middle-class communities are witnessing the arrival of professionals from many parts of the world whose children must learn English in order to succeed in school. Many of these same communities, moreover, are also witnessing the growth of nearby "immigrant ghettos" that are home to gardeners, hotel maids, hamburger flippers, dishwashers, vegetable pickers, seamstresses, and other workers who do many types of jobs that native-born Americans are no longer available to do. Their children too must learn English in order to succeed. For public schools, the result of these demographic changes is that many teachers are suddenly discovering English language learners in their classrooms. In some areas of the country, these students might be only a trickle of one or two children, but in other parts of the U.S., they are part of a quickly growing rivulet that threatens to flood entire schools. What becomes immediately clear to teachers is that they cannot pretend that these youngsters are not there. Not educating them is not an option, but the challenge involves giving them access to the curriculum while they are still in the process of learning English.

In this chapter, we have presented demographic data to highlight the characteristics of the immigrant population. We have also focused on the changing composition of the school-age population and highlighted the academic achievement gaps that characterize the performance of ELL students in schools around the country. We have emphasized the fact that the largest group of immigrant-origin students are Latinos, many of whom are of working-class origin. We have also sought to emphasize that, in spite of popular misconceptions, newly arrived immigrants and their children *are* learning English.

Such background information is important for teachers because, for the country in general and for public schools in particular, these are difficult times. The political environment surrounding Spanish-speaking persons in the United States is particularly hostile. For a number of years, we have been living in an anti-immigrant climate in which the image of Latino immigrants has been deeply tainted by debates about the number of both authorized and unauthorized immigrants currently living in this country, and the lack of a coherent national policy on immigration. Not surprisingly, given hostility toward immigrants in general and toward Latino immigrants in particular, there is a fear—especially in states where recent influxes of Latino immigrants have increased dramatically—that Spanish might replace English and that the dominant culture will be "polluted" by foreigners. In a recent article, a distinguished Harvard University scholar, for example, argued that Mexican immigrants pose special challenges to the American state. He speaks of immigration from Mexico as "a unique, disturbing, and looming challenge to our cultural integrity, our national identity, and potentially to our future as a country" (Huntington, 2004, p. 8). These views and fears touch the lives of teachers and schools in many parts of the U.S. Many middle-class parents do not want children like Lizet, Teng, and Alejandro in the same classrooms with their children. At the same time, teachers who come into contact with such children worry that they are not prepared to work with students who speak little English, who, like Lizet, have endured many difficulties in their young lives, or who, like Alejandro, may have had an interrupted education in two languages.

As Bransford, Darling-Hammond, and LePage (2005) have argued, preparing teachers for a changing world will require them "to understand their roles and responsibilities as professionals in schools that must prepare all students for equitable participation in a democratic society" (p. 11). Whether or not they personally work with immigrant-origin children, public school teachers in the United States are part of a unique educational system in which the free common school has been seen as "the most American thing about America"

(Tyack, 2003, p. 1). Our own position is that those who are committed to American public schools and those who plan to teach in such schools must commit to carrying out the hard work involved in creating "civic cohesion through education in a socially diverse and contentious democracy" (Tyack, 2003, p. 3). Teacher preparation, then, cannot focus exclusively on pedagogical knowledge and skills. It must also engage teachers in examining the broader issues that surround them, as well as the national and local debates that shape and inform policies and decisions enacted in their schools and classrooms. As Persell (1977) has pointed out, educational inequality is a function of (1) structures of dominance in society and societal ideologies, (2) educational structures and educational ideologies and concepts, and (3) teacher expectations and educational interactions. Societal, institutional, and interpersonal variables together result in intrapsychic educational outcomes that we recognize as academic success and failure for individual students.

In order to understand education and inequality in our increasingly diverse society and to support the ideals that must shape our democratic society in the future, teachers must be committed to carrying out the work required to educate all students. This work includes attending to the number and distribution of new immigrants across the country, in their states, and in their regions, as well as to the achievement gaps between immigrant-origin children and mainstream children. It also includes examining the tensions between educational ideals and actual practice, and perhaps playing an advocacy role for vulnerable children when participating in discussions about the role of the "best" schools in educating at-risk immigrant-origin students. It means committing to learning about immigrant-origin children and their communities, and to broadening and strengthening their own pedagogical skills in order to work with English language learners.

In order to best educate children like Lizet, Teng, and Alejandro well, for example, teachers need to become familiar with their backgrounds, their communities, their histories, and their culture. It would be important for Lizet's teachers to obtain information about the community where she lives, the educational background of her uncles and their wives, the types of work in which members of the community are engaged, and the availability of educated Spanish-speaking persons in the community. Should such persons be present, they could be recruited to provide information about the Mexican curriculum (e.g., what subjects third- and fourth-graders study in school). They might also be able to provide subject-matter after-school support for subjects such as mathematics and science *in Spanish* while Lizet is in the process of acquiring English. In this case, census data on educational attainment by persons of Mexican background in the region might be an important place to start.

Similarly, Alejandro's teachers would gain much from examining information about secondary school Hispanic students around the country, their patterns of success and failure, and the special challenges faced by students who have interrupted educations. Given what is known about the challenges facing adolescent students, several of his teachers may need to play an advocacy role in obtaining appropriate support and placement for Alejandro. Both his academic subject-matter knowledge and his English language proficiency need to be assessed and diagnosed. His interactions with classmates also need to be observed closely by someone who can understand Spanish, and a discussion needs to take place about appropriate interventions that will prevent this becoming a victim of adolescent mischievousness. The dilemma of giving Alejandro access to the curriculum in the particular charter school he attends–where there is no support for English language learners—needs to be discussed frankly by administrators, teachers, and persons knowledgeable about such students as quickly as possible.

In the case of Teng, knowledge that the Hmong are here because they fought for the U.S. in the Vietnam War would be particularly important. Understanding that many Hmong people who were resettled in this country were originally from Laos, where their life was spent in agricultural work and where rates of literacy were low, would also be helpful for Teng's teacher. However, it would be important that the teacher not generalize about Teng and his family from limited information. Many websites are available that provide data about the history and culture of the Hmong, and are excellent points of departure. Teng's teachers would be greatly helped by learning how the Hmong people are different from "model minority" Asians such as upper-class Chinese and Korean students with whom they might be already familiar. They would also gain much from learning about the local group of Hmong residents, finding out when they arrived in the area, the size of the community, and the availability of community members to provide just-in-time translation assistance to the family. It would also be important for the teacher to obtain information about the size of the Hmong enrollment in the district, the availability of Hmong language school information (forms, general school information), and types of assistance that the district might provide for the teacher in working with Teng and his family.

Preparing teachers for a changing society that will integrate, educate, and celebrate very diverse children is a major challenge. For teacher educators, preparing teachers for such a society will require structuring classes so that honest explorations about difference, diversity, and a changing society can take place. Future teachers need a space where it is safe for them to examine fears about changing communities, children who look and are different, and visions about a future that may seem both different and threatening. While it is tempting for both teacher educators and teachers to focus exclusively on pedagogies and practices, we argue that a deep understanding and exploration of the place in society of children who require new practices and pedagogies is fundamental and essential. Numbers matter for many reasons. They help us begin to understand emerging changes, existing misconceptions, and the choices we must make if we are to avoid educational failure for a very large number of immigrant-origin Americans.

Notes

1. Language Use, English Ability, and Linguistic Isolation data were collected in the 2000, 1990, and 1980 decennial censuses using a three-part series of questions:

   A. Does this person speak a language other than English at home?
   (For those who speak another language)
   B. What is this language? _____
   C. How well does this person speak English?—very well, well, not well, not at all.

   (US Census Bureau, 2000)

2. Households considered to be "linguistically isolated" by the US Census are those households where no person aged 14 or over speaks only English at home or speaks English "very well" in addition to another language. Any person living in such a household is classified as linguistically isolated, including children under 14 years of age, even though they themselves may be English monolinguals.

3. We use the term "English language learner" unless reporting on publications that explicitly used the term "limited English proficient" students.

4. The National Assessment of Educational Progress (NAEP) is a test administered to a random sample of all students at ages nine, thirteen, and seventeen. NAEP was designed, not as a measure to hold local schools accountable but simply as a yardstick that is often referred to as the "Nation's Report Card."

5. Lee (2006) and Ngo and Lee (2007) argue that the stereotype of Asians as model minorities underestimates the differences among these students, and results in their needs not being met by educators who assume that they need little support.

References

Abedi, J. (2007). English language proficiency assessment and accountability under NCLB Title III: An overview. In *English language proficiency assessment in the nation: Current status and future practice* (chapter 1). Davis, CA: University of California. Retrieved June 8, 2008, from http://education.ucdavis.edu/research/ELP_Report.pdf.

Abedi, J., & Dietel, R. (2004). *Policy brief 7: Challenges in the No Child Left Behind Act for English language learners.* National Center for Research on Evaluation Standards and Student Testing (CRESST)/UCLA. Retrieved from www.cse.ucla.edu/products/policy/cresst_policy7.pdf.

August, D., & Hakuta, K. (1997). Student assessment. In D. August & K. Hakuta (Eds.), *Improving schooling for minority language children* (pp. 113–131). Washington, D.C.: National Academy Press.

Batalova, J., Fix, M., & Murray, J. (2007). Measures of change: The demography and literacy of adolescent English learners: A report to the Carnegie Corporation of New York. Washington, D.C.: Migration Policy Institute.

Bendixsen, S., & Guchteneire, P. (2004). *Best practices in immigration services planning.* New York: UNESCO. Retrieved from www.unesco.org/most/migration/article_bpimm.htm.

Bransford, J., Darling-Hammond, L., & LePage, P. (2005). Introduction. In L. Darling-Hammond & J. Bransford (Eds.), *Preparing teachers for a changing world* (pp. 1–39). San Francisco: Jossey-Bass.

Capps, R., Fix, M., Murray, J., Ost, J., Herwantoro, S., Zimmerman, W., et al. (2004). *Promise or peril: Immigrants, LEP students and the No Child Left Behind Act.* Washington, D.C.: The Urban Institute.

Capps, R., Fix, M., Murray, J., Ost, J., Passel, J.S., & Herwantoro, S. (2005). *The new demography of America's schools: Immigration and the No Child Left Behind Act.* Washington, D.C.: The Urban Institute.

Consentino de Cohen, C., & Clewell, B.C. (2007). *Putting English language learners on the educational map: The No Child Left Behind Act Implemented.* Washington, D.C.: The Urban Institute.

Fry, R. (2007a). *The changing racial and ethnic composition of U.S. public schools.* Washington, D.C.: Pew Hispanic Center.

Fry, R. (2007b). *How far behind in math and reading are English language learners?* Washington, D.C.: Pew Hispanic Center.

Hakimzadeh, S., & Cohn, D.V. (2007). *English usage among Hispanics in the United States.* Washington, D.C.: Pew Hispanic Center.

Huntington, S.P. (2004). *Who are we? The challenges to America's national identity.* New York: Simon & Schuster.

KewalRamani, A., Gilbertson, L., Fox, M.A., & Provasnik, S. (2007). *Status and trends in the education of racial and ethnic minorities.* Washington, D.C.: Institute for Educational Sciences. National Center for Education Statistics.

Kiang, P.N.-C. (2006). Policy challenges for Asian Americans and Pacific Islanders in education. *Race, Ethnicity and Education, 9*(1), 103–115.

Lee, S. (2006). Additional complexities: Social class, ethnicity, generation and gender in Asian American student experiences. *Race, Ethnicity and Education, 9*(1), 17–28.

Migration Policy Institute. (2007). *Ten source countries with the largest populations in the United States as percentages of the total foreign-born population, 1960.* Washington, D.C.: Author. Retrieved from www.migrationinformation.org/datahub/charts/10.60.shtml.

National Clearinghouse for English Language Acquisition. (n.d.). *NCELA FastFaqs.* Retrieved from www.ncela.gwu.edu/.

Ngo, B., & Lee, S. (2007). Complicating the image of model minority success: A review of Southeast Asian American education. *Review of Educational Research, 77*(4), 415–453.

Persell, C.H. (1977). *Education and inequality: The roots and results of stratification in America's schools.* New York: The Free Press.

Pew Hispanic Center. (2008). *Statistical portrait of the foreign-born population of the United States, 2006* [Electronic Version]. Washington, D.C.: Pew Research Center. Retrieved from http://pewhispanic.org/factsheets/factsheet.php?FactsheetID=36.

Shin, H.B., & Bruno, R. (2003). *Language use and English-speaking ability: 2000. Census 2000 Brief.* Washington, D.C.: US Census Bureau.

Short, D., & Fitzsimmons, S. (2007). *Double the work: Challenges and solutions to acquiring language and academic literacy for adolescent English language learners— A report to Carnegie Corporation of New York.* Washington, D.C.: Alliance for Excellent Education.

Solano-Flores, G. (2008). Who is given tests in what language by whom, when and where? The need for probabilistic view of language in the testing of English language learners. *Educational Researcher, 37*(4), 189–199.

Solórzano, R.W. (2008). High stakes testing: Issues, implications, and remedies for English language learners. *Review of Educational Research, 78*(2), 260–329.

Terrazas, A., Batalova, J., & Fan, V. (2007). *Frequently requested statistics on immigrants in the United States.* Washington, D.C.: Migration Policy Institute. Retrieved from www.migrationinformation.org/USfocus/display.cfm?id=649.

Tyack, D. (2003). *Seeking common ground: Public schools in a diverse society.* Cambridge, MA: Harvard University Press.

U.S. Census Bureau. (2000). *Twenty languages most frequently spoken at home by English ability for the population 5 years and over: 1990 and 2000.* Retrieved from www.census.gov/prod/2003pubs/c2kbr-29.pdf.

U.S. Census Bureau. (2007). *The American community—Hispanics 2004 American Community Survey Reports.* Washington, D.C.: Author.

Chapter 3

Preparing Classroom Teachers for English Language Learners

The Policy Context

Ana María Villegas and Tamara Lucas

The rapidly growing number of students in U.S. schools who speak languages other than English at home and their increasing inclusion in mainstream classrooms is raising urgent questions, not only about the type of schooling provided to them, but also about how mainstream classroom teachers are and should be prepared to educate them. Normative questions such as the latter are of special interest to policy-makers responsible for establishing guidelines and requirements for the preparation of teachers in U.S. schools. While the relationship between policy and practice is always indirect, policies do have major—if sometimes unanticipated—consequences. For that reason, an examination of the policy context is an essential part of the foundation for understanding the preparation of teachers for teaching English language learners (ELLs).

Consistent with the notion that dimensions of policy are like layers of an onion to be peeled away (Ricento & Hornberger, 1996), we view policy-making as a complex phenomenon with inter-related levels influencing each other in often unanticipated ways. Local implementation rarely mirrors the vision of those who conceive policy at national or state levels; policies inevitably evolve as they are interpreted and implemented both across bureaucratic boundaries and over time. When they conflict with the values and beliefs of those charged with implementing them, policies may not be implemented at all. The application of language-related policies is especially likely to be shaped by school-based educators, given the deeply entrenched attitudes toward languages other than English within local communities in the United States (Varghese & Stritikus, 2005).

The conception, design, and implementation of policies related to the preparation of classroom teachers for teaching ELLs are greatly influenced by the prevailing demographic and political contexts, as well as by other policies and practices related to teacher certification and to the K-12 education of language minority students. Even when policies are in place, teacher educators may not have the knowledge of ELL education needed to implement them effectively. The task of understanding this multifaceted policy domain is made even more complex by the fact that, "because human society is constituted of, by, and through language, all acts and actions mediated by language are opportunities for the implicit (or explicit) expression of language policies" (Ricento & Horngerber, 1996, p. 420). Further complicating an analysis of teacher education policy is the variability in the nature and quality of teacher education programs and the typical lack of coherence across such programs (Darling-Hammond, Pacheco, Michelli, LePage, & Hammerness, 2005).

We cannot hope to fully explore the multitude of dimensions or influences on policy here. Our approach in this chapter is to examine the role played by the policy context in intensifying the need to prepare teachers to teach ELLs and the influence of existing policies on the nature and extent of that preparation. We briefly discuss relevant aspects of the demographic landscape, the political climate, and the national policy context that constitute the larger environment within which teacher education policies are situated. We then examine particular national and state policies that directly and indirectly influence the preparation of mainstream teachers for teaching ELLs. We conclude with recommendations for policy and research based on our analysis of the realities of the policy context and of teacher education.

The Demographic Landscape

The demographic factor of primary relevance to our analysis is the increasing number of speakers of languages other than English in the United States. Because much has been written about changing demographics in the U.S., it is easy to become inured to reports of the rapidly growing proportion of students learning English as a second (or third) language. But the changes in this population are already having a major impact on schools and teachers across the country, even in many areas that have historically been monolingual and had few immigrants (*Education Week*, 2009; Fix & Capps, 2005). The rising numbers of ELLs, along with the prevailing trend to minimize the time ELLs spend in special language-related classes and programs, have given classroom teachers increasing responsibility for educating students they might not have had in their classes in decades past (Evans & Hornberger, 2004; Freeman & Riley, 2005).

Between 1979 and 2004, the proportion of five-to-seventeen-year-olds in the U.S. who spoke a language other than English at home increased from 9% to 19% (3.8 to 9.9 million) (U.S. Department of Education, 2006). The proportion who spoke English with difficulty increased from 3% (1.3 million) to 5% (2.8 million). This 15-year period saw a 162% increase in the number of young people who spoke a language other than English at home, compared to just an 18% increase in the total number of school-age children and youth. While most ELLs continue to be concentrated in a few states, a "new diaspora" is occurring through which immigrants are moving to many areas where they have not lived in great numbers in the past (Fix & Capps, 2005). Between 1995 and 2005, the states with more than 200% growth in ELL enrollment were Alabama, Arkansas, Colorado, Georgia, Indiana, Kentucky, Nebraska, North Carolina, Tennessee, and Virginia (Maxwell, 2009). Compared to states with a long history of ELLs (e.g., California, Texas, Florida, Illinois, New York, New Jersey), these states have fewer teachers and other educators with expertise in the education of ELLs, and fewer options for placing ELLs in special language-related classes or programs.

Speaking a language other than English is often equated with being an immigrant, leading to the assumption that the majority of speakers of home languages other than English in the U.S. are immigrants. However, the opposite is true. According to the 2000 Census, 76% of limited English proficient (LEP) students in elementary schools and 56% of secondary LEP students were born in the U.S. (Fix & Capps, 2005). These data clearly show that ELLs are not temporary visitors but are in fact "American" students, part of the fabric of "mainstream" schools and classrooms.

The Political Climate

The political context plays an integral role in all education policies, no less so in teacher preparation. As Darling-Hammond et al. (2005) point out, "standards for accreditation, licensing, and certification [in teacher education] are substantially governed by political bodies rather than by the profession itself" (p. 451). Politicization is intensified for issues regarding the education of ELLs (and their teachers) because of the always volatile debates about immigration and prevalent negative attitudes toward languages other than English.

Despite the fact that the United States is largely a country of immigrants, a sizeable segment of the U.S.-born population has long been unwelcoming to new immigrants. Throughout the history of the U.S., efforts have been made to restrict immigrants' rights and access to jobs and benefits (Crawford, 1992). The fear of outsiders increased after the events of September 11, 2001, and in recent years immigration has become an increasingly prominent political issue. Several recent presidents have attempted to reform immigration laws, so far to no avail. Between 2005 and 2009, more than one unsuccessful attempt was made to pass a bill to establish a guest worker program for undocumented immigrants. The only immigrant bill that passed Congress in those years, however, was the bill ordering construction of a 670-mile-long fence along the U.S.–Mexico border (see Archbold & Preston, 2008). Thus, the hard-line anti-immigrant forces prevailed, and federal and state governments took measures to curb "illegal" immigration and to deport undocumented immigrants (*New York Times*, 2009).

Attitudes toward immigrants are integrally related to attitudes toward languages other than English inside and outside schools (Crawford, 1992, 2000; Evans & Hornberger, 2004). The modern English-only movement that began in the early 1980s has been closely associated with the movement to restrict immigration. Crawford (2000) points out that, while the lobbying organization

"U.S. English" has repeatedly denied a connection, it has in fact shared several key staff members with the restrictionist Federation for American Immigrant Reform (FAIR), including a common founder and chairman. Crawford concludes that the "covert agenda" of U.S. English is "to resist racial and cultural diversity in the United States" (p. 23), using language as an acceptable issue through which to highlight the presumed threat from large numbers of immigrants.

The close connection between attitudes toward language and attitudes toward race and ethnicity is also reflected in the differential perceptions of U.S.-born European-Americans who are fluent in English and another language, on the one hand, and people of other ethnic backgrounds who are fluent in English and a home language other than English, on the other hand (Lo Bianco, 2004; Macedo, Dendrinos, & Gounari, 2003). "The bilingualism of immigrants and poor people [in the U.S.] is often construed as a major social problem threatening national cohesion and endangering security," while fluency in more than one language among "elites" is "an esteemed accomplishment ... and a resource for advancing national security" (Lo Bianco, 2004, p. 22). In fact, there is considerable irony in the fact that, after 9–11, the federal government called for more Americans to fulfill their "patriotic duty" to become fluent in other languages while simultaneously enacting policy that led to the demise of the Bilingual Education Act (Lo Bianco, 2004, p. 19).

As this discussion suggests, policies restricting language use generally have their roots in concerns that are not linguistic or educational, but political—particularly worries about the impact of "outsiders" (Ricento & Hornberger, 1996). The persistent myth that immigrants—especially those who speak Spanish—do not want to learn English (Evans & Hornberger, 2004) has bolstered political support for an exclusive focus on English proficiency in schools and a turn away from support for the development of proficiency in other languages as well as English. These moves have important implications for teacher preparation—by reducing the number of bilingual programs and therefore teachers, by increasing the number of ELLs in mainstream classes, and by subtly fostering a resistance to providing "special treatment" for ELLs.

No Child Left Behind and the Inclusion of ELLs in Mainstream Classrooms

In 2002, the U.S. Department of Education's Office of Bilingual Education and Minority Languages Affairs (OBEMLA) became the Office of English Language Acquisition (OELA). This new title was indicative of a sea change in federal policies regarding the education of English language learners in U.S. schools implemented during the G.W. Bush Administration. Some elements of this shift had begun in the previous two Administrations, including a greater focus on standards, assessment, and accountability. But the passage of the No Child Left Behind (NCLB) Act in 2002 made a number of far-reaching changes in policies for the education of ELLs that have led to more inclusion of ELLs in mainstream classes and therefore a greater need for all teachers to be prepared to teach them. It can be argued that NCLB has had a positive impact on the education of ELLs in that, by requiring their test scores to be disaggregated and reported with all other students' scores, it gives them increased attention (Evans & Hornberger, 2004). However, a number of NCLB provisions have been problematic for ELL education.

One of the key changes was NCLB's exclusive focus on English language development and complete silence on the use and development of other languages in schools. The legislation replaced by NCLB (the 1994 Improving America's Schools Act) gave extensive attention not only to English language development but also to the use of ELLs' home languages to give them access to academic content in a language they could understand. The 1994 Act incorporated *Title VII: Bilingual Education, Language Enhancement, and Language Acquisition Programs*, first instituted in 1968, which officially acknowledged the inherent inequity in placing "limited English proficient" students in mainstream classes if no accommodations were made to give them access to the curriculum. In NCLB, Title VII was replaced by *Title III: Language Instruction for Limited English Proficient and Immigrant Students*. While instruction in languages other than English is not explicitly prohibited in NCLB, the word "bilingual" does not appear in the Act (Crawford, 2008); "English language development is taken as the *sine qua non* of academic achievement" and students' home languages are not given a role in their education, as they were in the 1994 Act (Evans & Hornberger, 2004, p. 89). In effect, NCLB makes the rapid development of English proficiency the most important goal for ELLs— apparently more important than developing content knowledge or academic skills (Ardila-Rey, 2008).

The timeframes established by NCLB have also had an impact on ELL education. NCLB allows a shorter time for ELLs to learn English before entering mainstream classes. While the previous legislation imposed no limit on the time ELLs could remain in bilingual or ESL programs, NCLB allows a maximum of three years, thus providing less access to academic content taught in a language students can understand or through special instructional approaches for ELLs. It also allows less time before ELLs must take the same standardized tests as non-ELLs, requiring them to take those tests in English after they have been in U.S. schools for three or more years. One of the ironies of this requirement is that, while NCLB defines limited English proficient (LEP) students as those whose "difficulties" with English do not allow them to reach the proficient level on state assessments (Title IX, Section 9101), it requires LEP students to take those tests after three years whether they are deemed to have sufficiently overcome those difficulties or not (Wright, 2006). Another irony is that, despite the nominally greater emphasis on "scientifically-based research" in NCLB, it ignores years of research showing that ELLs require seven to ten years to develop academic proficiency in English equivalent to native English speakers (Cummins, 2008; Evans & Hornberger, 2004; Thomas & Collier, 2002). While the above changes have reduced the number of students who become long-term residents of programs originally intended to prepare them for the mainstream, the short time allowed before leaving special programs and before taking standardized tests assumes a homogeneity in ELL learning that is not consistent with knowledge from research or practice about how long it takes ELLs to become proficient at academic English (Harper, de Jong, & Platt, 2008).

Another change in national policy with implications for the education of ELLs and of their teachers is the NCLB requirement related to "highly qualified teachers" (HQTs). NCLB defines HQTs primarily according to their knowledge of content in the core curriculum subjects (Title IX, Section 9101). It does not mention language or culture in delineating knowledge and skills of HQTs and does not require ESL teachers to be "highly qualified" because ESL is not a core subject (Ardila-Rey, 2008; Harper et al., 2008). Thus, the linguistic and cultural knowledge, skills, and dispositions for teaching ELLs, as well as the expertise of ESL teachers for making content more accessible to ELLs, are accorded marginal status, as school districts focus on meeting the HQT subject area requirements for teachers. This marginalization sends the message that teachers need little special expertise for teaching ELLs, suggesting that instructional approaches to teaching ELLs can be reduced to the application of a simple set of instructional modifications (Harper et al., 2008). This perspective, in turn, contributes to the belief that teaching ELLs is "just good teaching" (de Jong & Harper, 2005, 2007). To the extent that teacher educators hold this view, they are not likely to devote attention and resources to making modifications in teacher preparation to give teachers the depth and breadth of knowledge and skills they will really need to effectively differentiate instruction for ELLs.

The above changes in national policy have led to an emphasis on the inclusion of ELLs in mainstream classes taught by teachers without sufficient preparation to teach them well (Freeman & Riley, 2005; Lucas & Grinberg, 2008). Inclusion is the logical result of the reduced time ELLs can remain in ESL or bilingual programs, the fact that they must take standardized tests in English after three years, the silence of NCLB on teacher expertise in language and culture and its emphasis on core content knowledge, and the implication that teaching ELLs involves learning how to make simple instructional modifications. These policy shifts have resulted not only in greater numbers of ELLs in mainstream classes, but greater variability in their level of English proficiency and academic preparation, as students who would have remained in special language-related programs are now pushed more quickly into mainstream classes (Gándara, Maxwell-Jolly, & Driscoll, 2005). While the inclusion "megatrend" (Platt, Harper, & Mendoza, 2003, p. 112) may seem on the surface to be a move toward greater equity, it too often becomes a means of reducing resources spent on students with "special" needs and standardizing education for all students. It can, in fact, result in the exclusion of ELLs from full participation and success in school if their teachers are not well-prepared to understand their language- and content-related needs and to differentiate instruction for them. Harper and Platt (1998) suggest that before continuing toward greater inclusion of ELLs, educators should draw on the special education literature to develop clear criteria for successful inclusion. Until that happens, increasing numbers of classroom teachers will be expected to make important decisions about the nature and extent of ELL inclusion in mainstream classrooms without criteria or preparation to guide those decisions.

Policies of Relevance to the Preparation of Classroom Teachers to Teach ELLs

A host of policies have important direct and indirect influence on the preparation of classroom teachers to teach ELLs. These include accreditation requirements, professional standards, and state certification policies, which we discuss below.

Accreditation Requirements

While Federal legislation establishes policies and practices that must be followed by institutions and individuals, accreditation requirements are under the purview of the states. There is no universal accreditation requirement or process for teacher education, as there is for other professions (Darling-Hammond et al., 2005). Some states require all teacher education programs to be nationally accredited, while others require only state accreditation. If institutions seek national accreditation, they do so from one of two federally approved teacher education accrediting agencies: the National Council for the Accreditation of Teacher Education (NCATE) or the Teacher Education Accreditation Council (TEAC). Because an institution's curriculum and assessments must be designed to directly address the accrediting agency's standards, the accreditation process has a powerful influence on the knowledge, skills, and dispositions teacher candidates are expected to develop in their teacher preparation programs, including those for teaching ELLs.

Established in 1954, NCATE is the primary accrediting agency for teacher education programs in the U.S. NCATE reported the following information about its relationships with states and institutions in 2009 (www.ncate.org):

- 632 departments, colleges, and schools of education were accredited by NCATE.
- In 17 states, all teacher education programs were accredited by NCATE.
- In 49 states (all except Arizona), at least one program was accredited.

- In 28 states, the majority of teacher education programs were accredited by NCATE.
- 25 states have adopted or adapted NCATE standards for teacher education programs throughout the state, even though some do not require formal accreditation by NCATE.

To be NCATE accredited, institutions must provide evidence that they meet six standards related to: (1) Candidate knowledge, skills, and dispositions; (2) Assessment system and unit evaluation; (3) Field experiences and clinical practice; (4) Diversity; (5) Faculty qualifications, performance, and development; and (6) Unit governance and resources. In 2001, NCATE began requiring institutions to submit evidence of teacher candidate performance showing that they meet the performance-based criteria in Standard 1—that is, to submit outcome data for teacher candidates in addition to syllabi and other institutional documents showing program "inputs."

The NCATE mission asserts that, "NCATE believes every student deserves a caring, competent, and highly qualified teacher." The NCATE Standard relevant to the preparation of teachers of ELLs is number 4, Diversity: "The unit designs, implements, and evaluates curriculum and experiences for candidates to acquire and apply the knowledge, skills, and dispositions necessary to help all students learn." The explanations for three of the four components of Standard 4 refer to students from "diverse groups," and the explanation for the first component explicitly mentions English language learners: "Candidates learn to contextualize teaching and draw effectively on representations from the students' own experiences and cultures. They challenge students toward cognitive complexity and engage all students, *including English language learners* and students with exceptionalities, through instructional conversation" (emphasis added). The Supporting Explanation for Standard 4 as a whole, which includes three explicit references to language diversity, acknowledges that "many [students speak] native languages other than English," asserts that teacher candidates should learn about English language learners and language acquisition, and specifies that they should be aware of the potential for discrimination based on language.

As the above shows, NCATE leaves no doubt about the need for teacher candidates to be prepared for ELLs. By explicitly referring to English language learners, language acquisition, language discrimination, and students of diverse language groups in the rubrics and explanation for Standard 4, NCATE assures that ELLs will not be forgotten in NCATE-accredited teacher preparation programs. As with all policies, however, NCATE's references to ELLs in Standard 4 do not ensure the nature, quality, or extent of that preparation. Despite the explicit attention to ELLs in the NCATE Standards, it is still possible for institutions to be accredited by NCATE with minimal attention to ELLs.

The Teacher Education Accreditation Council (TEAC) was established in 1997 as an alternative to NCATE. The TEAC website listed 66 TEAC-accredited teacher education programs in July 2009 (www.teac.org/index.php/membership/teac-members/). The primary goal of TEAC is very similar to that of NCATE: "TEAC's goal is to support the preparation of competent, caring, and qualified professional educators" (www.teac.org). TEAC requires evidence that institutions meet three Quality Principles for Teacher Education Programs: (1) Evidence of student learning, (2) Valid assessment of student learning, and (3) Institutional learning. An institution seeking TEAC accreditation conducts a self-study and then submits an Inquiry Brief that provides "evidence that it produces graduates who are competent, caring, and qualified educators, and that the program has the capacity to offer quality" (www.teac.org/wp-content/uploads/2009/03/iboverview-27.pdf). TEAC then determines whether the evidence is sufficient to show that the program meets TEAC's principles. TEAC does not specify the nature of the evidence to be presented, but states that, "The *Inquiry Brief* is based primarily on existing documents, such as reports of ongoing inquiry, other accrediting and state review reports, and institutional research and publications" (www.teac.org/wp-content/uploads/2009/03/ibcontent-28–31.pdf).

In contrast to NCATE, TEAC does not explicitly mention language, language acquisition, or ELLs anywhere in its Quality Principles. There are some general references to diversity and multiculturalism in Quality Principle 1, which requires evidence that teacher candidates "learn how to convert their knowledge of subject matter into compelling lessons that meet the needs of a wide range of students." "Multicultural Perspectives and Understandings" is one of the Cross-Cutting Dimensions of Principle 1, but there is no reference to language or ELLs in the explanatory material.

These two teacher education accrediting agencies play an important policy role, influencing the content and processes of teacher preparation in the institutions they accredit and contributing to the thinking in the field more broadly. There is ongoing debate among teacher education practitioners, researchers, and policy-makers about the merits of these two processes of accreditation. These debates and the charged political nature of accreditation led the NCATE and TEAC Boards to approve a resolution in 2009 to form one unified national accrediting agency that will offer institutions "a choice of comparable pathways to accreditation" (www.ncate.org/public/062509_NCA-TETEAC.asp). It is still to be seen how the outcome of that merger will affect the attention given in the accreditation process to preparing teachers to teach ELLs. Currently, there is a marked difference in the attention given by TEAC as compared to NCATE. Our analysis shows that NCATE requires institutions to give attention to ELLs in teacher preparation while TEAC is completely silent with regard to such preparation. It would appear institutions can be accredited by TEAC without devoting any attention at all to preparing classroom teachers to teach ELLs. If, in the future, the field is guided by the

TEAC Quality Principles, it is likely that classroom teachers will continue to complete their teacher preparation programs woefully unprepared to teach students who speak languages other than English.

Professional Association Standards and Position Statements

While NCATE and TEAC accredit teacher education programs at the institutional level, professional associations have developed standards, principles, and position statements that guide the development of discipline-specific programs within larger teacher preparation programs. NCATE has formal relationships with many of these professional associations, and most NCATE-accredited institutions require their individual programs to be "recognized" by the relevant association. Through formal agreements, NCATE conducts the review of programs for purposes of NCATE accreditation and state program approval in 29 states. Because professional associations play important leadership roles in their disciplines, their standards and other documents are influential, even for institutions not seeking formal recognition for their programs.

Some of these organizations require programs seeking formal recognition to give attention to preparing teachers to teach ELLs (Ardila-Rey, 2008). We examined the standards and accompanying explanatory texts of six key disciplinary associations for explicit references to teaching ELLs: Association for Childhood Education International (ACEI), International Reading Association (IRA), National Council for the Social Studies (NCSS), National Council of Teachers of English (NCTE), National Council of Teachers of Mathematics (NCTM), and National Science Teachers Association (NSTA). All except NCSS include some reference to preparing teachers with knowledge and/or skills for teaching ELLs. Because of the explicit focus of language in elementary education, reading, and English, ACEI, IRA, and NCTE include more explicit texts about ELLs than the others, but even those give relatively little attention to teaching ELLs within the disciplines. Most of the references in these standards include linguistic diversity in a list of other types of diversity to be addressed—for example, "Candidates create and sustain learning environments that promote respect for, and support of, individual differences of ethnicity, race, language, culture, gender and ability" (NCTE, Grades 7–12, Standard 4.4).

Beyond standards, some professional associations have issued position statements or resolutions explicitly addressing the teaching of ELLs. For instance, IRA (2001), NAEYC (1995), NCTE (2006), and NCTM (2008) have formal position statements articulating key issues facing teachers of ELLs in their disciplines and offering guidelines and suggestions for teachers and teacher preparation. NCTM also refers explicitly to ELLs in two Principles that guide the teaching of mathematics: The Equity Principle and The

Assessment Principle (see http://standards.nctm.org/document/chapter2/). These documents present more powerful statements about the need to prepare teachers in these disciplines to teach ELLs than do the associations' standards.

The largest professional association for teacher educators, the American Association of Colleges for Teacher Education (AACTE), has also weighed in on the need for all teachers to have the knowledge and skills necessary for teaching linguistic minority students well. AACTE issued a policy statement on preparing teachers for cultural and linguistic diversity (2002) and a resolution on preparing teachers for second language learners (initiated in 2001 and revised in 2006) (see www.aacte.org/?/About-Us/Governance-/-Structure/resolutions.html#53). Both articulate the need for teacher education programs to respond to the linguistic needs of ELLs. The policy document specifies that teacher preparation and professional development should help teachers learn about second language acquisition, "the realities of negotiating academic instruction in another language" (p. 6), the role of native language in academic success and English acquisition, and the distinction between social and academic language proficiency. It further recommends field experiences that give prospective teachers opportunities to observe and support language acquisition and literacy development in a second language. AACTE also sponsored the publication of a book focused on the preparation of teachers for linguistically and culturally diverse students, including but not limited to ELLs (see Brisk, 2008).

State-Level Teacher Education Policy

Besides specifying requirements governing the formal accreditation of teacher education programs, states also prescribe many of the particulars of the content, organization, and administration of teacher education through Administrative Codes and other documents (including teacher certification and teacher education program regulations). State licensure and programmatic requirements can serve as powerful "policy levers" to push teacher education programs to do what is necessary to provide well-prepared teachers for ELLs (Feldman, 2002, p. 117).

Some states have explicit policies regarding the preparation of classroom teachers to teach ELLs, but because of the decentralized nature of education policy and the dense language of Administrative Codes and policies, it is difficult to identify relevant state policies, and even more difficult to discern which are strictly enforced. Stevens (2008) examined secondary teacher certification requirements in each state regarding content area literacy, linguistics, and bilingualism/teaching English as a second language—areas which she argued are likely to offer opportunities for addressing instruction for ELLs. She found that 31 states require some or all teacher candidates to take courses in and/or demonstrate competency in content area literacy. While this expertise is important for all teachers, it is not safe to assume that learning about content area literacy necessarily involves learning about teaching ELLs. She also found that five states (Louisiana, Mississippi, Missouri, Pennsylvania, and Vermont) require teacher candidates to take a linguistics course, and four states (Arizona, California, Minnesota, and New York) require "knowledge of the needs of linguistically diverse students for all of their teachers" (p. 322). According to *Education Week's Quality Counts 2009*, 33 states have standards that describe what teachers should know and be able to do to instruct ELL students, although only three states (Arizona, Florida, and New York) require all prospective teachers to demonstrate competence in ELL instruction. It is difficult to tell from these mixed findings how much, if any, preparation related to teaching ELLs most teachers in U.S. schools are likely to have.

In an attempt to further clarify state policies regarding teacher knowledge and skills for teaching ELLs, we examined three other secondary sources.[1] Our analysis of these documents indicates that 39 states have formal policies specifying that teachers should be prepared (and teacher education programs should prepare them) to teach ELLs, and the other 11 do not. For some of those states, these policies derive solely or largely from an association with NCATE and the requirement to meet NCATE Standard 4 (including 12 of the 17 states that did not report having standards regarding ELL instruction in the *Education Week Quality Counts* survey referred to above). According to the information examined, 21 states require or strongly encourage all teacher education programs to seek accreditation through NCATE. In some of these, all programs must use NCATE standards even though they are not required to achieve NCATE accreditation. The remaining 18 states have other policies (in addition to or instead of NCATE Standard 4) regarding what teachers need to know and be able to do to teach ELLs. In a few states, these policies are elaborately described; in most there is simply a passing mention of linguistic diversity and ELLs.

The information from these sources is somewhat more hopeful than Stevens' (2008) findings discussed above, but still far from sufficient to ensure well-prepared classroom teachers for ELLs. Given the complexity of the NCATE accreditation process, it is quite possible that an institution could be accredited even if it gives very little attention to ELLs in the teacher education curriculum. Furthermore, the great majority of references to ELLs in these documents are minimal and therefore superficial. Thus, preparing all candidates in teacher education programs to teach ELLs depends, to a large extent, on the commitment of the teacher educators at an institution to this student population and on their individual and collective knowledge and skills to do so.

The states with the most extensive requirements for preparation and professional development of mainstream teachers of ELLs are Florida, Arizona, and California[2] (see de Jong & Harper, this volume). These states require all pre-service and in-service teachers to demonstrate particular types of knowledge and skills for teaching ELLs. Arizona and Florida specify the number of required pre-service credit hours and in-service clock hours (www.ade.state. az.us/certification/downloads/SEIFacts.pdf; Florida Department of Education, n.d.), while in California the required content and skills are embedded or infused into existing courses in the teacher education curriculum (Cadiero-Kaplan & Rodriguez, 2008). Yet, while these state requirements send a clear message that educators must have special preparation for teaching ELLs, they still do not ensure that ELLs have the teachers they need. For example, despite a two-decade history of extensive and ever-evolving policies in California requiring that all teachers have knowledge and skills for teaching ELLs, large numbers of California teachers continue to lack the appropriate credential. Rumberger (2003) found that 25% of California teachers with ELLs were not fully certified in 2001–2002. In 2005, Esch et al. (2005) found that while 87% of teachers in California reported having ELLs in their classes, only 48% had the required English Learner Authorization. This situation shows that the presence of state policies does not ensure their full implementation.

Making Sense of the Policy Context for Preparing Teachers for ELLs

In this chapter, we have examined the impact of the demographic and political contexts and of federal policy enacted in the No Child Left Behind Act on the need to prepare all teachers to teach English language learners. We have also considered the more direct influence of national and state policies related to teacher education accreditation and teacher preparation. The picture that emerges is of a changing context within which it is increasingly essential for all classroom teachers to begin their careers with an openness to teaching ELLs, an assumption that it is their responsibility to teach ELLs, the beginning knowledge and skills for doing so, and the commitment to continuing to develop the needed expertise.

As we have seen, the principal theme that emerges from an examination of contextual factors is that demographics, prevailing political views, and federal policies have led inexorably toward the increasing inclusion of ELLs in mainstream classes. Greater inclusion, in turn, has led to more pressure to ensure that classroom teachers at all stages in their careers are ready to teach ELLs. This trend toward inclusion poses something of a dilemma for ELL advocates. On one hand, ELLs need access to challenging, engaging curriculum and instruction usually associated with mainstream educational opportunities, and they need opportunities to interact with and learn from native speakers of English. Otherwise, they are likely to remain segregated and marginalized in society as adults. On the other hand, while inclusion of ELLs is usually presented as being motivated by concern for the students (the desire to provide greater access and opportunity), the true motivation may be pragmatic (to reduce expenditures on special language-related programs) or ethnocentric (fear of racial, ethnic, and cultural diversification of the U.S.) (Crawford, 2000; Platt et al., 2003).

A good indicator of the true impetus for inclusion of ELLs in mainstream classes is whether policies are in place to explicitly require mainstream teachers to develop the depth and breadth of knowledge and skills for teaching ELLs well. If mainstream educators are prepared as linguistically responsive teachers (see Lucas & Villegas, this volume), inclusion is likely to be appropriate and beneficial for many ELLs. However, even in this situation, carefully articulated criteria are needed to determine which ELLs will and will not benefit from inclusion in mainstream classes. The literature suggests that, before they can benefit from inclusion, students with limited educational backgrounds and minimal English proficiency, migrant students, and those who have had traumatic experiences in their home countries are likely to need more time in special language-related programs than they receive under NCLB (Platt et al., 2003).

Our analysis of existing policies of accreditation agencies and professional associations, and of official state standards and requirements for teacher certification and preparation, revealed that many (though not all) of these entities recognize the presence of ELLs in schools and acknowledge the importance of preparing teachers to educate them. Policies in many professional organizations and states focus at least some attention on ELLs and linguistic diversity in the preparation of teachers. NCATE, in particular, plays an influential role in preparing all classroom teachers to teach ELLs because of its national reach and the fact that its accreditation standards include explicit guidelines for such preparation. However, with a few exceptions, existing policies are diffuse and superficial. If they refer explicitly to ELLs at all, policies tend to include ELLs in lists of diverse groups of students. If policies are to serve as powerful levers for institutional decision makers (Feldman, 2002), they need to focus directly on ELLs instead of including them as one group in a string of underserved student populations. Position statements can further elaborate on the commitment of organizations and institutions to educate ELLs and prepare teachers to educate them well.

From our analysis, it is clear that a systematic and comprehensive study of policy related to preparing classroom teachers to teach ELLs is sorely needed—first, to get an accurate account of existing policies for preparing teachers to teach ELLs and then to systematically synthesize those policies into useful and professionally supported guidelines. Our review revealed contradictory information from usually reliable sources, unclear distinctions among different types of policies (teacher certification requirements, regulations for teacher education institutions, state standards for teachers, professional standards for teachers of different disciplines), and conflicting requirements across different policy entities. The policy context for preparing teachers to teach ELLs, in other words, reflects the variability and lack of coherence across teacher education in general (Darling-Hammond et al., 2005). A comprehensive analysis of relevant policies is needed to develop a clear view of the path we are on and the path we should follow to ensure that all teachers enter their teaching careers with beginning knowledge and skills for teaching ELLs, and continue to build this type of expertise in developmentally appropriate ways throughout their careers.

As the previous statement suggests, the systematic study of relevant policies related to preparing teachers to teach ELLs we are calling for should be viewed through the lens of the teacher development continuum (Feiman-Nemser, 2001)—that is, the central tasks of pre-service teacher preparation, new teacher induction, and professional development of practicing teachers. Pre-service programs cannot carry the full responsibility for this preparation for a number of reasons, including constraints on the number of credits allowed in teacher education and the large body of knowledge and skills teachers need to develop, and the limitations inherent in learning about teaching ELLs for those with minimal experience (as adults) in schools and with speakers of other languages. An analysis that yields well-grounded recommendations regarding how to distribute the necessary learning across preservice programs (including liberal arts pre-requisites to formal teacher preparation), the induction years, and ongoing professional development is needed (Baca & Escamilla, 2002; Feldman, 2002; Gollnick, 2002). The results of such an analysis could have a major impact by laying out a realistic plan for all entities engaged in teacher preparation and professional development. A comprehensive policy recommendation would clarify what is essential and realistic at different stages along the teacher development path.

Our analysis has exposed the complex and sometimes contradictory influences on and repercussions of policy related to the preparation of classroom teachers for teaching ELLs in the United States. There are some promising signs that policy-makers and educational leaders recognize the necessity of such preparation. At the same time, it is clear that we have a long way to go to develop a vision that can guide the development of coherent, well-grounded policy and practice in this area and the will to enact that vision. We hope this analysis can contribute in some small way to that project.

Notes

1. (1) NCATE State Partnership Features—2009. (Retrieved from www.ncate.org/documents/stateRelations/NCATEStatePartFeatures2008.pdf); (2) Teacher Preparation State Policy Database: Preparation Program Requirements—Course Work Requirements Related to Diversity (2006–2007). (Education Commission of the States, National Comprehensive Center for Teacher Quality) (Retrieved from www.ecs.org/ecsmain.asp?page=/html/statesTerritories/state_map.htm?am=2); (3) Teacher Preparation State Policy Database: State Requirements for Accreditation of Teacher Education Institutions (2006–2007). (Education Commission of the States, National Comprehensive Center for Teacher Quality) (see previous website.)

   It was beyond the scope of this chapter to conduct a study of the details of policy for all 50 states or to examine the extent to which relevant policies are implemented.

2. This fact contradicts the *Education Week Quality Counts* survey, which indicates that CA teachers are not required to demonstrate competence in teaching ELLs. It appears that CA did not fully respond to the survey.

References

American Association of Colleges for Teacher Education, Committee on Multicultural Education. (2002). *Educators' preparation for cultural and linguistic diversity: A call to action*, March. Retrieved from www.aacte.org/Programs/Multicultural/cultural-linguistic.pdf.

Archbold, R.C., & Preston, J. (2008). Homeland security stands by its fence. *New York Times*, May 21. Retrieved from www.nytimes.com/2008/05/21/washington/21fence.html.

Ardila-Rey, A. (2008). Language, culture, policy, and standards in teacher preparation: Lessons from research and model practices addressing the needs of CLD children and their teachers. In M.E. Brisk (Ed.), *Language, culture, and community in teacher education* (pp. 331–351). New York, NY: Lawrence Erlbaum.

Baca, L., & Escamilla, K. (2002). Educating teachers about language. In C. Adger, C.E. Snow, & D. Christian (Eds.), *What teachers need to know about language* (pp. 71–83). Mahwah, NJ: Lawrence Erlbaum.

Brisk, M.E. (Ed.). (2008). *Language, culture, and community in teacher education.* New York, NY: Lawrence Erlbaum.

Cadiero-Kaplan, K., & Rodríguez, J.L. (2008). The preparation of highly qualified teachers of English language learners: Educational responsiveness for unmet needs. *Equity & Excellence in Education, 41*(3), 372–387.

Crawford, J. (1992). *Hold your tongue: Bilingualism and the politics of English-only.* Reading, MA: Addison-Wesley.

Crawford, J. (2000). *At war with diversity: U.S. language policy in an age of anxiety.* Cleveland, U.K.: Multilingual Matters.

Crawford, J. (2008). *Advocating for English learners: Selected essays.* Clevedon, U.K.: Multilingual Matters.

Cummins, J. (2008). BICS and CALP: Empirical and theoretical status of the distinction. In B. Street & N.H. Hornberger (Eds.), *Encyclopedia of language and education* (2nd ed.), *Volume 2: Literacy* (pp. 71–83). New York, NY: Springer Science + Business Media LLC.

Darling-Hammond, L., Pacheco, A., Michelli, N., LePage, P., & Hammerness, K. (2005). Implementing curriculum renewal in teacher education: Organizational and policy change. In L. Darling-Hammond & J. Bransford (Eds.), *Preparing teachers for a changing world: What teachers should learn and be able to do* (pp. 442–479). San Francisco, CA: Jossey-Bass.

de Jong, E.J., & Harper, C.A. (2005). Preparing mainstream teachers for English-language learners: Is being a good teacher good enough? *Teacher Education Quarterly, 32*(2), 101–124.

de Jong, E.J., & Harper, C.A. (2007). ESL is good teaching "plus." In M.E. Brisk (Ed.), *Language, culture, and community in teacher education* (pp. 127–148). New York, NY: Lawrence Erlbaum.

Education Week. (2009). Quality counts 2009: Portrait of a population. *Education Week, 28*(17).

Esch, C.E., Chang-Ross, C.M., Guha, R., Humphrey, D.C., Shields, P.M., Tiffany-Morales, J.D., Wechsler, M.E., & Woodworth, K.R. (2005). *The status of the teaching profession 2005.* Santa Cruz, CA: The Center for the Future of Teaching and Learning.

Evans, B.A., & Hornberger, N.H. (2004). No Child Left Behind: Repealing and unpeeling federal language education policy in the United States. *Language Policy, 4,* 87–106.

Feiman-Nemser, S. (2001). From preparation to practice: Designing a continuum to strengthen and sustain teaching. *Teachers College Record, 103*(6), 1013–1055.

Feldman, S. (2002). Preparing teachers to guide children's language development. In C. Adger, C.E. Snow, & D. Christian (Eds.), *What teachers need to know about language* (pp. 113–122). Mahwah, NJ: Lawrence Erlbaum.

Fix, M., & Capps, R. (2005). *Immigrant children, urban schools, and the No Child Left Behind Act.* Washington, D.C.: Migration Policy Institute. Retrieved from www.migrationinformation.org/Feature/display.cfm?id=347.

Florida Department of Education. (n.d.). *Bureau of Student Achievement Through Language Acquisition: Settlement agreement.* Retrieved from www.fldoe.org/aala/lulac.asp.

Freeman, D., & Riley, K. (2005). When the law goes local: One state's view on NCLB in practice. *Modern Language Journal, 89*(3), 264–268.

Gándara, P., Maxwell-Jolly, J., & Driscoll, A. (2005). *Listening to teachers of English language learners: A survey of California teachers' challenges, experiences, and professional development needs.* Santa Cruz, CA: The Center for the Future of Teaching and Learning.

Gollnick, D. (2002). Incorporating linguistic knowledge in standards for teacher performance. In C. Adger, C.E. Snow, & D. Christian (Eds.), *What teachers need to know about language* (pp. 103–112). Mahwah, NJ: Lawrence Erlbaum.

Harper, C., & Platt, E. (1998). Full inclusion for secondary school ESOL students: Some concerns from Florida. *TESOL Journal, 5*(7), 30–36.

Harper, C.A., de Jong, E.J., & Platt, E.J. (2008). Marginalizing English as a second language teacher expertise: The exclusionary consequences of *No Child Left Behind. Language Policy, 7,* 267–284.

International Reading Association. (2001). *Second-language literacy instruction: A position statement of the International Reading Association.* Newark, DE: Author.

Lo Bianco, J. (2004). Uncle Sam and Mr. Unz. *English Today, 20*(3), 16–22.

Lucas, T., & Grinberg, J. (2008). Responding to the linguistic reality of mainstream classrooms: Preparing all teachers to teach English language learners. In M. Cochran-Smith, S. Feiman-Nemser, & J. McIntyre (Eds.), *Handbook of research on teacher education: Enduring issues in changing contexts* (3rd ed., pp. 606–636). Mahwah, NJ: Lawrence Erlbaum.

Macedo, D., Dendrinos, B., & Gounari, P. (2003). *The hegemony of English.* Boulder, CO: Paradigm Publishers.

Maxwell, L.A. (2009). Shifting landscape: Immigration transforms communities. *Quality Counts 2009: Portrait of a Population. Education Week, 28*(17), 10.

National Association for the Education of Young Children. (1995). *Responding to linguistic and cultural diversity: Recommendations for effective early childhood education.* Washington, D.C.: Author.

National Council of Teachers of English. (2006). *NCTE position paper on the role of English teachers in educating English language learners (ELLs).* Urbana, IL: Author.

National Council of Teachers of Mathematics. (2008). *Teaching mathematics to English language learners: A position of the National Council of Teachers of Mathematics.* Retrieved from www.nctm.org/about/content.aspx?id=16135.

New York Times. (2009). Times topics: Immigration and emigration. Retrieved from http://topics.nytimes.com/top/reference/timestopics/subjects/i/immigration_and_refugees/index.html?inline=nyt-classifier.

Platt, E., Harper, C., & Mendoza, M.B. (2003). Dueling philosophies: Inclusion or separation for Florida's English language learners. *TESOL Quarterly, 37*(1), 105–133.

Ricento, T.K., & Hornberger, N.H. (1996). Unpeeling the onion: Language planning and policy and the ELT professional. *TESOL Quarterly, 30*(3), 401–427.

Rumberger, R.W. (2003). One quarter of California's teachers for English learners not fully certified. *UC LMRI EL Facts 3.* Retrieved from www.lmri.ucsb.edu/publications/elfacts-3.pdf.

Stevens, L.P. (2008). Educational policy and linguistic diversity: A critical analysis of teacher certification requirements. In M.E. Brisk (Ed.), *Language, culture, and community in teacher education* (pp. 315–330). New York, NY: Lawrence Erlbaum.

Thomas, W.P., & Collier, V.P. (2002). *A national study of school effectiveness for language minority students' long-term academic achievement.* University of California, Santa Cruz: Center for Research on Education, Diversity, and Excellence.

United States Department of Education. (2006). *The condition of education 2006.* Washington, D.C.: Author. Retrieved from http://nces.ed.gov/pubs2006/2006071.pdf.

Varghese, M.M., & Stritikus, T. (2005). "Nadie me dijo (Nobody told me)": Language policy negotiation and implications for teacher education. *Journal of Teacher Education, 56*(1), 73–87.

Wright, W.E. (2006). A catch-22 for language learners. *Educational Leadership, 64*(3), 22–27.

Part II

Developing Teacher Expertise for Educating English Language Learners

Chapter 4

A Framework for Preparing Linguistically Responsive Teachers

Tamara Lucas and Ana María Villegas

The experience of Melissa, a recent graduate of a well-established teacher education program, is all too familiar. When she completed her elementary teacher certification program, Melissa had a solid understanding of child development and learning theory and was prepared to organize the classroom to foster student learning and to use varied instructional approaches to teach academic content and skills. But she had had little opportunity to learn how to teach students who are learning English as a second (or third) language. While some of her instructors had mentioned ways to adapt particular activities for students with different needs, including English language learners (ELLs), she could not recall any class sessions that focused primarily on teaching ELLs. One student in the class where she did her student teaching was an English language learner, but the teacher felt unprepared to teach that student and had arranged to have him pulled out for ESL classes for a large portion of each day. Melissa noted that when the student was in the class he mostly sat by himself and seemed lost. When she discovered she had three ELLs in her first class as a new teacher, Melissa felt panic. She realized she was not at all prepared to design instruction to incorporate them into the classroom learning community. While some teacher education programs are taking concrete steps to prepare classroom teachers like Melissa to teach ELLs (Lucas & Grinberg, 2008; see also chapters 5–12 in this volume), most programs continue to give little if any attention to doing so.

This situation must change. Students who speak languages other than English are a growing presence in U.S. schools (see Valdés & Castellón, this volume). Between 1979 and 2003, the proportion of 5-to-17-year-olds in the United States speaking a language other than English increased by 161% (from 8.5% to 18.7%) (NCES, 2005). The enrollment of students with limited proficiency in English increased by 105% between 1990 and 2000, compared to a 12% overall enrollment increase (Kindler, 2002). ELLs are enrolled in classrooms across the United States—not just in coastal metropolitan areas historically home to immigrants. While some of these students are linguistically prepared to participate in mainstream classes, many continue to face challenges to learning in those contexts. Most classroom teachers, like Melissa, have had little or no preparation for providing the types of assistance ELLs need to successfully meet those challenges (Lucas & Grinberg, 2008; Zeichner, 2003).

While the increasing cultural diversity in schools has led teacher education programs to give heightened attention to preparing teachers to teach in ways that incorporate students' cultural backgrounds (e.g., Cochran-Smith, Davis, & Fries, 2004; Gay, 2000; Ladson-Billings, 1995; Villegas, 1991; Villegas & Lucas, 2002a, 2002b), for the most part these efforts give inadequate attention to educating students of linguistically diverse backgrounds. Programs typically treat language only peripherally as one of many aspects of culture (Lucas & Grinberg, 2008). While language and culture are interrelated in a number of ways, they are also distinct. Embedding the preparation of teachers to teach ELLs within broad efforts to prepare teachers for culturally diverse populations does not ensure that teachers can draw on students' linguistic resources and help them develop academic facility in English. To do so, teachers need specific language-related preparation.

In this chapter, we present a conception of linguistically responsive teaching that extends our framework for culturally responsive teaching (Villegas & Lucas, 2002a, 2002b, 2007). We have argued that to teach students of diverse cultural backgrounds well, teachers need to develop six qualities: sociocultural consciousness, affirming views of diversity, commitment and skills for promoting change in schools, understanding of how learners construct knowledge, skills for learning about their students, and ability to use appropriate instructional approaches for diverse students. In this chapter, we bring the notion of language from the periphery into the center of the discussion of teaching and, by extension, teacher preparation. We suggest a framework for preparing linguistically responsive teachers, articulating the special types of expertise needed for teaching ELLs.

Expertise of Linguistically Responsive Teachers

The expertise of linguistically responsive teachers is reflected in a set of orientations toward language and ELLs, and in particular language-related knowledge and skills (see Figure 4.1). By "orientations," we mean inclinations or tendencies toward particular ideas and actions, influenced by attitudes and beliefs (Richardson, 1996). By "knowledge and skills," we are referring to the complex and interconnected disciplinary knowledge, pedagogical content knowledge, knowledge of learners, and pedagogical skills needed by successful teachers.

Orientations of Linguistically Responsive Teachers

Sociolinguistic Consciousness

The first orientation in our framework of linguistically responsive teachers is sociolinguistic consciousness. Our conception of sociolinguistic consciousness entails (1) an understanding that language, culture, and identity are

I. Orientations of Linguistically Responsive Teachers

   1. Sociolinguistic consciousness:
      a. Understanding of the connection between language, culture, and identity
      b. Awareness of the sociopolitical dimensions of language use and language education

   2. Value for linguistic diversity

   3. Inclination to advocate for ELL students

II. Knowledge and Skills of Linguistically Responsive Teachers

   1. Learning about ELL students' language backgrounds, experiences, and proficiencies

   2. Identifying the language demands of classroom tasks

   3. Applying key principles of second language learning
      a. Conversational language proficiency is fundamentally different from academic language proficiency.
      b. ELLs need comprehensible input just beyond their current level of proficiency.
      c. Social interaction for authentic communicative purposes fosters ELL learning.
      d. Skills and concepts learned in the first language transfer to the second language.
      e. Anxiety about performing in a second language can interfere with learning.

   4. Scaffolding instruction to promote ELL students' learning

Figure 4.1 Qualities of Linguistically Responsive Teachers.

deeply interconnected, and (2) an awareness of the sociopolitical dimensions of language use and language education. (See Valdés & Castellón, and Gort, Glenn, & Settlage, this volume, for related discussions.)

    Language is the medium through which the norms and values of a cultural group are passed on from one generation to the next and are expressed. The language each of us speaks is therefore deeply entwined with our sense of identity and our affiliations with social and cultural groups (Valdés, Bunch, Snow, & Lee, 2005). This connection is evident, for example, when two speakers of Spanish or another language shift to their common mother tongue, even though both are fluent in English. It is also evident when speakers of "standard" English transition into their childhood dialects when they interact with family members. Language is also the primary medium through which we construct our personal identities in interaction with people in our lives as children. Lisa Delpit (1998) has powerfully described this dimension of language in discussing Ebonics:

> I can be neither for Ebonics nor against Ebonics any more than I can be for or against air. It exists. It is the language ... many of our African-American children ... heard as their mothers nursed them and changed their diapers and played peek-a-boo with them. It is the language through which they first encountered love, nurturance, and joy.
>
> (p. 17)

In the U.S. context, most adults who speak the language of the dominant social group—usually called Standard English—are unaware of the link between their identities and their language. They take the seamlessness of this connection for granted. Those whose mother tongue is a subordinated language or language variety, however, learn soon enough that their language is considered inferior (Baugh, 2005; Nieto, 2002). This realization can cause them considerable pain and anger since, as Delpit makes clear, our language is closely associated with people we care about and with whom we identify.

Miscommunication can result from cultural differences expressed through language (Wolfram, Adger, & Christian, 1999). An influential body of research in the 1970s and 1980s identified cross-cultural differences in communication and interaction patterns that can interfere with student learning, including approaches to story-telling, expectations about teacher–student interactions, and uses of literacy (Au, 1980; Heath, 1983; Michaels, 1981; Philips, 1972, 1983). In schools and classes where these differences are not understood, where students' "non-mainstream" linguistic backgrounds are ignored, or where teachers and other students denigrate non-English languages or treat them as inconsequential, students' "competing linguistic loyalties" (Baugh, 2005, p. 1143) come to the forefront. These feelings can result in students' silence and disengagement, or their distancing themselves from their home language, culture, and families in an effort to assimilate to mainstream norms.

Teachers sensitive to the connection between language and identity—teachers who understand that students' ways of expressing themselves and using language reflect cultural values and expectations—can learn not to make assumptions about students' intentions based on their own cultural frameworks (Price & Osborne, 2000; Valdés, 2001). They understand that students cannot simply leave their home languages and dialects behind as they develop facility with the language of school. They understand the importance of taking students' linguistic backgrounds into account in their instruction and can help ELLs become confidently bilingual and bicultural, rather than silent or alienated.

A second important aspect of sociolinguistic consciousness is awareness of the sociopolitical dimension of language—the understanding that no language or language variety is inherently better than another, and that the dominant position of a language or language variety within a particular social context derives solely from the power of the speakers of that language (Fasold, 1990). Language is intimately tied to its sociopolitical context. The languages of wealthy and powerful groups come to be seen as superior to the languages of poor and powerless groups (Dicker, 2006). Language discrimination, intentional or not, is one means for speakers of the dominant language in a particular sociopolitical context to maintain their privileged position (Nieto, 2002).

This sociopolitical dimension of language is reflected in historical and contemporary efforts to restrict the uses of languages other than English in schools (Crawford, 1992). The volatile debates regarding language policies ostensibly focus on language, but the underlying issues are power and privilege associated with speakers of particular languages (Nieto, 2002). Forbidding students to use their home languages for communication and learning is a way of structuring inequality into the educational system. Few students can hope to benefit maximally from school in that situation.

Sociolinguistically conscious teachers understand their students' experiences as speakers of subordinated languages and recognize that the challenges they face are partly political, extending beyond the cognitive difficulties of learning a second language (see Olsen, 1997). Such teachers are vigilant in reflecting on their assumptions about ELLs, and cognizant that their perceptions of language, language use, and language learning are shaped by their own and their students' socio-cultural positioning.

Value for Linguistic Diversity

The second fundamental orientation of linguistically responsive teachers is value for linguistic diversity. (See Villegas & Lucas, and Sakash & Rodriguez-Brown, this volume, for related discussions.) Teachers aware of the language–identity connection and the sociopolitical dimensions of language recognize the potential impact on students of their attitudes regarding students' languages and language proficiencies. Students are likely to interpret teachers' attitudes as indications of feelings about them and their families (Bartolomé, 2000). Teacher educators can foster positive attitudes toward ELLs by making it a priority to increase the racial, ethnic, and linguistic diversity of the teaching force; requiring foreign language and multicultural education courses; teaching future teachers about ESL instructional approaches; and selecting teacher candidates with international experiences and with bi-/multilingual communities in this country (see Byrnes, Kiger, & Manning, 1996, 1997; García-Nevarez, Stafford, & Arias, 2005; Marx, 2000; Reeves, 2006; Walker, Shafer, & Iiams, 2004). Educators argue that attitudes disrespectful or dismissive of students' languages can undermine the teacher–student relationship at the heart of learning (Nieto, 2000; Valdés, 2001). Exclusive focus on ELLs' imperfect English proficiency without acknowledging their proficiency in their home languages may make students reluctant to interact with or trust teachers.

Lack of value for and recognition of ELLs' linguistic resources may also translate into lowered expectations and unchallenging instructional practices (Villegas & Lucas, 2002a). Perceiving students as linguistically deficient, teachers are likely to ignore or marginalize them in class; provide them a simplified, unengaging curriculum emphasizing basic skills; and focus primarily on controlling their behavior. (Olsen (1997) and Valdés (2001) present powerful portraits illustrating how teacher values regarding language can impact their students.) On the other hand, when teachers show respect for and interest in students' home languages, they send a welcoming message. Even when teachers do not speak those languages, they can show their value for linguistic diversity by, for example, learning some basic greetings and social vocabulary in students' native languages; allowing students to use their native languages in class to support their learning of content; encouraging students to continue to develop literacy skills in their home languages; and advocating for language development support for ELLs (Hite & Evans, 2006; Lucas, Henze, & Donato, 1990; Lucas & Katz, 1994; Lucas, Villegas, & Freedson-Gonzalez, 2008; Mohr & Mohr, 2007).

Inclination to Advocate for ELL Students

The third fundamental orientation of linguistically responsive teachers is the inclination to advocate for ELLs. Advocacy involves actively working to improve one or more aspects of ELLs' educational experiences. (See Athaneses & de Oliveira, this volume, and de Oliveira & Athanases, 2007, for a discussion of how one program prepares teachers to be advocates for ELLs.) Important for all subordinated groups, advocating for greater equity is especially important for ELLs, who tend to be more marginalized and invisible than most other groups (Mohr & Mohr, 2007; Sharkey & Layzer, 2000) because they are both culturally and linguistically outside the mainstream. Equity for ELLs must be the explicit focus of advocacy efforts to ensure that language-related issues do not continue to be minimized or ignored.

Empathy for ELLs and a desire to take action to improve their education can grow out of an understanding of the sociopolitical dimensions of language and the common disregard for languages other than English in schools. Advocacy can occur in one classroom or an entire district or state; it can focus on one small aspect of the educational experiences of ELLs or on policies with far-reaching consequences. Advocacy can focus on any of an array of issues— including adapting instructional materials and teaching practices to meet ELL learning needs (de Oliveira & Athanases, 2007; Hite & Evans, 2006);

interrogating policies and the extent to which they perpetuate or challenge inequities (Varghese & Stritikus, 2005); or engaging ELLs' families and community members in the educational system (Lucas et al., 1990).

Knowledge and Skills of Linguistically Responsive Teachers

Learning About ELL Students' Language Backgrounds, Experiences, and Proficiencies

Linguistically responsive teachers recognize the importance of knowing ELLs as individuals and have a repertoire of strategies for learning about them. To successfully (re)present school knowledge, teachers need to help students make connections between their prior knowledge and experience and new ideas to be learned. They need to know about students' lives outside school, prior experiences with school subject matter, and community life (Villegas & Lucas, 2002a). For teaching ELLs, they also should know about their language backgrounds, experiences, and proficiencies. (See Brisk & Zisselsberger, and Gebhard, Willett, Jimenez, & Piedra, this volume, for case studies that draw on ELLs' language and academic backgrounds.)

Although ELLs are typically discussed (even in this chapter) as if they were a homogeneous group, they are not (see Valdés & Castellón, this volume). They enter U.S. schools with varying levels of oral proficiency and literacy in English and their native language as well as prior knowledge of and experiences with the subject matter. These factors affect their success in learning academic content in English. While oral, reading, and writing proficiencies in English play a major role in academic success (Gibbons, 2002), linguistic and academic competence in the primary language is also important and can serve as a rich resource for learning in a second language (Cummins, 2000). Students' prior educational experiences are also influential. Some ELLs enter U.S. schools with strong academic backgrounds from their native countries, while others have interrupted schooling or have attended schools in the U.S. or elsewhere that have failed to educate them well.

To anticipate aspects of learning tasks likely to be especially challenging for ELL students, linguistically responsive teachers learn about each student's language and academic background in English and the home language. They can learn about students' oral English proficiency by interacting with them one-on-one, listening carefully when they interact with others (Yedlin, 2007), and observing their interactions outside class (Verplaetse, 2008). Depending on a student's age and English proficiency, a teacher can ask him/her directly to describe, in writing or orally, previous experiences in school or ask the student's parents about those experiences. Bilingual adults who know the students—such as classroom aides—can provide information about their home language abilities (Lenski, Ehlers-Zavala, Daniel, & Sun-Irminger, 2006). The ESL teacher can be another source of information about students' proficiency in English since ELLs tend to be more outgoing and interactive in ESL classes than regular classes (Verplaetse, 2008). Teachers can develop even deeper insights into their students' lives, including language use, by visiting their homes and talking to family members (González, 2005). Linguistically responsive teachers use all viable methods to learn about their ELL students' language backgrounds, experiences, and proficiencies to better tailor instruction for them.

Identifying the Language Demands of Classroom Tasks

To promote language development as well as academic content and skills development, teachers of ELLs must also be able to analyze the linguistic demands of oral and written discourse (Cummins, 2000; Wong-Fillmore & Snow, 2005). This involves identifying key vocabulary, understanding the semantic and syntactic complexity of language used in written materials, and knowing specific ways students are expected to use language to complete each learning task. For instance, are students required to listen to a lecture and take notes from it? Are they being asked to read expository text and draw conclusions from the material read? If a written report is required, what form of text are students expected to produce? The more detailed teachers can be in their analysis, the better able they will be to identify aspects of tasks and texts that could interfere with ELLs' understanding. To develop the ability to do these kinds of analyses, future teachers can engage in varied learning activities across the teacher education curriculum focused on language—e.g., examining the linguistic features of written texts in their academic areas, considering the purposes for different language activities, and examining the features of academic English (Lucas et al., 2008; see also Brisk & Zisselsberger, Gebhard et al., and Walker & Stone, this volume). While these types of learning activities can be incorporated into teacher education courses, teacher candidates would be well served by taking a linguistics course designed especially for teachers where they would learn about language forms and functions and the fundamentals of linguistic analysis.

Applying Key Principles of Second Language Learning

In U.S. schools, students must be able to read, understand, and write academic English in different subjects; and understand and communicate in oral English. This connection between language and school success is especially significant for ELLs, who are learning English as a language while simultaneously learning academic content and skills through English. Linguistically responsive teachers understand the process of learning a second language and can apply this understanding in teaching ELLs. Elsewhere, we have identified principles of second language learning with special relevance to teachers (Lucas & Grinberg, 2008; Lucas et al., 2008). Here, we further refine our thinking, highlighting five key principles of second language learning, briefly discussed below. (See Walker & Stone, Gort et al., and Walqui, this volume, for relevant examples and discussions.)

Principle 1: Conversational language proficiency is fundamentally different from academic language proficiency. In everyday conversation, speakers gain meaning from cues in the setting (e.g., facial expressions, gestures) as well as from words. Because such conversations are often predictable and focus on the speakers' personal experiences, they are relatively accessible to ELLs. However, communication less connected to personal and shared experiences—including academic discourse—relies increasingly on language alone to convey meaning, becoming more impersonal, technical, and abstract (Gibbons, 2002). The use of written text, which makes meaning still more dependent on language, adds another layer of abstraction. Thus, academic language is particularly challenging for ELLs. Not only must they derive understanding solely from language itself, but also the purposes for using language (e.g., arguing a point, making hypotheses) and the language forms (e.g., passive voice, formal connecting words) differ from those in conversation. Given these factors, it is not surprising that second language learners take several years longer to develop fluency in academic English than in conversational English (Cummins, 2008). Linguistically responsive teachers understand the difference between conversational proficiency and academic language proficiency and are therefore better prepared to provide ELLs with support to successfully complete academic tasks.

Principle 2: ELLs need comprehensible input just beyond their current level of competence. While it may seem obvious, this principle is a reminder that the quality and nature of language to which ELLs are exposed—not just exposure itself—play important roles in their learning (Wong-Fillmore & Valadez, 1986). Classroom language should not be so challenging that ELLs cannot access it at all, but, at the same time, it should stretch them beyond their current proficiency (Krashen, 1982, 2003). In determining how to modify English to make it comprehensible and appropriately challenging to ELLs, teachers need to consider the linguistic demands of school texts and tasks, the strengths and weaknesses their students bring to the tasks, and principles of second language learning. They also need to be able to provide appropriate instructional scaffolding (see below, pp. 65–67).

Principle 3: Social interaction for authentic communicative purposes fosters ELL learning. Learning a second language requires more than linguistic input; it also requires direct and frequent interactions with people who are fluent in that language (Gass, 1997; Wong-Fillmore & Snow, 2005). Through the negotiation of meaning that occurs in interaction, ELLs gain access to comprehensible input and extend their productive capabilities (Ellis, 1985; Swain, 1995). As Gibbons (2002) explains, when working in groups ELLs are exposed to more language, have more language directed toward them, and produce more language than in whole-class interactions.

Linguistically responsive teachers organize their classes so that "language learners [are] in situations where they have access to rich and meaningful input and where they are motivated to produce output" (Trumbull & Farr, 2005, p. 124). They build in opportunities for ELLs to work with English-proficient, academically capable peers in groups of different configurations on academic tasks that require extensive language use. They ensure that ELLs actively participate in the interactions (Walqui, 2007, p. 114) in which they are seeking to achieve a purpose that has meaning for them (Chamot & O'Malley, 1996) and are involved in the negotiation of meaning, not just carrying out an exercise (Schleppegrell, 2004). Verplaeste (2008) advises teachers to use activities in which students must collaborate and to modify their talk to ask *how* and *why* questions, respond to student comments in non-evaluative ways, and use instructional conversations in which the teacher acts as a facilitator rather than a questioner.

Principle 4: Skills and concepts learned in the first language transfer to the second language. The politicization of the uses of languages other than English in schools has obscured the well-supported fact that proficiency in one's home language is a significant resource for learning a second language. ELLs with strong home language skills, especially literacy skills, tend to do better in English-language instruction than those with weak home language and literacy skills (Thomas & Collier, 2002). If a student is already literate in Spanish, for example, many of the skills developed in the process of learning to read and write in that language will support learning to read and write in English (e.g., sound–symbol correspondence, strategies for making sense of text) (Cummins, 2000). Similarly, students who are academically strong in their first language have a broad range of subject matter knowledge and skills to draw on while learning in a second language, thereby easing the burden of learning content and a new language simultaneously.

Linguistically responsive teachers build on ELLs' home language as a resource for learning rather than treating it as an obstacle. To give ELLs greater access to content, teachers encourage them to use books and other materials in their native language, and to interact with and help other students in their native language inside and outside class. They encourage students to develop their native language and literacy abilities, and emphasize the social and psychological value of bilingualism. They encourage ELLs' families to cultivate their children's native language skills through oral and written activities and interactions. They reach out to community members and agencies, engaging them in school activities and connecting them with students. Because of their understanding of the role of the home language in learning, linguistically responsive teachers are also prepared to discern whether problems stem from lack of literacy skills in the home language, learning difficulties unrelated to language, or simply the normal challenges of learning a second language.

Principle 5: Anxiety about performing in a second language can interfere with learning. U.S. schools are anxiety-provoking even for many well-prepared "mainstream" students. They are all the more stressful for ELLs. It is not uncommon for ELLs to feel stigmatized, anxious, unwelcome, and ignored in U.S. classrooms (see Olsen, 1997; Valdés, 2001)—feelings that can interfere with learning. Krashen (1982, 2003) offered a powerful metaphor, the affective filter, to explain how anxiety can interfere with language learning. According to this theory, when a language learner feels anxious, the affective filter prevents her/him from making optimal use of the language s/he is hearing or reading. Such anxiety can come from many sources—unfamiliarity with U.S. culture and the institution of schooling, feeling invisible and out of place, peer harassment and ostracism. To promote optimal learning of ELLs, teachers must be especially vigilant to minimize anxiety and provide a safe, welcoming classroom environment for ELLs.

Scaffolding Instruction to Promote ELL Students' Learning

The final element of our framework for linguistically responsive teaching is instructional scaffolding. Teachers who are socio-culturally conscious, value linguistic diversity, see themselves as advocates for ELLs, have a clear sense of their students' linguistic backgrounds and resources, understand the linguistic demands of classroom tasks, and can apply key principles of second language learning are well equipped to provide the types of instructional scaffolding essential for ELL learning of academic content and English. (See Gort et al., and Walqui, this volume, for relevant discussions.)

Scaffolding, widely recognized as fundamental to the teaching and learning of ELLs (Echevarria, Vogt, & Short, 2004; Gibbons, 2002; Schleppegrell, 2004; Verplaetse & Migliacci, 2008), is the instructional response to Vygotsky's (1978) theory of the zone of proximal development—that is, the metaphorical space in which a learner can accomplish, with the assistance of a more capable peer, tasks s/he could not accomplish alone. Scaffolding, in the form of temporary support, helps a learner carry out learning tasks beyond her/his current capability. The goal is to help the learner "move toward new skills, concepts, or levels of understanding" (Gibbons, 2002, p. 10) so the support can ultimately be removed. Scaffolding is, therefore, not remedial assistance that simplifies tasks and minimizes the challenge to the learner; instead, it is the means through which teachers "amplify and enrich the linguistic and extralinguistic context" of a learning task (Walqui, 2007, p. 107) to make it accessible to ELLs. There is a growing body of literature on ways to scaffold learning for ELLs to make English comprehensible (e.g., Echevarria et al., 2004; Gibbons, 2002; Hite & Evans, 2006; Lucas et al., 2008). Below, we highlight four types of instructional scaffolding—summarized in Figure 4.2—that can foster ELLs' learning. Linguistically responsive teachers consider which of these types of scaffolding would enhance their students' learning and plan instruction that incorporates the appropriate strategies.

1. *Use extra-linguistic supports*

   - Visual cues (pictures, illustrations, videos, slides, realia)
   - Graphic organizers (charts, graphs, timelines, semantic webs)
   - Hands-on activities (role playing, dramatizations, simulations, games)
   - Alternative assignments (drawing maps, charts, or graphs; doing picture presentations)

2. *Supplement and modify written text*

   - Study guides (lists of important vocabulary and outlines of major concepts to be studied)
   - Adapted text (reduced readability demands that remain faithful to the meaning of concepts)
   - Highlighted texts (highlight key vocabulary, central ideas, major concepts, summary statements)
   - Notes in the margins of the textbook
   - Summary of central ideas on the board, overhead, or LCD panel

3. *Supplement and modify oral language*

   - Minimize the use of idiomatic expressions
   - Translate key concepts into students' language
   - Explain difficult words and ideas
   - Provide outlines of lectures/lessons
   - Give examples
   - Pause more frequently and for longer periods of time
   - Build repetition and redundancy into instruction

4. *Provide clear and explicit instructions*

   - List procedures for completing a required task on paper or on the board
   - Ask students to repeat directions in their own words
   - Include all details in the instructions; do not take shortcuts

Figure 4.2 Instructional Scaffolding for ELLs.

Use extra-linguistic supports. Extra-linguistic supports can give ELLs access to academic content they might have difficulty understanding if they had to rely solely on language (Echevarria et al., 2004; Gibbons, 2002). Visual cues such as pictures, illustrations, videos, and objects convey information that might be unclear if conveyed without those supports. Graphic organizers such as charts and timelines help students to see relationships between ideas and events. Role-playing, dramatizations, and games bring content to life in ways that reading or hearing about it would not. Visuals can also serve as alternative ways to complete assignments that rely less heavily on language—e.g., drawing maps or illustrations, designing charts or graphs.

Supplement and modify written texts. Scaffolding can also involve supplementing and modifying challenging written language. Teachers can develop study guides that might include key questions, important vocabulary, and outlines of key concepts (Brown, 2007). They can highlight important ideas or add notes in textbook margins for ELLs or summarize key ideas on the board or overhead. Though more time-consuming, teachers can also rewrite portions of text to reduce the linguistic demands on students (Hite & Evans, 2006; Verplaetse & Migliacci, 2008).

Supplement and modify oral language. Several strategies can reduce the burden of having to process fast-moving oral language through which academic content is being conveyed. These include minimizing the use of idiomatic expressions (Hite & Evans, 2006), translating key concepts into students' native languages (Lucas & Katz, 1994; Yedlin, 2007), explaining difficult words and ideas, providing lesson outlines, giving examples to illustrate important or difficult ideas, pausing more frequently and for longer than usual (Verplaetse & Migliacci, 2008), and building repetition and redundancy into instruction to give students multiple opportunities to grasp ideas (Yedlin, 2007).

Give clear and explicit instructions. Lack of familiarity with classroom procedures or lack of understanding of English may lead ELLs to misinterpret instructions for classroom activities or assignments. Linguistically responsive teachers provide clear and explicit instructions for carrying out tasks (Gibbons, 2002). They include the details of activities to be carried out, avoiding shortcuts that assume students are familiar with the way things are done in U.S. schools. Depending on the task, teachers may write procedures on paper or on the board, or ask students to take notes and repeat instructions in their own words. They double-check to make sure ELL students have fully understood what is expected of them.

Conclusion

The education of ELLs has until recently been viewed as the responsibility of specialists in ESL and bilingual education. For that reason, few teacher educators outside those specialized programs have had the opportunity to cultivate expertise in linguistically responsive teaching themselves. We envision the framework for preparing linguistically responsive teachers presented in this chapter as a tool for teacher educators. It places language at the center of the discussion rather than at the margin, articulating essential orientations, knowledge, and skills for teaching ELLs. It can serve as a guide for teacher educators as they reshape the curriculum to enhance the preparation of all teachers for teaching language minority students.

While precisely how the framework can inform curriculum revision depends on the particulars of each teacher education context, we offer some practical suggestions for infusing the elements of linguistically responsive teaching, drawing on our experience of infusing principles of culturally responsive teaching into the teacher education curriculum (see Villegas & Lucas, 2001). Before taking steps to revise the curriculum, teacher educators must first agree on the substance of the needed revision. A group of faculty members—perhaps a task force or ad hoc committee charged with leading the effort (or taking it upon themselves) to improve the preparation of teachers for teaching ELLs—can use the framework presented in this chapter as a starting point for discussions about what teachers of ELLs need to know and be able to do. Whether these teacher educators embrace the framework as it is or revise it in major or minor ways, the resulting conception of linguistically responsive teaching can then serve as the foundation for the infusion process. The next step is to broaden faculty involvement by engaging them in sustained dialogue about the conception, with the goal of achieving a broad consensus among the faculty about the vision of linguistically responsive teaching and the ways the curriculum needs to be modified to reflect that conception. With that consensus, faculty members are ready to engage in the work of deciding in what courses and field experiences particular elements of linguistically responsive teaching will be addressed and how they will be addressed. To make the necessary changes in the curriculum and realize their goal of preparing all classroom teachers to teach ELLs well, most teacher educators need to build their own knowledge and skills related to the education of ELLs. For that reason, professional development for teacher educators is essential throughout all phases of the curriculum revision process. Successfully using the framework for preparing linguistically responsive teachers in the ways we have proposed here requires thoughtful planning and strategizing, collaboration, and dialogue among all those involved in preparing teachers in particular institutions.

While there is some evidence regarding the importance and impact of elements of this framework (see, for example, chapters in this volume), there is a great need for research on all aspects of the preparation of classroom teachers for teaching of ELLs. Research is needed to document efforts to apply this or other similar frameworks in teacher education programs, to examine the factors that influence those efforts, and to determine the impact of teacher preparation that incorporates the identified orientations, knowledge, and skills. Questions to be addressed include: What factors within the larger teacher education program, the institution, and the surrounding school districts support and impede the incorporation of attention to linguistically responsive teaching in the teacher education curriculum? What specific roles do these factors play in the process? What evidence would be needed to show that the framework has been sufficiently infused into a curriculum? What impact does that infusion have on the readiness and effectiveness of teacher candidates in pre-service programs and practicing teachers in in-service programs for teaching ELLs?

Answers to these and other critical questions can inform teacher educators as we embark on the journey to build our own knowledge and change our programs to prepare teachers. Without question, such change is needed, as increasing numbers of classroom teachers are and will continue to be expected to educate ELLs, and teacher educators must take responsibility for preparing them to do so. We hope the framework for preparing linguistically responsive teachers we have presented in this chapter will support them in their efforts.

References

Au, K.H. (1980). Participation structures in a reading lesson with Hawaiian children: An analysis of a culturally appropriate instructional event. *Anthropology and Education Quarterly, 11*(2), 93–115.

Bartolomé, L.I. (2000). Democratizing bilingualism: The role of critical teacher education. In Z.F. Beykont (Ed.), *Lifting every voice: Pedagogy and politics of bilingualism* (pp. 167–186). Cambridge, MA: Harvard Education Publishing Group.

Baugh, J. (2005). Linguistics and education in multilingual America. In K. Denham & A. Lobeck (Eds.), *Language in the schools: Integrating linguistic knowledge into K-12 teaching* (pp. 5–16). Mahwah, NJ: Lawrence Erlbaum.

Brown, L.C. (2007). Strategies for making social studies texts more comprehensible for English-language learners. *The Social Studies, 98*(5), 185–188.

Byrnes, D.A., Kiger, G., & Manning, L. (1996). Social psychological correlates of teachers' language attitudes. *Journal of Applied Social Psychology, 26*(5), 455–467.

Byrnes, D.A., Kiger, G., & Manning, L. (1997). Teachers' attitudes about language diversity. *Teaching and Teacher Education, 13*(6), 637–644.

Chamot, A.U., & O'Malley, J.M. (1996). The cognitive academic language learning approach: A model for linguistically diverse classrooms. *The Elementary School Journal, 96*(3), 259–273.

Cochran-Smith, M., Davis, D., & Fries, K. (2004). Multicultural teacher education: Research, practice, and policy. In J.A. Banks & C.M. Banks (Eds.), *Handbook of research on multicultural education* (2nd ed., pp. 931–975). San Francisco, CA: Jossey-Bass.

Crawford, J. (1992). *Hold your tongue: The politics of "English Only."* Reading, MA: Addison Wesley.

Cummins, J. (2000). *Language, power, and pedagogy: Bilingual children in the crossfire.* Clevedon, U.K.: Multilingual Matters.

Cummins, J. (2008). BICS and CALP: Empirical and theoretical status of the distinction. In B. Street & N.H. Hornberger (Eds.), *Encyclopedia of language and education* (2nd ed.), *Volume 2: Literacy* (pp. 71–83). New York, NY: Springer Science + Business Media LLC.

Delpit, L. (1998). What should teachers do? Ebonics and culturally responsive instruction. In T. Perry & L. Delpit (Eds.), *The real Ebonics debate: Power, language, and the education of African-American children* (pp. 17–26). Boston, MA: Beacon Press.

de Oliveira, L.C., & Athanases, S.Z. (2007). Graduates' reports of advocating for English language learners. *Journal of Teacher Education, 58*(3), 202–215.

Dicker, S.J. (2006). *Languages in America: A pluralist view* (2nd ed.). Clevedon, U.K.: Multilingual Matters.

Echevarria, J., Vogt, M., & Short, D.J. (2004). *Making content comprehensible for English language learners: The SIOP model* (2nd ed.). Boston, MA: Allyn & Bacon.

Ellis, R. (1985). Teacher–pupil interaction in second language development. In S.M. Gass & C.G. Madden (Eds.), *Input in second language acquisition* (pp. 69–85). Rowley, MA: Newbury House.

Fasold, R. (1990). *The sociolinguistics of language*. Oxford, U.K.: Blackwell.

García-Nevarez, A.G., Stafford, M.E., & Arias, B. (2005). Arizona elementary teachers' attitudes toward English language learners and the use of Spanish in classroom instruction. *Bilingual Research Journal, 29*(2), 295–317.

Gass, S.M. (1997). *Input, interaction, and the second language learner*. Mahwah, NJ: Lawrence Erlbaum.

Gay, G. (2000). *Culturally responsive teaching: Theory, research, and practice*. New York, NY: Teachers College Press.

Gibbons, P. (2002). *Scaffolding language, scaffolding learning: Teaching second language learners in the mainstream classroom*. Portsmouth, NH: Heinemann.

González, N. (2005). *Funds of knowledge: Theorizing practices in households and classrooms*. Mahwah, NJ: Lawrence Erlbaum.

Heath, S.B. (1983). *Ways with words: Language, life, and work in communities and classrooms*. London, U.K.: Cambridge University Press.

Hite, C.E., & Evans, L.S. (2006). Mainstream first-grade teachers' understanding of strategies for accommodating the needs of English language learners. *Teacher Education Quarterly, 33*(2), 89–110.

Kindler, A.L. (2002). *Survey of the states' limited English proficient students and available educational programs and services: 2000–2001 summary report*. Washington, D.C.: National Clearinghouse for English Language Acquisition.

Krashen, S.D. (1982). *Principles and practices in second language acquisition*. New York, NY: Pergamon Press.

Krashen, S.D. (2003). *Explorations in language acquisition and use*. Portsmouth, NH: Heinemann.

Ladson-Billings, G. (1995). Multicultural teacher education: Research, practice, and policy. In J.A. Banks & C.M. Banks (Eds.), *Handbook of research on multicultural education* (pp. 747–759). New York, NY: Macmillan.

Lenski, S.D., Ehlers-Zavala, F., Daniel, M.C., & Sun-Irminger, X. (2006). Assessing English-language learners in mainstream classrooms. *The Reading Teacher, 60*(1), 24–34.

Lucas, T., & Grinberg, J. (2008). Responding to the linguistic reality of mainstream classrooms: Preparing all teachers to teach English language learners. In M. Cochran-Smith, S. Feiman-Nemser, & J. McIntyre (Eds.), *Handbook of research on teacher education: Enduring issues in changing contexts* (3rd ed., pp. 606–636). Mahwah, NJ: Lawrence Erlbaum.

Lucas, T., & Katz, A. (1994). Reframing the debate: The Roles of native languages in "English-Only" programs for language minority students. *TESOL Quarterly, 28*(3), 537–561.

Lucas, T., Henze, R., & Donato, R. (1990). Promoting the success of Latino language minority students: An exploratory study of six high schools. *Harvard Educational Review, 60*(3), 315–340.

Lucas, T., Villegas, A.M., & Freedson-Gonzalez, M. (2008). Linguistically responsive teacher education: Preparing classroom teachers to teach English language learners. *Journal of Teacher Education, 59*(4), 361–373.

Marx, S. (2000). An exploration of pre-service teacher perceptions of second language learners in the mainstream classroom. *Texas Papers in Foreign Language Education, 5*(1), 207–221.

Michaels, S. (1981). Sharing time: Children's narrative styles and differential access to literacy. *Language in Society 10*(3), 423–442.

Mohr, K.A.J., & Mohr, E.S. (2007). Extending English-language learners' classroom interactions using the Response Protocol. *The Reading Teacher, 60*(5), 440–450.

National Center for Educational Statistics. (2005). *The condition of education 2005.* Indicator 5: Language minority school-age children. Washington, D.C.: U.S. Department of Education. Retrieved from http://nces.ed.gov/programs/coe/2005/section1/indicator05.asp.

Nieto, S. (2000). Bringing bilingual education out of the basement, and other imperatives for teacher education. In Z.F. Beykont (Ed.), *Lifting every voice: Pedagogy and politics of bilingualism* (pp. 187–207). Cambridge, MA: Harvard Education Publishing Group.

Nieto, S. (2002). *Language, culture, and teaching: Critical perspectives for a new century.* Mahwah, NJ: Lawrence Erlbaum.

Olsen, L. (1997). *Made in America: Immigrant students in our public schools.* New York, NY: The New Press.

Philips, S. (1972). Participant structures and communicative competence: Warm Springs children in community and classroom. In C. Cazden, V. John, & D. Hymes (Eds.), *Functions of language in the classroom* (pp. 370–394). New York, NY: Teachers College Press.

Philips, S. (1983). *The invisible culture: Communication in classroom and community on the Warm Springs Indian Reservation.* New York, NY: Longman.

Price, J.N., & Osborne, M.D. (2000). Challenges of forging a humanizing pedagogy in teacher education. *Curriculum and Teaching, 15*(1), 27–51.

Reeves, J.R. (2006). Secondary teacher attitudes toward including English language learners in mainstream classrooms. *Journal of Educational Research, 99*(3), 131–142.

Richardson, V. (1996). The role of attitudes and beliefs in learning to teach. In J. Sikula (Ed.), *Handbook of research on teacher education* (2nd ed., pp. 102–119). New York, NY: Macmillan.

Schleppegrell, M.J. (2004). *The language of schooling: A functional linguistics perspective.* Mahwah, NJ: Lawrence Erlbaum.

Sharkey, J., & Layzer, C. (2000). Identity factors that affect English language learners' access to academic success and resources. *TESOL Quarterly, 23*(2), 352–368.

Swain, M. (1995). Three functions of output in second language learning. In G. Cook & B. Seidlehofer (Eds.), *Principle and practice in applied linguistics: Studies in honour of H.G. Widdowson* (pp. 125–144). Oxford, U.K.: Oxford University Press.

Thomas, W.P., & Collier, V.P. (2002). *A national study of school effectiveness for language minority students' long-term academic achievement.* University of California, Santa Cruz: Center for Research on Education, Diversity, and Excellence.

Trumbull, E., & Farr, B. (2005). *Language and learning: What teachers need to know.* Norwood, MA: Christopher-Gordon Publishers.

Valdés, G. (2001). *Learning and not learning English: Latino students in American schools.* New York, NY: SUNY Press.

Valdés, G., Bunch, G., Snow, C., & Lee, C., with Matos, L. (2005). Enhancing the development of students' language(s). In L. Darling-Hammond & J. Bransford (Eds.),

Preparing teachers for a changing world: What teachers should learn and be able to do (pp. 126–168). San Francisco, CA: Jossey-Bass.

Varghese, M.M., & Stritikus, T. (2005). "Nadie me dijo (Nobody told me)": Language policy negotiation and implications for teacher education. *Journal of Teacher Education, 56*(1), 73–87.

Verplaetse, L.S. (2008). Developing academic language through an abundance of interaction. In L.S. Verplaetse & N. Migliacci (Eds.), *Inclusive pedagogy for English language learners: A handbook of research-informed practices* (pp. 167–180). New York, NY: Lawrence Erlbaum.

Verplaetse, L.S., & Migliacci, N. (2008). Making mainstream content comprehensible through sheltered instruction. In L.S. Verplaetse & N. Migliacci (Eds.), *Inclusive pedagogy for English language learners: A handbook of research-informed practices* (pp. 127–165). New York, NY: Lawrence Erlbaum.

Villegas, A.M. (1991). *Culturally responsive teaching for the 1990s and beyond.* Washington, D.C.: American Association of Colleges for Teacher Education.

Villegas, A.M., & Lucas, T. (2001). *Preparing culturally responsive teachers: How can we teach what we don't know?* Paper presented at the Annual Conference of the American Educational Research Association, Chicago, April.

Villegas, A.M., & Lucas, T. (2002a). *Educating culturally responsive teachers: A coherent approach.* Albany, NY: SUNY Press.

Villegas, A.M., & Lucas, T. (2002b). Preparing culturally responsive teachers: Rethinking the curriculum. *Journal of Teacher Education, 53*(1), 20–32.

Villegas, A.M., & Lucas, T. (2007). The culturally responsive teacher. *Educational Leadership, 64*(6), 28–33.

Vygotsky, L. (1978). *Mind in society.* Cambridge, U.K.: Cambridge University Press.

Walker, A., Shafer, J., & Iiams, M. (2004). "Not in my classroom": Teacher attitudes towards English language learners in the mainstream classroom. *NABE Journal of Research and Practice, 2*(1), 130–160.

Walqui, A. (2007). The development of teacher expertise to work with adolescent English learners: A model and a few priorities. In L.S. Verplaetse & N. Migliacci (Eds.), *Inclusive pedagogy for English language learners: A handbook of research-informed practices* (pp. 103–125). New York, NY: Lawrence Erlbaum.

Wolfram, W., Adger, C.T., & Christian, D. (1999). *Dialects in schools and communities* (2nd ed.). Mahwah, NJ: Lawrence Erlbaum.

Wong-Fillmore, L., & Snow, C. (2005). What teachers need to know about language. In C.T. Adger, C.E. Snow, & D. Christian (Eds.), *What teachers need to know about language* (pp. 7–54). Washington, D.C.: Center for Applied Linguistics.

Wong-Fillmore, L., & Valadez, C. (1986). Teaching bilingual learners. In M.C. Wittrock (Ed.), *Handbook of research on teaching* (3rd ed., pp. 648–685). New York, NY: Macmillan.

Yedlin, J. (2007). Pedagogical thinking and teacher talk in a first-grade ELL classroom. In L.S. Verplaetse & N. Migliacci (Eds.), *Inclusive pedagogy for English language learners: A handbook of research-informed practices* (pp. 55–77). New York, NY: Lawrence Erlbaum.

Zeichner, K.M. (2003). The adequacies and inadequacies of three current strategies to recruit, prepare, and retain the best teachers for all students. *Teachers College Record, 105*(3), 490–519.

Chapter 5

"Accommodating Diversity"

Pre-Service Teachers' Views on Effective Practices for English Language Learners

Ester J. de Jong and Candace A. Harper

According to the 2000 U.S. Census, 25% of students aged 5–17 come from homes where a language other than English is spoken. An estimated 15% of these students have limited proficiency in English, and are commonly referred to as English language learners (ELLs). In the past, ELLs' language learning needs were addressed in special bilingual or English as a second language (ESL) programs or classes. In 1993 only 3% of ELLs were reported as having no access to special language services. By 2003 that number had risen to almost 12%, and nearly one-fourth (24%) of all ELLs received fewer than 10 hours per week of ESL instruction (Zehler et al., 2003). As their number and diversity grow steadily, K-12 ELLs are increasingly placed in mainstream settings for the majority (if not the entirety) of the school day.

In spite of several decades of demographic projections of increasing linguistic and cultural diversity in U.S. schools, pre-service teacher education programs have not kept pace with the challenges of diverse classrooms. For example, Menken and Antunez (2001) reported that in-service teachers had fewer than 10 hours of professional development specifically related to ELLs. The U.S. Department of Education reported that, as early as 1997, 39% of teachers surveyed had ELLs in their classrooms, but only one-quarter of these teachers had received any professional development targeted to meet their needs (Gándara, Maxwell-Jolly, & Driscoll, 2005). Until recently, few states required any ELL-specific preparation in initial teacher certification programs. (Florida and California were the first states to mandate such preparation for all teachers in 2001 and 2003, respectively. ESL/bilingual teacher specialist—in contrast to general educator—preparation has, of course, existed since the late 1960s.) Even in teacher preparation programs that emphasize culturally responsive teaching (Cochran-Smith, 2004; Gay, 2000, 2002), issues of second language development and bilingualism are not addressed systematically (Au, 1998; Nieto, 2002). Moreover, textbooks for general educators typically address ELL-specific information through marginal notes, if at all (Bernhardt, 1994).

The recognition that linguistically and culturally diverse students are today's mainstream students is not recent (e.g., Cummins & Cameron, 1994), but it does raise important questions about general educator preparation and ELLs. In this chapter, we report on the findings from a survey at a large public institution that elicited pre-service teachers' (henceforth, PTs) views about what teachers of ELLs need to know and be able to do, how teaching classes with such students differs from teaching classes with (only) monolingual English speakers, and how confident they are in their ability to teach ELLs well. Before reporting the context of the study and survey results, we briefly discuss the knowledge, skills, and dispositions needed by mainstream teachers of ELLs. We conclude with implications for initial teacher preparation of mainstream teachers of ELLs.

ESL Expertise and General Education Teachers

The pressure to ensure mainstream educators' preparation to teach ELLs is not only the result of demographic changes. It has also been influenced by the inclusion movement in special education and by the standards movement in general education (e.g., *Goals 2000* and national content standards). The emphasis on universal student achievement by No Child Left Behind (U.S. Department of Education, 2001) has also had a major impact (see Villegas & Lucas, this volume). The fact that ELLs are one subgroup for whom schools, districts, and states must demonstrate annual yearly progress has highlighted their presence in schools in unprecedented ways. Further, developments in ESL teaching that emphasize content-based language learning have positioned the mainstream classroom as the preferred learning environment for all students, including ELLs (for a more detailed discussion of these trends, see de Jong & Harper, 2005; Harper & de Jong, 2009).

An important discussion that has emerged from these developments is what aspects of ESL teacher expertise must be included in general teacher preparation in order to ensure that the "mainstreaming" or "inclusion" of ELLs does not mean a return to the submersion ("sink or swim") classrooms of previous generations in which teachers failed to provide the instruction necessary to allow ELLs equal access to the curriculum (for one perspective, see Lucas & Villegas, this volume). As the Supreme Court clearly articulated in *Lau v. Nichols* (1974): "Under these state-imposed standards there is no equality of treatment merely by providing students with the same facilities, textbooks, teachers, and curriculum; for students who do not understand English are effectively foreclosed from any meaningful education."

Lau and its aftermath resulted in the expectation that specialized programs and bilingual and ESL teacher preparation might be necessary means to providing equal access to schooling. What is different today is the realization that general educators—not just specialist teachers—must be well prepared to work with ELLs. The implications of this shift for initial teacher preparation are only beginning to be considered (Brisk, 2007; Lucas & Grinberg, 2008; Mora & Grisham, 2001).

Elsewhere, we have argued that ESL teacher expertise can be conceptualized in terms of core knowledge, essential skills, and key dispositions in the general domains of language and culture (Figure 5.1) (de Jong & Harper, 2005; Harper & de Jong, 2009). First, teachers must understand the process of second language acquisition and acculturation, i.e., how native (L1) and second (L2) language oral and literacy development are both similar and different. Additionally, teachers must develop an understanding of how bilingual processes are manifested in ELLs' oral language and literacy development, and they should know how they can support an ELL student's native language and culture as resources for learning.

Teachers must also develop an awareness of the role that language and culture play as a medium of teaching and learning. In terms of language, this entails a basic understanding of the structure of English and of the oral/ written and colloquial/academic dimensions of English (Fillmore & Snow, 2002). It includes understanding the challenges that ELLs face in learning academic content through a language they do not yet control. From a cultural perspective, teachers need to understand how opportunities for learning are mediated through culturally based assumptions regarding classroom and literacy conventions that may not be shared by all students. They also need to be able to respond to the instructional implications of this awareness.

The third dimension of ESL teacher knowledge considers the inclusion of linguistic and cultural diversity as explicit goals of curriculum and instruction.

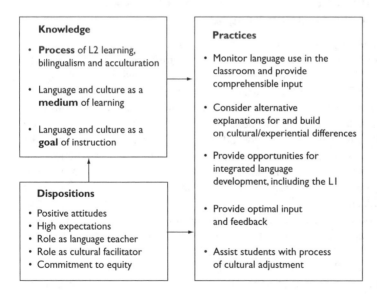

Figure 5.1 The Specialized Expertise of ESL Teachers (source: adapted from de Jong & Harper, 2005).

Mainstream teachers need to be able to identify the language demands inherent in their curriculum and organize their classrooms to support the development of academic language proficiency by integrating language and content objectives (Gibbons, 2002, 2003). Cross-cultural experiences and practices must also inform curriculum planning and implementation.

Teachers' understandings of these dimensions, culture and language as process, medium, and goal of schooling, affect classroom practices (see Figure 5.1). For example, effective teachers of ELLs not only make their instruction more comprehensible, they also explicitly and purposefully scaffold for diverse opportunities to use and practice the second language meaningfully, building on students' background knowledge and expertise. They provide frequent and thoughtful feedback and realize that ELLs' "funds of knowledge" (González, Moll, & Amanti, 2005) may differ from those of other students.

However, changes in pedagogy will be insufficient unless teachers' dispositions toward ELLs also change. Nieto (2000) notes: "Teaching language minority students successfully means above all challenging one's attitudes toward the students, their languages and cultures, and their communities. Anything short of this will result in repeating the pattern of failure that currently exists" (p. 196). Good teachers of ELLs embrace their roles as language teachers and cultural facilitators in order to ensure equitable classrooms (Brisk, 2006).

The Context of the Study: State Policies and the Teacher Preparation Program

Florida has some of the most extensive professional development requirements for teachers of ELLs in the U.S. This emphasis on teacher preparation for ELLs stems from the settlement of a 1990 lawsuit brought against the Florida Department of Education (FDOE) alleging inadequate and discriminatory identification, placement, and instruction of ELLs, limiting their access to an education. The Consent Agreement signed by the FDOE included requirements to assess and identify students' language and literacy needs in English, provide appropriate grade-level instruction and access to special programs, monitor their achievement, and prepare all instructional and support personnel to work effectively with ELLs (www.fldoe.org/aala/).

The Consent Decree defines qualifications for teachers of ELLs in terms of professional development units organized around five curricular areas: ESL Methods, ESL Curriculum and Materials Development, Cross-cultural Communication, ESL Testing and Evaluation, and Applied Linguistics. The specific content and quantity of the ESL "training" required by the Consent Decree are determined by a teacher's instructional assignment in classes that include ELLs. For example, elementary teachers and secondary teachers of

English Language Arts in classrooms including ELLs are required to earn an ESL endorsement equivalent to 300 hours of ESL in-service work; (secondary) teachers of math, science, and social studies are required to take a 60-hour course in ESL Strategies; and teachers of all other subjects, such as music, art, and physical education, need 18 hours of professional development in ESL.

In 2001, the Florida legislature extended this in-service requirement to include all PTs, who must now complete ESL competencies prior to graduation from any teacher education program. The FDOE considers mainstream teachers who have completed the 300-hour ESL endorsement requirement through these "ESL infused" pre-service programs to be as qualified to teach ELLs as specialist ESL teachers, who have developed disciplinary expertise through professional teacher certification in ESL or who have earned graduate degrees in ESL/bilingual education.

The teacher preparation program considered in this study uses an infused model with two ESL-specific anchor courses taught by ESL faculty. Additional ESL competencies are addressed in general education (primarily methods) courses. The first ESL anchor course focuses on foundational aspects of language and culture and is taken in the PTs' third semester in the program (first semester of their senior year). Issues of the structure of language, second language acquisition, the role of culture in schooling, and acculturation are central in this course. The second anchor course stresses the application of theory for curriculum, methods, and assessment. This course is taken at the end of the program in the PTs' fifth (graduate) year and, with a few exceptions, in their final semester before graduation. This course focuses on comprehensible input strategies, second language literacy development, and lesson planning for ELLs at different proficiency levels, including setting language objectives. The extent to which ESL teacher competencies are addressed in other courses varies and depends on course content and instructor variables. Another important program characteristic is the limited access to ELLs in clinical/field experiences in surrounding schools. Opportunities to work directly with ELLs (approximately 20 contact hours) occur almost exclusively in the context of the two dedicated ESL courses.

Data Collection and Analysis

The study was conducted in a five-year elementary education program at a Florida university between 2002 and 2004, and in 2007. Following national trends, the overwhelming majority of pre-service teacher candidates in this program are White, female, and native (monolingual) speakers of English. Graduates from this teacher preparation program intend to teach in general education settings, though they are required to fulfill the "infused ESL endorsement" program requirements. They do not think of themselves as (future) ESL teachers.

Multiple cohorts of elementary education PTs in this teacher education program completed a survey during the semester in which they took the second ESL-specific course. One survey was administered each semester between Fall 2002 and Fall 2004. The survey responses ($n = 128$) were analyzed with a focus on the PTs' responses to two open-ended survey questions: (1) What do good teachers of ELLs need to know and be able to do when working with linguistically and culturally diverse students? (2) What is the difference between teaching in an integrated ELL/native-English speaker classroom versus a classroom with (only) proficient English speakers? In addition, we analyzed preservice teacher candidates' responses to an item in which they were asked to rate their level of confidence in 10 specific areas of teaching ELLs, including their ability to set language objectives, scaffold language development, use language proficiency assessment results to inform their teaching, meet the needs of ESOL students (as ELLs are called in Florida) at different levels of English proficiency, and make their classroom welcoming for ELLs.

A second, slightly modified survey (Survey 2) was administered in the fall semester of 2007 to PTs ($n = 52$) at the same point in their program. Survey 2 asked similar questions, with slight variations to frame responses in terms of teacher knowledge and skills. For example, Survey 2 asked PTs to complete the following sentences: (1) *A teacher of ESOL students must definitely have knowledge about* ... (2) *A teacher of ESOL students must definitely be able to* ... A third question asked them to respond to the prompt: *Teaching in a classroom with only native English speakers is/is not (circle your answer) different from teaching in a classroom with both native English speakers and ESOL students because* ... As with Survey 1, Survey 2 asked PTs to rate the extent to which they felt prepared in specific areas of teaching ELLs.

We analyzed and coded the teacher candidates' responses to the targeted items from Survey 1 and Survey 2 (Total $n = 180$) according to broad conceptual categories. For example, the analysis of responses to the survey items asking what teachers need to know and be able to do when working with ELLs resulted in multiple categories, including second language acquisition, cultural differences, classroom environment, instructional strategies, comprehensible input, language development, and assessment. A majority of students (153 of 180) indicated that there were differences in the two instructional settings. Analysis of the responses to this question produced the following categories: making more accommodations, providing more comprehensible input, scaffolding English language development, using group work, building background knowledge, dealing with cultural differences, and changing assessment practices. We next looked for connecting themes within and across the coded categories of teacher candidate responses. This process led to the identification of two dominant themes, which we discuss in more detail below: the central role of culture and the characterization of teaching ELLs as the application of strategies.

General Education Pre-Service Teachers' Views Regarding Teaching ELLs

The Visibility of Cultural Issues

Cultural factors dominated the PTs' responses to the questions asking them to identify the essential knowledge and skills in teaching ELLs (Table 5.1). Almost half (44%) of their comments related to culture, with specific classroom practices the second most frequently mentioned response (33%). Comments focused in particular on affective factors for teachers, such as being patient, creating a comfortable learning environment, and showing respect for ELLs. As one pre-service teacher wrote, "They need to feel comfortable. They need to feel their culture and language is valued."

Comments about classroom-based practices (33%) focused on knowing how to make instruction more comprehensible for students at different proficiency levels. A typical response in this category was "[teachers need to know] how to teach them, specifically how to contextualize the learning and make it meaningful." Finally, responses addressing language-related teacher knowledge and skill were mentioned least frequently (25%). PTs commented on the need to know students' language proficiency level (including native language proficiency) and cross-linguistic differences as aspects of student information useful for designing instruction. One teacher candidate wrote, "It's important to know and respect the students [sic] background and culture and their stage of language proficiency."[1]

Similar observations emerged in relation to the areas in which teacher candidates felt most confident or prepared. At the beginning of the semester, students indicated their agreement with statements related to classroom practices. As Tables 5.2 and 5.3 show, students reported relatively high confidence/preparedness in making newcomer ESOL students feel welcome in their classrooms ($M = 3.4$, both surveys), connecting with families and communities ($M = 3.0$, Survey 1), and supporting the acculturation process ($M = 3.1$, Survey 2). In contrast, students rated themselves lower in language and literacy instruction. On Survey 1 (Table 5.2), respondents reported feeling least confident in their ability to "teach English as a second language, including aspects of English syntax and discourse" ($M = 2.2$) and to "set language objectives for ESOL students in [their] content classes" ($M = 2.3$). Similarly, on Survey 2 (Table 5.3), students felt least prepared to teach reading ($M = 2.2$), content ($M = 2.2$), and writing ($M = 2.3$) to ELLs.[2]

In short, the survey responses revealed that cultural issues were most prominent in these PTs' thinking about essential knowledge and skills for teaching ELLs. The survey results also reflect the skill areas in which the teacher candidates felt most confident or most prepared.

Table 5.1 Most Important Knowledge and Skills for Working with ELLs (Surveys 1 and 2)

Category	Description	Number (%) of Comments
CULTURE (44% of all comments)		
Creating a welcoming classroom environment	Be patient, have respect for other cultures, do not single out or segregate students, know what it is like, low anxiety	90 (29%)
Cultural differences	Know your students' background, differences in prior knowledge	45 (15%)
SPECIFIC CLASSROOM PRACTICES (33% of all comments)		
Comprehensible input	Contextualization, visuals, pictures, lowering language demand, scaffolding, extended wait time, knowing how to communicate with students	48 (16%)
Language or literacy development	Language objectives, practicing language, increased interaction	20 (7%)
Assessment	Authentic assessment, need to change assessments or tasks	12 (4%)
Expectations	Not confusing cognitive and language ability	17 (6%)
LANGUAGE (25% of all comments)		
Second language acquisition	Knowing students' proficiency levels, stages of second language development	35 (11%)
Language differences	Language acquisition processes and influencing factors	20 (7%)
	Students' native language, cross-linguistic differences	21 (7%)

Table 5.2 Mean Scores for Level of Confidence, Ranked from Most to Least Confident (Survey 1; Maximum Score = 4.0)

I feel confident in my ability to …	Mean Score (1–4)
Make newcomer ESOL students feel welcome in my classroom.	3.4
Work with and reach out to family and community members who do not speak English very well.	3.0
Locate resources and adapt and select materials appropriate for ESOL students.	2.9
Understand and respond appropriately to culturally diverse learners who have been raised and schooled in countries other than the U.S.	2.9
Contextualize my lessons for ESOL students.	2.6
Meet the language, culture, and content matter needs of ESOL students at the beginning and intermediate proficiency levels.	2.5
Assess what ESOL students can do and understand in my content class, taking language demands into consideration.	2.5
Use language proficiency assessment results to inform my teaching practice.	2.5
Set language objectives for ESOL students in my content classes.	2.3
Teach English as a second language, including aspects of English syntax and discourse.	2.2

Table 5.3 Mean Scores for Level of Preparedness, Ranked from Most to Least Prepared (Survey 2; Maximum Score = 4)

I feel prepared to ...	Mean Score (1–4)
Make my classroom a welcoming environment for ESOL students.	3.4
Support the acculturation of ESOL students.	3.1
Assess ESOL students fairly, even when they still have limited proficiency in English.	2.8
Find appropriate materials for ESOL students.	2.7
Support oral language development for ESOL students.	2.6
Teach reading to ESOL students.	2.3
Teach writing to ESOL students.	2.2
Teach content (math, science, social studies) to ESOL students.	2.2

Teaching ELLs as Strategy Application

A slightly different picture emerged when we asked the teacher candidates to reflect on how teaching an integrated native/non-native speaker classroom might be different from teaching a native-speaker-only classroom. In their responses to this question, many PTs gave generic responses about the need to make "accommodations" or "adaptations" and to use "strategies." Almost 30% of all comments in response to this question were of this generic nature. For example, one of the PTs wrote: "You have to always be consciously thinking about how to adapt your instruction and if it is accessible to ELLs."

When listing specific instructional differences, participants emphasized having to provide (more) comprehensible input through contextualization, visuals, and hands-on instruction (Table 5.4). One teacher candidate wrote: "Teaching a mix would mean I would have to make more adaptations for ELLs in order to make input more comprehensible." A total of 66% of the comments related to mediating comprehensibility of instruction due to the ELLs' language barrier. Responses that focused on specific efforts to support language development in the classroom and negotiate cultural differences, particularly prior knowledge, were less prominent (5% and 14%, respectively).

Those PTs who indicated that they did not see any difference between teaching native speakers and an integrated native/non-native speaker group (15% of the respondents) stressed that the common thread was to make accommodations. They argued that a good teacher treats students as individuals and makes accommodations to meet their individual needs, regardless of their language status. As one of them explained,

Table 5.4 Comparing Native Speaker (Only) and Native Speaker/ELL Classroom Teaching (Surveys 1 and 2)

Category	Description	Number (%) of Comments
SPECIFIC CLASSROOM PRACTICES (66% of all comments)		
Comprehensible input	Contextualization, visuals, pictures, lowering language demand, scaffolding, extended wait time, knowing how to communicate with students	72 (41%)
Language or literacy development	Language objectives, practicing language, increased interaction	31 (17%)
Assessment	Authentic assessment, need to change assessments or tasks	14 (8%)
CULTURE (14% of all comments)		
Cultural differences	Know your students' background, differences in prior knowledge	25 (14%)
LANGUAGE (5% of all comments)		
Second language acquisition	Knowing students' proficiency levels, stages of language development	9 (5%)
NO DIFFERENCE (15% of all comments)		
	There is no real difference.	27 (15%)

> There is [sic] not a lot of differences, to be honest. All students need accommodations, ESOL students are no different. Each child is different and needs different things. As teachers, we need to realize this and look at all learners as equals.

In other words, when thinking about what teachers of ELLs *do*, these PTs considered their task in terms of making adjustments for ELLs, especially overcoming the language barrier by providing comprehensible instruction. These instructional adjustments do not necessarily represent a different approach to their teaching.

Discussion and Implications for Teacher Education

Discussion of Key Findings

This study addressed pre-service elementary (mainstream) teacher candidates' understandings of what teachers must know and be able to do for ELLs in the context of a mainstream classroom. The results of this study cannot be generalized to other contexts or other groups of PTs. However, our analysis of 180 surveys of fifth-year PTs generated two findings that warrant consideration by all teacher educators engaged in preparing mainstream teachers.

The first finding suggests that the expertise of teachers of ELLs was construed as largely a set of cultural knowledge and skills. Linguistic knowledge and skills occupied a less prominent place in the respondents' idea of what it takes to teach ELLs well. Regarding what is important for teachers of ELLs to know and be able to do, the PTs stressed providing a welcoming learning environment respectful of ELLs' cultures. Teacher knowledge of ELLs' backgrounds (such as home country, family background, language spoken at home) was also highlighted, albeit to a lesser extent. Teacher candidates indicated that they felt most prepared and confident in this area. In contrast, issues related to second language acquisition were mentioned less frequently, and the pre-service candidates felt less prepared and confident in teaching language and literacy to ELLs. When second language learning was mentioned, responses centered particularly on knowing a student's stage of English language development.

These PTs' awareness of cultural variables that may affect ELLs' performance in school is encouraging and can become an important base for their practice (Mullock, 2006). Moreover, affective variables play an important role in ELLs' adjustment and can influence their performance in the classroom (Igoa, 1995). At the same time, the dominance of culture over language in ELL teacher expertise highlights two important issues.

First, the PTs' representation of ELL teacher expertise stands in contrast to the knowledge base typically advocated by and for specialist ESL teachers. In

ESL specialist preparation and practice, teacher knowledge and skill related to the structure of (the English) language and the process of second language learning are central (e.g., Fillmore & Snow, 2002; Harper & de Jong, 2009; TESOL, 2002). Similarly, in a survey conducted in the context of a TESOL webcast presentation ($n = 38$), respondents mentioned knowing the structure of English and being able to facilitate language acquisition processes most frequently as the distinctive knowledge and skill base for ESL teachers (Harper & de Jong, 2007). This difference suggests that the PTs may not (yet) be fully aware of the central role of language as a medium of instruction. This role is not always apparent in a general education setting with fluent English speakers (with the possible exception of vocabulary development). In a mainstream classroom, learning activities, class discussions, and homework assignments are typically designed with the assumption that students have a developmentally appropriate command over oral and written language. This English language base cannot be assumed, however, when ELLs are members of the classroom, and instructional changes become necessary. The comments of a secondary Language Arts teacher about her use of a pre-writing strategy as an introduction to a book her students were preparing to read illustrate this point:

> I read them ... *Ira Sleeps Over* and it's about a little boy's first sleepover and I read that as a pre-writing activity, writing about a child's own experience. And then after reading it I talked about a childhood experience of my own and then we start talking about a childhood experience of their own. Well, that worked for my mainstream class. For [the] second language learners it was just reading a story without showing pictures. You know, it was just a lot of language without any ... so it was pre-writing activities, but it wasn't ideal for a second language learner in that class.
>
> (Harper & de Jong, 2004)

The finding that the PTs were more confident and felt more prepared in relation to cultural and affective issues than linguistic ones points to the importance of helping mainstream teachers look *at* language (rather than simply *through* language) in order to effectively mediate student learning (Harper & de Jong, 2004). Mainstream teachers must develop a deeper understanding of the role of linguistic scaffolding in supporting second language development and helping ELLs to succeed in their classrooms (Gersten, 1999; Platt & Troudi, 1997).

Our second major finding considers how the PTs described the difference between teaching (only) fluent English speakers and teaching both ELLs and fluent English speakers. The majority defined this difference in terms of instructional strategies, or accommodations, with a particular emphasis on making modifications to increase comprehensibility of instruction. Background knowledge and opportunities for language practice through increased peer interaction were mentioned, but did not emerge as prominent practices. The responses may reflect what Bartolomé (1994) refers to as "the methods fetish," a preoccupation with practical strategies and less interest in why the strategies are appropriate or in the wider sociopolitical context of teaching. Multicultural education scholars argue that culturally responsive teaching requires a restructuring of power and status within the classroom, not merely the addition of specific teaching techniques or discrete items to the curriculum (Cummins, 2001; Gay, 2002). Simply "tweaking" standard curriculum practices for native English speakers by using techniques to increase comprehensible input will not sufficiently, or necessarily, scaffold ELLs' socio-cultural, academic, language, and literacy development. The PTs' emphasis on accommodations for ELLs may also reflect a non-discriminatory rather than a transformative approach to diversity (Miller, 1996, cited in Buck, Mast, Ehlers, & Franklin, 2005). These PTs seem to accept that they have to make changes to their classrooms for ELLs, but they do not question the de facto curriculum. The accommodations they advocate are not intended to change the mainstream classroom but, rather, function to help ELLs overcome the language barrier to be able to reach mainstream (native English speaker) expectations.

The PTs' focus on comprehensible input as the main strategy to support ELLs in their classrooms prompts us to question their views on the role of teachers of ELLs. The use of visuals and adjustments in teacher talk reflect an understanding of comprehensible input as a way to mediate the language barrier (for beginning students) for access to content, but not necessarily as a means for language development. These PTs may not perceive language *development* as an integral part of their role in teaching ELLs, though language development is central to the identity of the specialist ESL teacher (Harper & de Jong, 2009). Many mainstream teachers do not consider the role of language teacher as their responsibility, but rather ascribe that role exclusively to the ESL teacher, who is also expected to provide any necessary curricular or instructional adaptations for ELLs (Clair, 1995; Harklau, 1999; Short, 2002; Youngs & Youngs, 2001). In a survey of 422 mainstream teachers in the Midwest, Walker, Shafer, and Iiams (2004) found that a large proportion (84%) of teachers in their study were either not interested in or directly objected to having ELLs in their classroom. Almost half of these teachers (47%) objected to or were neutral toward making instructional accommodations when needed. Our study suggests that these future elementary teachers may not see themselves as active planners for language development. Instead, they may consider the mere placement of ELLs in their classroom sufficient for natural second language learning opportunities and, thus, may not see the need to play a proactive role in social and academic language scaffolding (Harper & de Jong, 2004; Platt & Troudi, 1997).

Implications for Teacher Education

Our study provides a snapshot of a group of White, female PTs who are being prepared to address the cultural and linguistic diversity that ELLs bring to their mainstream classrooms. This teacher preparation context is quite specific: an infused ESL preparation program in a city with a small K-12 ELL student population. When any teacher preparation program begins to consider including ELL-specific knowledge and skills, teacher educators must ensure that ELLs are a visible and integral part of their pre-service candidates' education. That is, they need to prevent the "infusion" of ELL-specific knowledge and skills from becoming a "diffusion" of this linguistic and cultural expertise under a generic cover of "diversity" (cf. Costa, McPhail, Smith, & Brisk, 2005; Leung & Franson, 2001).

While more research is needed on effective preparation of teachers of ELLs, we draw on the results of our study as the basis for the following recommendations. First, the prevalence of cultural issues in these PTs' pedagogical knowledge suggests that teacher preparation programs may need to take additional steps to make linguistic issues equally visible for teacher candidates. This may be accomplished by:

- Helping mainstream teacher candidates to look *at* rather than *through* the language demands of the classroom in order to support language scaffolding for English language and literacy development (Gibbons, 2003) (see also Gebhard, Willett, Jimenez, & Piedra, and Brisk & Zisselsberger, this volume).
- Explicitly addressing the implications of second language development for curriculum, pedagogy, and assessment practices. For example, mainstream teachers must be able to identify goals and structure opportunities for second language and literacy development. They also should be able to distinguish how strategies or activities designed for native speakers need to be modified or extended for ELLs (Brisk, Dawson, Hartgering, MacDonald, & Zehr, 2002; Harper & de Jong, 2005).

Second, our study suggests that shifting from an "accommodation" stance with a focus on strategy (methods) to an inclusive classroom perspective where cultural and linguistic differences are acknowledged and negotiated equitably by teachers and students alike is challenging. To mediate this challenge, teacher preparation programs can:

- Help PTs understand the relevance of the "why" as well as the "how" of teaching in general and with ELLs in particular. Mainstream teachers must be able to advocate for practices that acknowledge the linguistic and cultural needs of ELLs (Varghese & Stritikus, 2005).
- Link practices for ELLs with a broader social justice agenda through which teachers avoid limiting their view of diversity as an accommodation to be made to a monolingual, monocultural classroom (Creese, 2003).

The current interest in mainstream teacher preparation programs in preparing future teachers to work with ELLs is a long overdue response to the changing demographics of U.S. schools. Our study suggests that linguistic diversity and its implications for language and content learning must become visible throughout a teacher preparation program. Awareness of the role of language is especially important given the tendency of policy-makers and mainstream educators to assume that what works for (struggling) native speakers will also work for ELLs. The standardization and homogenization of curriculum and instruction through national and state standards (Sleeter & Stillman, 2005) and of school outcomes through standardized tests have largely ignored the unique cultural and linguistic needs of bilingual learners. Like specialist ESL or bilingual teachers, mainstream teachers must have the knowledge, skills, and dispositions to critically reflect on their own practices and move beyond generic "just good teaching" for ELLs.

Notes

1. The latter comment references stages of second language development—i.e., preproduction, early production, speech emergence, intermediate fluency (Krashen & Terrell, 1983)—taught in the ESL classes.
2. By the end of the second ESOL course, the PTs felt more confident in aspects of language but still rated culture-related skills more highly.

References

Au, K.H. (1998). Social constructivism and the school literacy learning of students of diverse backgrounds. *Journal of Literacy Research, 30*, 297–319.

Bartolomé, L.I. (1994). Beyond the methods fetish: Toward a humanizing pedagogy. *Harvard Educational Review, 64*(2), 173–194.

Bernhardt, E.B. (1994). A content analysis of reading methods texts: What are we told about the nonnative speaker of English? *Journal of Reading Behavior, 26*(2), 159–189.

Brisk, M.E. (2006). *Quality bilingual education: From compensatory to quality schooling* (2nd ed.). Mahwah, NJ: Lawrence Erlbaum.

Brisk, M.E. (Ed.). (2007). *Language, culture, and community in teacher education.* Mahwah, NJ: Lawrence Erlbaum.

Brisk, M.E., Dawson, M., Hartgering, M., MacDonald, E., & Zehr, L. (2002). Teaching bilingual students in mainstream classrooms. In Z.F. Beykont (Ed.), *The power of culture: Teaching across language differences* (pp. 89–120). Cambridge, MA: Harvard Education Publishing Group.

Buck, G., Mast, C., Ehlers, N., & Franklin, E. (2005). Preparing teachers to create a mainstream science classroom conducive to the needs of English-language learners: A feminist action research project. *Journal of Research in Science Teaching, 42*(9), 1013–1031.

Clair, N. (1995). Mainstream classroom teachers and ESL students. *TESOL Quarterly, 29*, 189–196.

Cochran-Smith, M. (2004). *Walking the road: Race, diversity, and social justice in teacher education.* New York, NY: Teachers College Press.

Costa, J., McPhail, G., Smith, J., & Brisk, M. (2005). Faculty first. *Journal of Teacher Education, 56,* 104–118.

Creese, A. (2003). Language, ethnicity, and the mediation of allegations of racism: Negotiating diversity and sameness in multilingual school discourses. *International Journal of Bilingual Education and Bilingualism, 6*(3–4), 221–236.

Cummins, J. (2001). *Negotiating identities: Education for empowerment in a diverse society* (2nd ed.). Los Angeles, CA: California Association of Bilingual Education.

Cummins, J., & Cameron, L. (1994). The ESL student IS the mainstream: The marginalization of diversity in current Canadian educational debates. *English Quarterly, 26*(3), 30–33.

de Jong, E.J., & Harper, C.A. (2005). Preparing mainstream teachers for English language learners: Is being a good teacher good enough? *Teacher Education Quarterly, 32*(2), 101–124.

Fillmore, L.W., & Snow, C.E. (2002). What teachers need to know about language. In C.A. Adger, C.E. Snow, & D. Christian (Eds.), *What teachers need to know about language* (pp. 7–54). McHenry, IL and Washington, D.C.: Delta Systems, and Center for Applied Linguistics.

Gándara, P., Maxwell-Jolly, J., & Driscoll, A. (2005). *Listening to teachers of English language learners: A survey of California teachers' challenges, experiences, and professional development needs.* The Center for the Future of Teaching and Learning, April. Retrieved from www.cftl.org/publications_latest.php.

Gay, G. (2000). *Culturally responsive teaching: Theory, research, & practice.* New York, NY: Teachers College Press.

Gay, G. (2002). Preparing for culturally responsive teaching. *Journal of Teacher Education, 53*(2), 106–116.

Gersten, R. (1999). Lost opportunities: Challenges confronting four teachers of English-language learners. *The Elementary School Journal, 100*(1), 37–56.

Gibbons, P. (2002). *Scaffolding language, scaffolding learning.* Portsmouth, NH: Heinemann.

Gibbons, P. (2003). Mediating language learning: Teacher interactions with ESL students in a content-based classroom. *TESOL Quarterly, 3,* 247–273.

González, N., Moll, L.C., & Amanti, C. (2005). *Funds of knowledge: Theorizing practices in households, communities, and classrooms.* Mahwah, NJ: Lawrence Erlbaum.

Harklau, L. (1999). The ESL learning environment in secondary school. In C.J. Faltis & P. Wolfe (Eds.), *So much to say: Adolescents, bilingualism & ESL in the secondary school* (pp. 42–60). New York, NY: Teachers College Press.

Harper, C.A., & de Jong, E.J. (2004). Misconceptions about teaching ELLs. *Journal of Adolescent and Adult Literacy, 48*(2), 152–162.

Harper, C.A., & de Jong, E.J. (2005). Working with ELLs: What's the difference? In A. Huerta Macias (Ed.), *Working with English language learners: Perspectives and practice* (pp. 107–135). Dubuque, IA: Kendall Hunt.

Harper, C.A., & de Jong, E.J. (2007). Is the emperor wearing any clothes? Is ESL just good teaching? [Webcast Presentation]. Alexandria, VA: TESOL.

Harper, C.A., & de Jong, E.J. (2009). English language teacher expertise: The elephant in the room. *Language and Education, 23*(2), 137–151.

Igoa, C. (1995). *The inner world of the immigrant child.* Mahwah, NJ: Lawrence Erlbaum.

Krashen, S., & Terrell, T. (1983). *The natural approach: Language acquisition in the classroom*. San Francisco, CA: Alemany Press.

Leung, C., & Franson, C. (2001). Mainstreaming: ESL as a diffused curriculum concern. In B. Mohan, C. Leung, & C. Davison (Eds.), *English as a second language in the mainstream: Teaching, learning and identity* (pp. 11–29). London: Pearson.

Lucas, T., & Grinberg, J. (2008). Responding to the linguistic reality of mainstream classrooms: Preparing all teachers to teach English language learners. In M. Cochran-Smith, S. Feiman-Nemser, & D.J. McIntyre (Eds.), *Handbook of research on teacher education: Enduring questions in changing contexts* (3rd ed., pp. 606–636). New York, NY: Routledge.

Menken, K., & Antunez, B. (2001). *An overview of the preparation and certification of teachers working with limited English proficient (LEP) students*. Washington, D.C.: National Clearinghouse for Bilingual Education.

Mora, J.K., & Grisham, D.L. (2001). ¡What deliches tortillas! Preparing teachers for literacy instruction in linguistically diverse classrooms. *Teacher Education Quarterly, 28*(4), 51–70.

Mullock, B. (2006). The pedagogical knowledge base of four TESOL teachers. *The Modern Language Journal, 90*(1), 48–66.

Nieto, S. (2000). *Affirming diversity: The sociopolitical context of multicultural education* (3rd ed.). New York, NY: Longman.

Nieto, S. (2002). *Language, culture, and teaching: Critical perspectives for a new century*. Mahwah, NJ: Lawrence Erlbaum.

Platt, E., & Troudi, S. (1997). Mary and her teachers: A Grebo-speaking child's place in the mainstream classroom. *Modern Language Journal, 81*, 28–49.

Short, D. (2002). Language learning in sheltered social studies classes. *TESOL Journal, 11*(1), 18–24.

Sleeter, C.E., & Stillman, J. (2005). Standardizing knowledge in a multicultural society. *Curriculum Inquiry, 35*(1), 27–46.

TESOL. (2002). *TESOL/NCATE P-12 Standards for Teacher Education Programs*. Alexandria, VA. Retrieved from www.ncate.org/documents/ProgramStandards/tesol.pdf.

U.S. Department of Education (2001). No Child Left Behind Act (2002). Retrieved from www.ed.gov/policy/elsec/leg/esea02/index.html.

Varghese, M.M., & Stritikus, T.T. (2005). "Nadie me dijo: (Nobody told me)": Language policy negotiation and implications for teacher education. *Journal of Teacher Education, 56*(1), 73–87.

Walker, A., Shafer, J., & Iiams, M. (2004). "Not in my classroom": Teacher attitudes towards English language learners in the mainstream classroom. *NABE Journal of Research and Practice, 2*(1), 130–160.

Wong-Fillmore, L., & Snow, C.E. (2002). What teachers need to know about language. In C.T. Adger, C.E. Snow, & D. Christian, (Eds.), *What teachers need to know about language* (pp. 7–53). Washington, D.C.: Center for Applied Linguistics.

Youngs, C.S., & Youngs, G.A., Jr. (2001). Predictors of mainstream teachers' attitudes toward ESL students. *TESOL Quarterly, 35*(1), 97–120.

Zehler, A., Fleischman, H., Hopstock, P., Stephenson, T., Pendizick, M., & Sapru, S. (2003). *Descriptive study of services to LEP students and LEP students with disabilities. Vol. 1. Research Report*. Retrieved from www.ncela.gwu.edu/resabout/research/descriptivestudyfiles/volI_research_fulltxt.pdf.

Chapter 6

Systemic Functional Linguistics, Teachers' Professional Development, and ELLs' Academic Literacy Practices

Meg Gebhard, Jerri Willett, Juan Pablo Jiménez Caicedo, and Amy Piedra

Changing demographics, in combination with state and federal policies such as No Child Left Behind legislation, English-only mandates, and high-stakes testing practices, have placed new demands on all educators (e.g., August & Shanahan, 2006). In response, content-area teachers and teacher educators are asking fundamentally different questions about the nature of their work given the demand for *all* educators to meet the needs of an increasing number of English language learners (ELLs) and students who speak non-dominant varieties of English. The purpose of this chapter is to describe how a district–university partnership supported teachers in exploring how they can teach *all* of their students, including ELLs, to use content-based language in ways that value and build on what students already know and can do with language by introducing them to an approach to content-based literacy development based on the work of M.A.K. Halliday (1978, 1996) and using this approach to design, implement, and reflect on curriculum and instruction. To achieve this purpose, we begin by describing a district–university partnership called the ACCELA Alliance (Access to Critical Content and English Language Acquisition) and ways in which Halliday's theory of Systemic Functional Linguistics (SFL) informs its work. Next, we illustrate the workings of this partnership by providing an ethnographic case study of the literacy practices enacted by a fourth-grade teacher and one of her students over the course of an academic year. We conclude by discussing the implications of this work for teachers' professional development.

The ACCELA Alliance[1]

ACCELA is a professional development partnership between the University of Massachusetts and two urban school districts. Designed by faculty members in the Language, Literacy, and Culture Concentration (LLC),[2] this partnership was established in 2002 with federal funds to support in-service teachers, administrators, teacher educators, and researchers in understanding and responding to the combined influences of No Child Left Behind legislation, state-wide curriculum frameworks, high-stakes tests, mandated approaches to literacy instruction, and the passage of a state-wide English-only referendum. The broad goal of this partnership is to provide sustained and reciprocal professional development to all participants by engaging in collaborative and action-oriented research regarding the academic literacy development of ELLs in today's schools. In working toward this goal, the ACCELA Alliance has designed and implemented a number of institutional structures and practices, all of which focus on critically understanding the nature of teaching and learning in ACCELA teachers' classrooms.

First, ACCELA faculty developed an inquiry-based Master's degree program designed specifically for in-service classroom teachers working with large numbers of ELLs. Second, we created a weekly seminar for LLC doctoral students and faculty to support LLC doctoral students in acting as research assistants to ACCELA teachers. Third, we initiated the "ACCELA Dialogues," a local conference that provides a forum for school, district, and university administrators, Doctoral students, and faculty to explore more effective and equitable policies and practices for ELLs and their teachers.

The teachers who participate in ACCELA are in-service elementary and middle school teachers of Language Arts, Reading, Special Education, or ESL. All seek a graduate degree and some seek an additional state license in ESL and/or Reading. ACCELA courses are taught in the local schools by university faculty following district calendars. One course is offered each quarter so teachers can complete the program within three years. As part of this course-work, ACCELA teachers conduct inquiry projects in which they document and analyze their teaching practices in light of how these practices influence the learning of selected case study students. Data from these case studies inform discussions in courses and research seminars, which in turn inform the development of teachers' research projects. Doctoral students and faculty support teachers as they: develop research questions aligned with course objectives and connected to pressing local issues; analyze district, state, and national standards; design curriculum and instruction; collect and analyze student data (e.g., transcripts, writing samples, test scores); and present their research projects to colleagues in their districts, to other educators at national conferences, and in various publications (see www.umass.edu/accela).

ACCELA's practices are informed by a socio-cultural perspective of designing, implementing, and assessing standards-based instruction; a teacher-as-researcher stance to professional development; a functional view of language and language learning; and a recursive focus on issues concerning social justice and political forces influencing public education (Gebhard, Austin, Nieto, & Willett, 2002). Based on this framework, case study data are discussed by faculty and doctoral students in weekly seminars on campus to understand how the ACCELA curriculum is shaping teacher learning and to inform revisions in our teacher education program. For example, our analyses revealed early on that, although most ACCELA teachers were capable users of academic language themselves, they were not adequately prepared to provide their students with explicit instruction and feedback in how content-based language operates within the disciplinary genres they routinely ask students to read and write (e.g., narratives, reports, explanations). Thus a significant change in the ACCELA program early in its development was the introduction of Halliday's theory of Systemic Functional Linguistics (SFL) and genre-based pedagogy to support the academic literacy development of ELLs.

Systemic Functional Linguistics and Academic Literacy Development

Despite important differences among researchers using Halliday's theories, all share a socio-cultural perspective of language and language learning (Halliday, 1978, 1996; Vygotsky, 1978). From an SFL perspective, language is a dynamic system of linguistic choices that students learn to use to accomplish a wide variety of social, academic, and political goals in and out of school (New London Group, 1996). Therefore, from an SFL perspective, the job of the teacher is to broaden students' ability to use language more expertly across a variety of social and academic contexts to accomplish specific kinds of work. Teachers and students can explore the way language functions to enact relationships among participants, convey new meaning or ideas, and reflect the mode of communication (e.g., face-to-face, online, written). These three functions provide a basis for analyzing how texts vary in relation to who is communicating with whom, what they are communicating about, and the modes through which they are interacting (Christie & Martin, 1997; Cope & Kalantzis, 1993).

A brief example that reveals how SFL can support an analysis of academic language development comes from an interaction the first author, Meg, had with a sixth-grade girl regarding her science fair project. This student asked Meg for feedback on her investigation regarding which brand of bubble gum would yield the biggest bubble. This assignment was designed to teach students how to use the scientific method and the language of science. In reviewing this student's report, Meg drew the girl's attention to the last sentence that read, "So, in the end, we decided that Trident Sugarless Gum is best." Meg commented that scientists typically do not use "so" in their writing and they do not use language that suggests they decided the results of their experiments. Rather, part of understanding the scientific method is understanding that scientists try (and sometimes fail) to be more detached from the results of their experiments and to let the data "do the talking" (Lemke, 1990). Meg suggested the following alternative, "In conclusion, the data suggest that Trident Sugarless Gum is best for bubble-blowing." Interestingly, the student laughed out loud, almost fell out of her chair, and said, "There is no way I'm talking like that! What do you think I am, a geek!" This response suggests that she understood that linguistic choices not only construct ideas (e.g., an understanding of the scientific method and the results of an experiment) and reflect modes of interacting (oral/everyday and written/formal), but also convey aspects of identity. In other words, she understood the meaning of the changes Meg suggested on multiple levels, but she was not willing to play around with her 12-year-old-girl voice by trying on a new, more "scientific" one.

This example also illustrates how SFL-based pedagogy focuses on expanding the range of linguistic choices available to students in performing essential school-based tasks such as writing laboratory reports, narrating events, providing definitions, writing descriptions, describing a process, or making an argument (Schleppegrell, 2004). From this perspective, linguistic choices are understood to operate at the word, sentence, and discourse levels, and to reflect the degree to which students have been socialized into and wish to align themselves with valued ways of knowing and being in school (Gee, 1996). As many studies have shown, schooled ways of using language, knowing, and being differ from everyday practices in significant ways (Heath, 1983). For ELLs and speakers of non-dominant varieties of English, these differences are even greater and take on even more significance as students are required to read and write about unfamiliar topics, use technical language that differs from home or peer meaning-making practices, and assume new, often uncomfortable or contradictory, identities (Dyson, 1993). As such, one of the main goals of ACCELA (and subsequently our on-campus program) has been to support teachers in critically apprenticing students to using academic language to accomplish meaningful cognitive, social, and political work while also valuing community ways of using language, knowing, and being (Nieto & Bode, 2008).

To describe how ACCELA supports teachers in using SFL and SFL-based pedagogy, this chapter looks at a case study that involves the genre of narrative. Despite the fact that narrative is one of the most commonly assigned types of text in school, and that the story is one of the most powerful mediums for capturing important social issues, many teachers lack an explicit awareness of how the organizational, grammatical, and lexical features work in the texts they assign, or how to teach novice readers and writers to play with these features in learning to write their own narratives in more able and compelling ways (Hyland, 2007). SFL scholarship can assist teachers in supporting their students in this task by providing insights into how narratives work (Derewianka, 1990; Knapp & Watkins, 2005).

Thus, in order to foster the incorporation of SFL pedagogy in the teaching of reading and writing narratives, ACCELA supports teachers in understanding the features typical of the narrative genre:

- An "orientation" in which the writer attempts to situate the reader in a particular time, place, or social context, and to introduce the main characters.

- A "sequence of events" or series of "complications," in which the characters confront an issue or set of issues and explore possible solutions to the problem(s) at hand. Through these events, the reader develops a deeper sense of who the characters are and how they have been shaped by their experiences.
- A "resolution" phase in which the characters come to terms (or not) with the problem at hand. This phase often shows how the characters have been changed (or not) by their experiences and may contain an evaluation or comment on the narrative as a whole.

With regard to grammatical and lexical features, narratives typically rely on the use of particular types of verbs. These types include: (1) material processes expressing concrete actions central to the plot (e.g., run, fight, arrest, rescue); (2) verbal processes communicating how characters express themselves (e.g., say, scream, whisper); (3) mental processes communicating how characters think or feel (e.g., think, decide, wonder); and (4) relational processes showing relationships among characters and events (e.g., is, have). Narratives rely on the past tense and the use of "temporal connectives" to communicate the sequences of events (e.g., one day, next, then, suddenly, in the end). They also rely on the use of "logical connectives" to express the purposes, causes, or effects of actions (e.g., because, although, so).

As a way of illustrating how ACCELA uses SFL theory and SFL-based pedagogies, we present below an ethnographic case study of how a teacher named Amy Piedra learned to use SFL to teach narratives to her students. At the time of the study, Amy was teaching fourth grade, and nearly all of her students were ELLs and could be described as struggling readers and writers. We focus on changes in Amy's teaching practices and how these changes influenced the narratives produced by an academically struggling ELL student named "Eloy." (The names of students, schools, and neighborhoods are pseudonyms.)

An Ethnographic Case Study of SFL in Practice

Context

Both Amy and Eloy lived in "Milltown," Massachusetts—a once-thriving industrial city that has suffered greatly as it has undergone dramatic economic and demographic changes in the last 50 years. It is now one of the poorest school districts serving the highest numbers of Latino students in the state. For example, three of four students live below the poverty line, identify as "Hispanic" and speak a language other than English at home (http://profiles. doe.mass.edu). Amy was born in Milltown to recent immigrants from Puerto Rico and moved back and forth between Milltown and Puerto Rico as a child. She lived in a Puerto Rican community called the "Flats" and attended Lincoln Elementary School as a girl. After graduating from Milltown High

School, she attended Milltown Community College and a local four-year state college where she earned a Bachelor's Degree in Elementary Education. After graduating in 2000, she worked as a daycare provider, a long-term substitute teacher, and an ESL/bilingual paraprofessional. In 2003 Amy applied and was accepted into the ACCELA program and in 2004 she was offered her first full-time position as a fourth-grade teacher at Lincoln. Through her ACCELA course work, Amy became acquainted with Meg Gebhard and Jerri Willett, the co-directors of ACCELA. She had also worked with Juan Pablo Jiménez Caicedo, a doctoral student who supported the data collection activities related to her course work. While Amy was enrolled in Jerri's course on content-based instruction for ELLs, Amy, Meg, and Juan Pablo agreed to collaborate on researching questions regarding Amy's teaching practices and how these practices influenced the way ELLs analyzed and wrote narratives over the course of the year. We focused on narratives because this genre forms the foundation of Language Arts curriculum frameworks in Massachusetts and in other states (Schleppegrell, 2003). Narratives were also the focus of the first unit Amy was required to teach in adhering to a mandated textbook series in her school. Given these factors, our collaboration centered on the following questions:

- Over the course of the academic school year, how did Amy's approach to designing and implementing instruction related to supporting students in interpreting and producing narratives change?
- Over the course of the academic school year, how did ELLs' ability to produce written narratives change?

Eloy lived in the "Flats" of Milltown with his older brother, sister, mother, and aunt, all of whom he reported spoke mostly Spanish. He had a slight frame when compared to many of the other boys in his class, but made his presence known through his easy-going, light-hearted manner (despite often writing about weighty topics). He was rarely absent from school and participated actively in discussions, often chiming in with expressions that seemed to belong to another time (e.g., *that's the ticket, now you're talking*). Eloy had received bilingual instruction at Lincoln for grades K-3. In fourth grade, as a result of a statewide English-only mandate, he began receiving instruction in English despite the fact that his English proficiency was still limited. For example, he struggled to manage the English tense system in his speech and writing. In addition, as is typical of language learner discourse, it was often difficult to follow the thread of his ideas over longer stretches of talk without a good deal of negotiation, as he often relied on his audience to play a very active role in constructing meaning with him. In his discourse, he often searched for a word or a phrase and interrupted the flow of his talk to find alternatives. While, like all language learners, he had creative ways of using the linguistic resources at his disposal to construct new meanings, some structural, grammatical, and lexical aspects of this oral narrative were difficult to follow. These aspects of both Eloy's oral and written texts, not at all unusual for an ELL or an emergent reader/writer, provide a baseline "snapshot" for analyzing how his ability to produce narratives changed over the course of the year in the context of Amy's classroom. To present our analysis, we look at Amy's curricular and instructional practices and examine how these practices influenced Eloy's textual practices. Given the limits of this chapter, we focus specifically on units one and three.

Changes in Teaching and Writing Practices Over an Academic Year

Fall 2004: Amy and Eloy Follow the Script

In September, when we met with Amy to discuss how she was approaching Language Arts instruction, she made it clear that she did not have much room in her day to implement "ACCELA ideas" and that she wasn't sure her class-room was going to be a place where we could do "any interesting research." This response was one faculty and doctoral students working with ACCELA teachers were hearing a lot. When we followed up on the issue in the weekly ACCELA seminar, teachers reported that they were required to adhere faith-fully to a mandated textbook series and follow scripted lesson plans aligned to the state standards and exams. Teachers added that in some schools multicul-tural trade books and bilingual materials were being "thrown out." Amy echoed many of these concerns, adding that she did not think the mandated textbook materials were designed for ELLs and certainly not for bilingual, multicultural students of color living in urban areas. She described the first unit she was required to teach, which focused on the genre of "personal nar-ratives." The main text students were required to read and analyze was a chapter from *Addie Across the Prairie* by Laurie Lawlor. This story, set in the Midwest in the 1800s, describes the adventures of a nine-year-old girl who must protect herself and her brother when a fire breaks out on their farm. Amy did not feel this book "represented" her students. She also talked about how much she missed having access to sets of multicultural trade books that were available the year before when she was a classroom aide. She felt so strongly about this that she bought single copies of many of these books and decided to use them as short "read-alouds" in conjunction with the mandated readings.

Despite her willingness to depart from the prescribed curriculum, Amy still did not have the leeway she needed to experiment with using SFL-based pedagogy to support emergent readers and writers like Eloy. The first unit she was mandated to teach required that she introduce students to the "key fea-tures" of the genre of "personal narratives" as stipulated by the textbook. Somewhat erroneously, from an SFL perspective, this list indicates that personal narratives are about an "interesting event or experience in the writ-er's life"; use the pronouns "I" and "me"; "flow" from beginning, to middle, to end; provide "details"; and use "vivid words." As will become evident in an analysis of how Amy and her students worked with these key features, the list did more to constrain than support them in developing a deeper understand-ing of the features of narratives and in producing coherent texts.

From her ACCELA coursework, Amy was aware that children develop the ability to produce narratives with an identifiable setting, characters, a plot sequence, and a thematic moment. Also, in a class discussion of the prescribed list of key features, many of her students stated that narratives have "settings," have "characters," use descriptive words related to the "five senses," and have "a narrator." However, over the course of this discussion, driven by the teach-er's manual, Amy did not take up these valid contributions. Rather, with the teaching script in her hand at all times, she continued to reformulate her questions regarding what constitutes a personal narrative until she received responses that matched the features stipulated by the textbook authors. As a result, the interaction became less a discussion and more a protracted guess-ing game that left students, in Amy's words, feeling "antsy," and her feeling that she had done "a really bad job." Figure 6.1 shows part of this interaction, with Amy working to get students to say the next feature on the list related to the use of the pronouns *I* and *me*. This interaction became increasingly tense as Amy worked to lead them to this specific response and discounted or did not take up other responses that were both valid and provocative (e.g., the topic of "voice," writing "your way of thinking").

As a result of Amy's adherence to the script, this interaction nearly col-lapsed under the weight of her trying to "ventriloquate" the voices of the authors of the teacher's manual rather than attempting to author her own professional one (Bakhtin, 1981, p. 299).

The textbook's list also did little to support Eloy in improving his ability to write a more coherent and developed narrative. Despite his high level of engagement, his first attempt to write a narrative following this lesson func-tioned more like an expository text. This draft, which was about a karate class, opened with the narrative marker *One day*, but then moved to explaining the different kinds of "moves" he was learning rather than an event or series of events related to his experiences learning karate (e.g., *hand punch, hold punch*). Nonetheless, he diligently used the textbook's list to confirm, errone-ously, that he had written a well-formed personal narrative. For example, in reviewing his draft, he confirmed with confidence that the text was about an interesting event in his life and that he had used the pronouns *I* and *me*. In addition, he indicated that his text had a beginning, middle, and end by writing these words on the margins of his paper and concluded that he had given details and used vivid words (e.g., types of punches, reference to blood). Nonetheless, this first draft still had problems because he did not establish a central event or sequence of events as is typical of a narrative text.

1. **Amy:** When you write, when you're a narrator, okay, you tell a story by using what?
2. **Student:** Your voice
3. **Jesus:** Memories!
4. **Amy:** No, memories are (inaudible) now
5. **Jesus:** You're listening ... I mean your letters
6. **Students:** (inaudible)
7. **Amy:** Stop shouting out and think about it, raise your hands (pause). By using what Ramon?
8. **Ramon:** (Inaudible)
9. **Amy:** No! to describe you as a character in your narrative, in your personal narrative, what are you using?
10. **Student:** Your way, your way of thinking, you ...
11. **Amy:** How do you describe your character?
12. **Eveliz:** By yourself
13. **Amy:** Okay, by yourself, Okay, but what pronouns do you use to describe yourself in the story?

There are 19 turns-at-talk about characters as Amy reads a section of a story called Come on, Rain! *This section includes the use of the pronouns* I *and* me.

14. **Amy:** Yes, her Mamma says *"Is it ... is it thunder outside Tessie?"* That's how we know her name, but throughout the whole book, do we say "Tessie steps out into the rain, Tessie went to go get her xx ... Tessie." No, she is telling the story, so she is using two pronouns. What are they?
15. **Karina:** She and um ... um Tessie!
16. **Jaime:** I and her
17. **Amy:** I and ...
18. **Jaime:** Her!
19. **Amy:** No! I and ME, who said ME? I and Me

The interaction continues until Amy has been able to generate the required list of features.

Figure 6.1 Classroom transcript, Unit 1, Fall 2004.

Moreover, the prescribed list did little to highlight what the problem in his text might be or what he might do to address it. For example, the textbook did not provide Amy or her students with guidance in how to make the kinds of linguistic choices expert writers use to help their writing "flow" from "beginning, middle, to end." From an SFL perspective, this list did not draw Amy's and her students' attention to the fact that written narratives, unlike oral stories, typically do not connect new ideas with the word "and." Rather, written narratives typically connect ideas temporally and create "flow" by using words such as *next, then, suddenly, after that, in the end*, and *even now*.

In working on his second draft, Eloy did not develop the topic of learning karate, but initiated a new one about his mother buying two unruly Chihuahuas (see Figure 6.2).

Although Eloy established an orientation and provided a sequence of events, his text still lacked a resolution regarding the dogs and/or a comment on the experience as a whole. Hypothetically, with instruction, he might have concluded by writing, "Wow, am I glad those dogs are gone!" or "Now, we have a

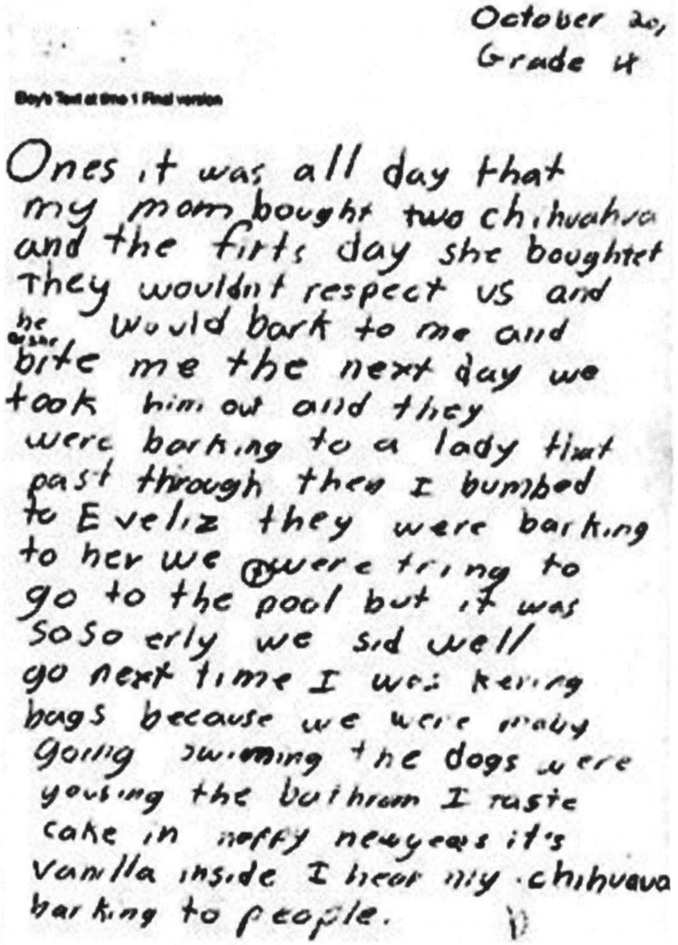

October 20,
Grade 4

Boy's Text at Drive 1 Final version

Ones it was all day that
my mom bought two chihuahua
and the firts day she boughtet
They wouldn't respect us and
he or she would bark to me and
bite me the next day we
took him out and they
were barking to a lady that
past through then I bumbed
to Eveliz they were barking
to her we were tring to
go to the pool but it was
so so erly we sid well
go next time I was kering
bags because we were maby
going swiming the dogs were
yousing the bathroom I taste
cake in hoffy newyeas it's
vanilla inside I hear my chihuava
barking to people.

Eloy's Text 1 (Oct. 2004)

Ones it was all day that my mom bought two chihuahua and the firts day she boughtet they wouldn't respect us and he or she would bark to me and bite me the next day we took him out and they were barking to a lady that past through then I bumbed to Eveliz they were barking to her we were tring to go to the pool but it was so so erly we sid well go next time I was kering bags because we were maby going swimming the dogs were yousing the bathroom I taste cake in happy newyears it's vanilla inside I hear my chihuaua barking to people.

Figure 6.2 Eloy's Final Draft of Dog Story, Unit 1, Fall 2004.

pit bull and I like him better," which in his oral reading he added. Rather, the narrative became incoherent as the text moved from describing how hard it was to walk two barking dogs while simultaneously carrying bags full of swimsuits and towels, to making a statement about the taste of a vanilla cake on New Year's.

In an end-of-the-unit interview with Eloy about this final draft, which he had edited with a peer (i.e., they attended to several unconventional spellings and looked up "Chihuahua" in the dictionary), he recognized that the "cake part" of his text was confusing and described how he might fix it, saying, "I will take that [the part about the cake] out and then keep going with the Chihuahuas." This interview provides evidence that Eloy had a meta-awareness of narrative structures, an awareness that might have led him to make more substantive revisions if the textbook had guided him in that direction or if Amy had had more knowledge and had felt more able to challenge the textbook's conception of the key genre features of a personal narrative. In addition, it is clear that Eloy also had a meta-awareness of textual aspects of his written work. For example, he commented that his text could be improved if it was punctuated and had illustrations.

In reflecting on the unit as a whole, Amy re-iterated her frustration with the mandated materials, the students' texts, and her inability to provide students with instruction that would "move them along as writers." In response to this frustration, for the second unit, and in the context of completing additional coursework, she delved deeper into the literature regarding the use of multicultural children's literature and SFL-based pedagogies to support the academic literacies of linguistically and culturally diverse students. She assigned a portion of the novel *My Name is Maria Isabel* by Alma Flor Ada, which explores issues of language and identity through the experiences of a young Puerto Rican girl whose teacher renames her Mary out of convenience. Amy was introduced to this novel in a course focusing on children's literature and the Puerto Rican experience. In designing this second unit, Amy followed a "backward design" approach (Wiggins & McTighe, 2004) to establish the main content and language goals of the unit and how she was going to provide students with both conceptual and linguistic scaffolding and would assess their final projects—an approach introduced by Jerri in the course Teaching Content for Language Development. Drawing on her ACCELA coursework, Amy assigned her students a unit project that required them to write a narrative about their names by drawing on insights from the Ada novel and focused on their developing understanding of the structural and linguistic features of narratives. Although Amy felt that the changes she implemented in unit two had benefited her students, she still expressed frustration with the quality of her students' narratives. In informal interviews, she recognized that she still was unclear about how to use SFL to design instruction, provide feedback, and assess students' writing. As the following analysis of unit three makes clear, Amy's third attempt at using SFL proved to be much more productive.

May 2005: Amy and Eloy Author Their Own Words

For unit three, Amy continued to strike a balance between adhering to the textbook and introducing students to multicultural children's literature. She also continued to hone her understanding of the linguistic features of written narratives and SFL pedagogy. She was supported in these activities by her continued participation in ACCELA courses and conversations with Meg and Juan Pablo. For example, we re-read parts of Kamberelis' 1999 article on children's knowledge of genres and talked more explicitly about how she was going to scaffold and assess students' developing knowledge of the linguistic features of narratives. In planning this unit, which centered on supporting students in writing a "narrative about a family story," Amy had five goals (as indicated in her unit plans and in an email to the course instructor).

First, she was committed to providing students with access to literature that might resonate with their experiences as Puerto Rican youth living in urban communities. She chose to focus the unit on another text to which she had been introduced during ACCELA coursework—*Grandma's Record* by Eric Velasquez, an autobiography that describes the author's introduction to the sounds and steps of merengue and conga during summers he spent in his grandmother's apartment in Spanish Harlem. Second, Amy wanted to engage students in a linguistic analysis of the language used by Velasquez in constructing his text—especially how he used language to establish setting, create characters, develop the plot, and explore themes related to family. Third, she wanted to support students in using "temporal" and "logical connectives" in revising their narratives to make their texts more coherent. Fourth, as part of an assignment for a seminar on Systemic Functional Linguistics for Teachers, she wanted to make students more aware of the linguistic differences between oral and written ways of telling stories without losing "their voice." Last, she wanted to continue to model her own writing process and provide students with exemplar texts she had written.

An example of how Amy united these five goals in classroom practice is evident in the following classroom interaction (see Figure 6.3). In this example, Amy led the class in a discussion of how temporal connectives in *Grandma's Records* functioned "to move the story along." Similar to the routines she established at the beginning of the year, she stood next to a dry-erase easel with a marker in her hand as students sat on the rug in a circle. Each student had a highlighter and typed copy of the text of *Grandma's Records*. Previously, Amy had instructed them to highlight all of the "plot sequence words" and report their lists back to the whole class. The words the class had generated were posted on a sheet of butcher paper, which was clipped to the easel (e.g., *every year, other times, sometimes, next, whenever, then, one day, while, after, the next day, all day, all of a sudden, over the next days and weeks, as I got older, even now*). Following the topic prescribed in the mandated text-

1. **Amy:** Okay, here Eric Velasquez used these words to move the sequence of events along. To tell us there were many events that happened throughout the summer. Okay? *(Amy reads aloud from the list of words they just generated. Most students joined her in an impromptu choral recitation of these words)*

2. **Amy and students:** Every year, other times, sometimes, next, whenever, then, one day, while, after, the next day, all day, all of the sudden

3. **Eloy:** Suddenly,

4. **Amy:** Suddenly, okay, over the next days and weeks, and as I got older, or even now.

5. **Eloy:** Even now.

6. **Amy:** Now the story, as the story goes on *(flips the butcher paper up to reveal a triangle. At the base is the word "plot" and at the top is the word "climax" as directed by the teacher's manual)* Eric Velasquez wrote about the setting *(writes the word setting on the bottom left of the triangle)*. He introduced us to the setting when we first read it, throughout the book he talks about characters *(writes characters above setting)*. But it starts with every year, every year *(writes every year on left leg of the triangle)* **this is how the story going.** Sometimes *(writes sometimes)* ... other times we danced ... Okay. Um, ONE DAY *(writes one day)* they got a visitor and WHILE *(writes while)* they were eating dessert, they got two tickets. Okay? Now they are on the way to the concert. Then SUDDENLY *(writes suddenly at the top of the triangle by the word climax)* BOOM! The concert went off! *(circles the top point of the triangle)*. So that is like our climax ... they are at a concert ... for the first time ... and then suddenly when the lights went dark// *(spreads arms wide)*

7. **Mark:**   //Everybody got (XXXX)//

8. **Amy:** When the grandma got sung to, Okay.

...

9. **Amy:** *(Pointing to the word suddenly)* Boom the climax ... Then it starts to calm down, then we are like, after the show,

10. **Mark:** The same day

11. **Amy:** *(Softer voice)* We found out ... over the next weeks *(writes over the next weeks)* as I got older *(writes as I got older)* and even now *(writes even now)*. Notice how that happens? *(Moves her hand up the left leg, to the top, and down the right leg of the triangle)*.

12. **Students:** Yeah!

13. **Mark:** A pyramid.

14. **Amy:** That was like our PLOT. This is like a sequence of events. And he uses these words to moves us along in the story *(finger hits each word up and down the pyramid as she speaks)*.

Figure 6.3 Classroom transcript, Unit 3, Spring 2005.

book, Amy provided students with a mini-lesson in how these words and phrases could also be mapped on to the structure of a narrative.

This transcript reveals how Amy supported all students, including ELLs, in analyzing the linguistic choices expert writers make in constructing the plot structure of a written narrative. Amy used this same routine to support students in analyzing how authors use language to establish the setting, develop characters, and convey thematic elements. For example, using their highlighters, the class made lists and analyzed the words and phrases Velasquez used to

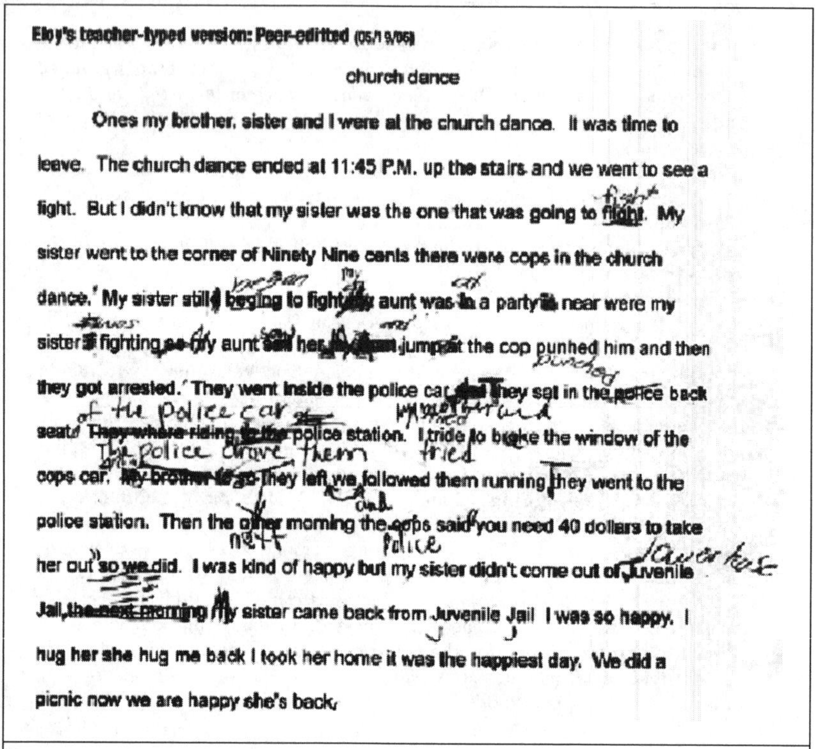

Eloy's teacher-typed version: Peer-edited (05/15/06)

church dance

Ones my brother, sister and I were at the church dance. It was time to leave. The church dance ended at 11:45 P.M. up the stairs and we went to see a fight. But I didn't know that my sister was the one that was going to fight. My sister went to the corner of Ninety Nine cents there were cops in the church dance.' My sister still began to fight my aunt was in a party near were my sister fighting my aunt saw her jumped the cop punhed him and then they got arrested.' They went inside the police car They sat in the police back seat of the Police car They where riding to the police station. I tride to brake the window of the cops car. My brother The police drove them They left we followed them running they went to the police station. Then the other morning the cops said you need 40 dollars to take her out so we did. I was kind of happy but my sister didn't come out of juvenile Jail the next morning My sister came back from Juvenile Jail I was so happy. I hug her she hug me back I took her home it was the happiest day. We did a picnic now we are happy she's back.

Church Dance

Ones my brother, sister and I were at the church dance. It was time to leave. The church dance ended at 11:45 P.M. up the stairs and we went to see a fight. But I didn't know that my sister was the one that was going to fight. My sister went to the corner of Ninety Nine cents there were cops in the church dance. My sister still began to fight, my aunt was at a party near were my sister was fighting. My aunt saw her and my aunt jumped at the cop punched him and then they got arrested! They went inside the police car. They sat in the back seat of the police car. The police drove them to the police station. My brother and I tried to brake the window of the cops car. They left and we followed them running. They went to the police station. Then the next morning the police said "you need 40 dollars to take her out" so we did. I was kind of happy but my sister didn't come out of juvenile jail. My sister came back from juvenile jail I was so happy. I hug her she hug me back I took her home it was the happiest day. We did a picnic now we are happy she's back.

Figure 6.4 Eloy's Third Draft of Church Dance Story, May Unit.

describe the setting (e.g., *"el barrio"* versus "Spanish Harlem," or "neighborhood"; "Grandma's apartment" versus *"abuela's* apartment"); the characters (describing himself as a "homebody" and his grandmother as "nervous on the subway"); the presence or absence of dialogue written in Spanish or varieties of Spanish; reasons for providing or not providing a translation of dialogue written in Spanish for non-Spanish-speakers; and the theme (e.g., family).

As the class began to write their own narratives, Amy provided them with two additional texts to analyze. The first text was one she had written about the boyhood adventures of her fiancé and his brother on a snowy day. The second text was written by Mrs. Rodriquez, a paraprofessional who frequently asked Amy for help with assignments for her adult ESL class. Mrs. Rodriquez' text related the story of when she was held responsible for her younger brother eating a cake intended for a family celebration of her first communion. Following the same routine as illustrated in Figure 6.3, Amy provided the students with highlighters and typed copies of these two additional texts. Next, she asked them to identify how she and Mrs. Rodriquez used words and phrases to establish the setting (e.g., *North Village on a snowy day; Grandma cooking in the kitchen*); to develop characters through description and the use of dialogue; to support the plot structure (*then the impossible happened, all of a sudden*); and to convey themes (e.g., *family responsibility*). Once the students had practiced analyzing and cataloging the words and phrases used by expert writers, they turned their attention to analyzing their own drafts. With highlighters in hands, they identified how they used words and phrases to establish the setting, develop characters through description and the use of dialogue, support the plot structure, and convey themes. If students noticed that their drafts lacked these linguistic features, they were encouraged to appropriate the language of more expert writers in developing their subsequent drafts.

As instructed, Eloy used this procedure to analyze his third draft of a narrative called *Church Dance* (see Figure 6.4). This text recounted the events associated with his sister and aunt getting arrested for fighting at a church dance. He identified the setting as *the church*; listed the characters as *his brother, sister, aunt,* and *the cops*; and described the sequence of events as *focusing on his sister* and *aunt getting arrested*. Although he did not indicate it on the worksheet, his draft included a resolution (i.e., *My sister came back from juvenile jail*) and an evaluation or coda (*We did a picnic now we are happy she's back*).

In his near-final typed draft shown in Figure 6.4, he attended to unconventional spellings (e.g., *punhed/punched*), difficulties in indicating tense (e.g., *my sister still beginning to fight*), the need for punctuation, and writing dialogue. While falling short of producing a fully developed narrative, Eloy did provide his readers with a simple, relatively coherent recount of an event he was invested in sharing. This investment was evident in the degree to which, relative to his other texts, he made linguistic choices to ensure his peers could read his text without a lot of face-to-face negotiation. Eloy's narrative included a brief orientation (e.g., *Ones my brother, sister and I were at the church dance*); a complication and sequence of events (e.g., *we went to see a fight. But I didn't know that my sister was the one that was going to fight*); a resolution (e.g., *My sister came back from juvenile jail*); and an evaluative comment that shifts from the narrative past to the present and brings the story to a close (e.g., *now we are happy she's back*). In addition, he exhibited greater control over a more written as opposed to oral register when compared to the narrative he produced during unit one. For example, this text shows greater control of the narrative past (e.g., *ended, went, saw, jumped, punched, sat, drove, left, followed, said, did*) and ability to use temporal connectives to support the plot structure (*Ones, then the next morning, now*). More striking, he initiated far fewer clauses with "and." Equally significant is his ability to use adverbial and adjectival clauses to pack more information into single clauses while also managing more complex aspects of tense (e.g., *But I didn't know that my sister was the one that was going to fight; my aunt was at a party near w*[h]*ere my sister was fighting*). Last, while he did not make use of paragraphs to signal moves in his narrative, he did make greater and more varied use of punctuation to support readers in pausing between clauses and in reading with intonation (e.g., periods, exclamation mark, quotations). In an end-of-the-unit interview, Eloy commented specifically on the function of punctuation in written texts. Pointing to an earlier draft, he said: "Right here was [*pointing to draft*] and this story was, I had to change stuff because I never put periods here and I keep talking and talking and talking, without no period, without no breathing."

In line with an SFL perspective of language learning, Eloy's work and comments indicate that over the course of the year he was developing not only an understanding of narrative as a specific genre, but also an understanding of the differences between oral and written registers and the function of punctuation in realizing these differences. For example, rather than reciting a rule such as "a period goes at the end of a sentence," he described using periods as a way to support his audience in reading his text.

In reflecting on this curricular unit, Amy also talked in SFL terms about how, in the future, she would support students in writing more developed orientations to situate the reader in a particular time, place, or social context, and to introduce the main characters. She described how she would teach students to notice how authors use language to open their narratives, introduce their characters, and write dialogue. With reference to students' texts, she pointed out that they tended to overuse the verbal process "said" and that they could learn to expand the choices available to them by making lists of how published authors use verbs to reveal how characters feel and express themselves. She also talked about how she would support ELLs in learning to combine simple sentences into compound ones as a way of supporting them in writing more varied and complex sentence structures. Last, Amy commented that an illuminating moment for her was how writing and analyzing her own texts with students made her much more aware of the linguistic features of narratives in a way that she could transform into concrete teaching practices. She also remarked on the ease with which her students, including ELLs, became "text analysts."

These insights were ones she shared with her ACCELA colleagues and her principal at a presentation of her work at the end of the year during one of the ACCELA Dialogues, emphasizing in her final slide that *Kids CAN analyze text.* While not all ACCELA teachers were as successful as Amy in exploring the potential of SFL in their classrooms (a few resisted it entirely), many found her approach to teaching both content and language compelling and began to explore how they could support ELLs in analyzing and appropriating the linguistic features of academic genres in their classrooms. In fact, Amy's work was used with later cohorts of teachers in ACCELA and in our on-campus program. In addition to benefitting from the growing expertise of faculty and doctoral students in using SFL in teacher education, later cohorts drew on Amy's example of how to use SFL-based pedagogy as they designed units of study focusing on such diverse topics and text types as recounts written by second graders for classmates and family members through a class blog (Shin, Gebhard, & Seger, in press); multicultural fairy tales written by third graders; bilingual poetry by fourth graders; published research regarding the benefits of recess read by fifth graders who then wrote persuasive letters to their principal to get their recess reinstated (Gebhard, Harman, & Seger, 2007); and a writer's notebook modeled after the work of Tupac Shakur written by eighth graders. Collectively, what is striking about many of these projects is how ACCELA teachers used their developing understanding of SFL-based pedagogy to support not just ELLs, but *all* students in learning new academic concepts and literacy practices. In addition, these projects supported students in attempting to meet state standards while simultaneously making a space in the curriculum for students to read, write, and take action about topics that were culturally and politically relevant to them and their families.

Summary and Implications

This chapter has analyzed how an ACCELA teacher learned to use SFL-based pedagogy to teach her fourth graders, most of whom were ELLs, to analyze literary texts and write narratives of their own over the course of an academic year. This study focused on analyzing changes in the teacher's instructional practices as mediated by her participation in ACCELA, and how these changes influenced the literacy practices of emergent ELL readers and writers. This analysis reveals that the teacher, Amy, gained a deeper understanding of the structural, lexical, and grammatical features of narratives, a fundamental genre within the Language Arts curriculum. She also developed a more sophisticated understanding of how to incorporate SFL-based pedagogy in her work with ELLs as a way of teaching them disciplinary knowledge and supporting their academic literacy development. She did this by teaching students to analyze the linguistic features of multicultural children's literature and to appropriate the textual practices of more-expert writers, particularly bilingual/bicultural Puerto Rican ones. The analysis also shows that emergent readers and writers, like Eloy, developed a greater ability to use words and phrases to signal essential genre moves found in narratives (e.g., use of lexical-grammatical words and phrases to construe the orientation, the sequence of events, and the resolution), and to shift from an oral to a written register (e.g., less use of *and* to initiate clauses and more use of conventional punctuation and spelling, the narrative past, and more complex clause structures). Finally, the analysis shows that Amy's critical use of SFL tools opened up a discursive space that allowed her to author her own teaching materials and to support students in authoring themselves as capable readers of literature and as writers of their own narratives. Over the year, these practices legitimated the use of multicultural children's literature and the display of bicultural identities while supporting the academic literacy development of ELLs.

The findings from this case study, in combination with the scholarship of other researchers, suggest a number of ways teacher educators can explore the potential of SFL in their work with pre- and in-service teachers (Brisk & Zisselsberger, this volume; Gebhard, Demers, & Castillo-Rosenthal, 2008; Gebhard et al., 2007; Gibbons, 2002; Schleppegrell, 2003, 2004, 2005; Schleppegrell & Go, 2007; Shin et al., in press). First, teacher educators can design a program of study that supports pre- and in-service teachers in developing a greater and more critical understanding of how language works in the texts they routinely ask their students to read and write by drawing on SFL scholarship. For example, teacher educators can develop a program that supports their candidates in: (1) analyzing state curricular frameworks and identifying the genres that are essential to their discipline; (2) analyzing the linguistic features of these discipline-specific text types; and (3) designing curricula, instruction, and assessment tools that explicitly attend to and support the development of both disciplinary knowledge and disciplinary literacy practices.

Second, this study illustrates that it is important for coursework to support teachers in critically engaging with state curricular frameworks as well as other state and federal mandates (e.g., English-only mandates, high-stakes testing practices, scripted lesson materials). In ACCELA, this engagement involves supporting teachers in coupling standards-based instruction with an SFL perspective of academic literacy development *and* a multicultural perspective of education (e.g., Nieto & Bode, 2008). Naturally, engaging in this three-pronged approach to professional development takes time and can be very challenging. However, teachers like Amy, who initially rejected SFL and was apprehensive about replacing required readings with multicultural ones, began to document that her students were less resistant, more engaged, and produced higher quality work when they were supported in working toward state standards by analyzing literature that resonated with them and their communities.

Last, this study suggests that teachers are more likely to develop a critical understanding of school reforms, SFL, and multicultural education if they engage in collaborative and sustained analyses of classroom data (e.g., video clips, curricular materials, transcripts, students' texts). This aspect of ACCELA underscores the importance of teachers, teacher educators, and researchers participating in joint research activities. As leading analysts of teachers' professional development have long argued, joint research projects can support the professional development of teachers and faculty as well as contribute to the production of new knowledge, practices, and policies in local schools and in the field of education more broadly defined (Darling Hammond, 1994).

Notes

1. The ACCELA Alliance (Access to Critical Content and English Language Acquisition) is a federally funded professional development partnership between the University of Massachusetts and two urban school districts in Massachusetts. This study also received support from the Healey Foundation.
2. Faculty from the University of Massachusetts who have been involved in designing and implementing the ACCELA Alliance include Theresa Austin, Francis Bangou, Costanza Eggers-Pierola, Meg Gebhard, Sonia Nieto, Pat Paugh, Fatima Pirbhai-Illich, and Jerri Willett.

References

Ada, A.F. (1995). *My name is María Isabel.* New York, NY: Aladdin Paperbacks.

August, D., & Shanahan, T. (Eds.). (2006). *Developing literacy in second-language learners: Report of the National Literacy Panel on Language-Minority Children and Youth.* Mahwah, NJ: Lawrence Erlbaum.

Bakhtin, M. (1981). *The dialogic imagination: Four essays.* Austin, TX: University of Texas.

Christie, F., & Martin, J.R. (1997). *Genre and institutions: Social processes in the workplace and school.* London: Cassell.

Cope, B., & Kalantzis, M. (1993). *The powers of literacy: A genre approach to teaching writing.* Pittsburgh, PA: University of Pittsburgh Press.

Darling-Hammond, L. (1994). *Professional development schools: Schools for a developing profession.* New York, NY: Teachers College Press.

Derewianka, B. (1990). *Exploring how texts work.* Sydney: Primary English Teaching Association.

Dyson, A. (1993). *Social worlds of children learning to write in an urban primary school.* New York, NY: Teachers College Press.

Gebhard, M., Austin, T., Nieto, S., & Willett, J. (2002). "You can't step on someone else's words": Preparing all teachers to teach language minority students. In Z. Beykont (Ed.), *The power of culture: Teaching across language difference* (pp. 219–243). Cambridge, MA: Harvard Educational Publishing Group.

Gebhard, M., Demers, J., & Castillo-Rosenthal, Z. (2008). Teachers as critical text analysts: L2 literacies and teachers' work in the context of high-stakes school reform. *Journal of Second Language Writing, 17,* 274–291.

Gebhard, M., Harman, R., & Seger, W. (2007). Reclaiming recess in urban schools: The potential of Systemic Functional Linguistics for ELLs and their teachers. *Language Arts, 84*(5), 419–430.

Gee, J. (1996). *Social linguistics and literacy: Ideology in discourse.* London: Taylor & Francis.

Gibbons, P. (2002). *Scaffolding language, scaffolding learning.* Portsmouth, NH: Heinemann.

Halliday, M.A.K. (1978). *Language as social semiotic.* London: Edward Arnold.

Halliday, M.A.K. (1996). Literacy and linguistics: A functional perspective. In R. Hasan & G. Williams (Eds.), *Literacy in society* (pp. 339–376). London: Longman.

Heath, S.B. (1983). *Ways with words.* New York, NY: Cambridge University Press.

Hyland, K. (2007). Genre-based pedagogy: Language, literacy, and L2 writing instruction. *Journal of Second Language Writing, 12*(1), 17–29.

Kamberelis, G. (1999). Genre development and learning: Children writing stories, reports, and poems. *Research in the Teaching of English, 33*(4), 403–460.

Knapp, P., & Watkins, M. (2005). *Genre, text, grammar: Technologies for teaching and assessing writing.* Sydney: University of New South Wales Press.

Lawlor, L. (1986). *Addie across the prairie.* Morton Grove, IL: Albert Whitman & Company.

Lemke, J. (1990). *Talking science: Language, learning, and value.* Norwood, NJ: Ablex Publishing.

Massachusetts Department of Elementary and Secondary Education. (2001). *Massachusetts Curriculum Frameworks for English Language Arts,* June. Retrieved from www.doe.mass.edu/frameworks/current.html.

Massachusetts Department of Elementary and Secondary Education. (2009). School/district profiles, June. Retrieved from http://profiles.doe.mass.edu.

New London Group. (1996). A pedagogy of multiliteracies: Designing social features. *Harvard Educational Review, 66*(1), 60–92.

Nieto, S., & Bode, P. (2008). *Affirming diversity: The sociopolitical context of multicultural education* (5th ed.). Boston, MA/New York, NY: Allyn & Bacon/Longman.

Schleppegrell, M. (2003). *Grammar for writing: Academic language and the ELD Standards.* Santa Barbara, CA: University of California's Linguistic Minorities Research Institute.

Schleppegrell, M. (2004). *The language of schooling: A functional linguistics perspective.* Mahwah, NJ: Lawrence Erlbaum.

Schleppegrell, M. (2005). *Helping content area teachers work with academic language: Promoting English language learners' literacy in History.* Santa Barbara, CA: University of California's Linguistic Minorities Research Institute.

Schleppegrell, M., & Go, A. (2007). Analyzing the writing of English learners: A functional approach. *Language Arts, 84*(6), 529–538.

Shin, D.S., Gebhard, M., & Seger, M. (in press). Weblogs and English language learners' academic literacy development: Expanding audiences, expanding identities. In S. Rilling & M. Dantas-Whitney (Eds.), *Authenticity in the classroom and beyond.* Alexandria, VA: TESOL, Inc.

Velasquez, E. (2004). *Grandma's records.* New York, NY: Walker Young Readers.

Vygotsky, L.S. (1978). *Mind in society.* Cambridge: Harvard University Press.

Wiggins, G., & McTighe, J. (2004). *Understanding by design.* Alexandria, VA: Association for Supervision and Curriculum Development.

Chapter 7

"We've Let Them in on the Secret"

Using SFL Theory to Improve the Teaching of Writing to Bilingual Learners

María Estela Brisk and Margarita Zisselsberger

Bilingual learners represent a growing population in Massachusetts classrooms, with a 13% increase in the last ten years. Approximately 50,000 students in Massachusetts, speaking 112 languages, were identified as limited English proficient in 2006 (National Clearinghouse for English Language Acquisition, 2006). In addition, Massachusetts is one of a number of states that passed legislation eliminating most forms of bilingual education, the only exception being two-way programs. This restrictive language policy, coupled with the barrage of standards and test requirements mandated to ensure accountability under the 2001 No Child Left Behind Act (NCLB), has placed an increasing strain on schools with large numbers of students acquiring English as a new language. In Massachusetts, as in other states, language policies that place bilingual students in mainstream classrooms increasingly create a context that generalizes the linguistic and cultural needs of bilingual learners, thereby operating under the assumption "that effective instruction for [English language learners] is little more than good teaching practices for a diverse group of native English speakers" (Harper & de Jong, 2005, p. 55). As a result of this assumption, the specific linguistic and cultural features of school writing remain invisible to those acquiring English as an additional language since most teachers do not explicitly teach those features to native English speakers.

Bilingual learners need to acquire the second language in addition to literacy and content knowledge (Bernhardt, 1991) to competently perform in the academic registers required of mainstream monolingual classrooms. If the specific teaching of language is ignored, students develop a dialect that allows them to cope with everyday communicative challenges (Fillmore & Snow, 2000), but "when lexical and grammatical development does not keep pace with school expectations, students are unable to meet the reading and writing demands of disciplinary learning" (Schleppegrell, 2004, p. 80). However, little is known about best practices for writing instruction for bilingual learners (Fitzgerald, 2006).

One approach to teaching writing ripe for research is the use of systemic functional linguistics (SFL) as the theoretical basis to describe what needs to be taught. Teaching writing based on SFL theory allows students to "uncover the secrets" of English academic writing (in the words of one of the teachers discussed below, p. 118). The cultural and linguistic norms of academic writing often remain implicit in the demands made of children in school. Language, from an SFL perspective, is viewed as a resource in connecting meaning and form (Schleppegrell, 2004) rather than as isolated grammatical rules. SFL makes the academic language demands explicit to students, thereby allowing them to manipulate language to create meaning.

The purpose of this chapter is to report on a professional development project that presented elementary teachers with an SFL-based approach to the teaching of writing. Data were collected to investigate how learning about SFL would impact the teaching of writing in mainstream elementary classrooms with bilingual learners. This chapter describes the project and then presents findings from the study—first through a brief analysis of the impact of the project on all the participating teachers and then through an analysis of one teacher's class and the writing development of three bilingual students in her class.

Systemic Functional Linguistics: An Overview

The systemic functional linguistics (SFL) tradition is rooted in Halliday's (1985) scholarship on social semiotics, which can be defined as the relationship between text and context. Halliday (1985) posits that systemic functional linguistics theory is "a theory of meaning as choice, by which a language, or any other semiotic system, is interpreted as networks of interlocking options" (p. xiv).

SFL focuses on texts—which exist in the context of culture and are further embedded in the context of situation. Context, register, and genre, in combination, guide the language choices made by users of language to create a particular text. Thus, the language choices made by a professor for a PowerPoint presentation for a college class in the United States will be different from the choices made by a first-grade student writing a fictional story in a classroom in Singapore. Second language (L2) learners need to learn the language demands of the particular cultural and situational context as well as the register and genre. For example, when calling the teacher, second language learners should say: "Mrs. Smith, could you please explain that again?" rather than "Teacher, could you please explain that again?" This form of address, frequently used by immigrant students, is considered inappropriate in the American cultural context. When talking on the playground with a friend, a second language speaker can say "He always cry." However, when writing the final version of a story for publication, this student should be able to write: "He always cries." Thus, L2 learners need to acquire the appropriate syntactic forms of the language, not because they are the correct rules but because they are essential for certain contexts.

Register is the use of language in a particular context for a particular purpose. The register of a text is defined by (a) the type of text (mode)—oral, written, or multimodal, (b) the audience/writer relationship (tenor), and (c) the topic (field). For SFL, a letter is a type of text (mode) as are PowerPoint presentations and short stories—each follows certain patterns. But a letter can be written for different purposes; it can persuade (exposition), inform (report), or tell what happened to an author (recount). The language used in a text is also shaped by the relative status of the writer and reader. Different academic registers in school require different linguistic choices. Through an SFL approach to looking at language, each of the socio-cultural functions of mode, tenor and field can be examined in more depth to understand how grammar and the organization of clauses impact meaning (Halliday, 1985).

Examining the *field*, or the content of a message, shows how language is made up of a set of resources that, when combined, create meaning. A clause typically creates meaning by describing what is going on (verbs or processes) involving things (nouns, participants) which sometimes have attributes (adjectives) that occur within a particular context involving time, place, and manner (adverbs or circumstances) (Thompson, 2004). Clauses in a discourse are connected through logical links, which allow for two or more clauses to be joined, creating a larger whole. The types of relationships between clauses determine the language choices available to create a coherent text. For example:

> The mother placed the baby gently in the crib. Later, she checked on the baby to make sure he was sleeping.

The mother, the baby and the crib are participants of the clause. Placing the baby and checking on the baby show the processes or actions that took place. The words "gently" and "to make sure he was sleeping in the crib" describe the circumstances or what was done given the time, place, and manner. The adverb "later" serves as a logical semantic link that enhances what was said in the first clause. Examining the specific grammatical resources and how these resources function is part of developing a greater understanding of language. This understanding is what an SFL approach offers to students in learning how language works in social and academic contexts.

Genre is defined by the purpose of the text, and texts in different genres are characterized by different structural organizations. SFL defines genre as the forms of texts that share the same general purpose in the culture, often sharing the same obligatory and optional structural elements (Butt, Fahey, Feez, Spinks, & Yallop, 2000). The most common genres in elementary settings include various types of recounts (personal, factual, procedural, historical, and imaginative), fictional narratives, procedures, reports, and expositions. Recounts relate a series of events based on personal experience, an observed incident, or observations of phenomena; they may take the point of view of the author or of someone else (Martin & Rothery, 1986; Schleppegrell, 2004). Recounts can also record historical events. By contrast, fictional narratives tell an imaginative story, although sometimes these are based on facts. Fictional narratives are structures meant to entertain and to teach cultural values (Martin & Rothery, 1986). Typically, procedures provide instructions for how something is done, whether general or scientific. A report is a factual text used to organize and store information clearly and succinctly (Schleppegrell, 2004). Finally, expositions persuade people to a particular point of view, with arguments introduced and supported with evidence. Another type of exposition presents both points of view (Butt et al., 2000; Dewsbury, 1994). Each of these genres can be produced using a number of text types such as letters, essays, responses to literature, story books, and plays.

SFL-based pedagogy makes the linguistic, lexical, grammatical, and schematic structure of texts within genres explicit, thus providing access for all learners (Cope & Kalantzis, 1993). This pedagogy shows students that there are explicit patterns within a culture, and that these patterns are not rigid but are used to achieve a certain purpose to express meaning (Christie, 1998; Halliday & Hasan, 1989). As such, SFL pedagogy emphasizes the development of a language to talk *about language* with students. This metalanguage gives students a deeper awareness of language features and offers students *and teachers* knowledge about when and how to use language (tenor) so that they can make informed choices when speaking/writing (mode) about different topics (field). SFL theory does not endorse fixed rules but shows how different choices serve different purposes and thus create different meanings (Christie, 1998; Halliday & Hasan, 1989). Understanding why genres are structured as they are and the role language plays for particular discourse patterns required of academic writing in school settings (Schleppegrell, 2004; Smith, Cheville, & Hillocks Jr., 2006) is particularly important for bilingual students learning both the language and cultural demands of writing in school.

Supported by this theory of language, we organized a university–school collaboration designed to prepare teachers to teach writing by calling attention to language through examination of student work and children's literature. The focus on language makes this approach particularly helpful to classrooms with English language learners.

Methods of Inquiry

Participants

Teachers from two elementary schools that have had a long-term partnership with the university were invited to participate in the collaborative project. Eight K-5 mainstream classroom teachers, a K-2 science teacher, an English as a second language teacher, and a literacy coach volunteered to participate. Shortly after the initial summer meeting, the fifth-grade teacher had to withdraw. A fifth-grade teacher with a long term relationship with the first author from a third school was invited to join in order to have all grade levels represented. The second-grade teacher was also the literacy coach for her school.

In the classes involved in the study, more than 80% of the students came from homes that use a language other than English for communication (although the district officially classifies 18% of its students as Limited English Proficient (LEP)). The teachers were asked to identify three bilingual learners in their classes whom they would observe and whose writing they would collect. The mainstream teachers in all three schools had received professional development to work with bilingual learners.

Both authors of this chapter had conducted professional development on teaching bilingual learners in the two schools before embarking on the project described in the chapter. The first author, referred to in this chapter as "the facilitator," organized the professional development (PD) materials, facilitated the PD meetings, and observed the classrooms between meetings. During these observations, she discussed with the teachers what she observed in their teaching and in the students' performances. The second author worked exclusively with the kindergarten teacher, assisting in planning the writing instruction and observing its implementation. The second author also observed the three focus students and collected their writing. A research assistant took field notes of the PD meetings and interviewed the teachers.

Context: The Professional Development Meetings

The 11 participants attended seven two-hour sessions in which the facilitator presented SFL theory applied to the teaching of writing. During the first session, which took place in the summer, three weeks prior to the start of the school year, participants were given an overview of the content. The group discussed and agreed on the process to be followed during the upcoming few months, deciding that the rest of the meetings would take place in the schools, alternating between the two schools where most of the participants worked. Each participant received a large binder with materials related to the main topics in SFL theory, including context of culture, context of situation, field, tenor, mode, and genres. For each of the selected genres found in elementary school texts, there was an explanation of the structural organization and language demands of the genre. The concepts of participants, processes, circumstances, and links were elaborated. The materials also included suggestions for teaching strategies for the various genres.

Data Collection and Analysis

Data were collected to document the PD meetings, teachers' perceptions of the PD, classroom implementation, and student work. The content of the PD meetings was documented through field notes of the meetings and meeting plans and materials. Teachers' perceptions of the PD and the impact on their teaching and their students' learning were identified through teacher interviews carried out and recorded by the graduate assistant. Both authors took field notes during classroom observations and collected the products from the three focus students that the teachers collected and copied. Content covered in classes, concerns raised by the teachers, and changes made from the original plans were identified through analysis of the PD field notes. Finally, the notes on observations served to illustrate how the theory discussed in the PD translated into practice. Notes from observations of the kindergarten teacher were also used to develop a detailed description of the implementation within one classroom. The products of the three kindergarten students were analyzed to find evidence of the impact of the implementation on students' writing.

Results

This section presents findings from the analysis of the work with all 11 participants with respect to the content of the PD meetings, participants' perceptions of the project, the implementation of the new ideas about teaching writing, and the impact on three students in one kindergarten classroom. The classroom practices and student learning in this kindergarten classroom are described in some depth.

Responsiveness of Professional Development to Participants' Needs and Interests

Although the facilitator had a clear plan for the PD, she constantly made adjustments based on the participants' reactions. Changes were made in the syllabus, the content of the individual sessions, and the logistics. The final syllabus was revised to focus on specific genres after the meeting with the second-grade teacher/literacy coach. The PD meetings were allowed to flow freely in response to teachers' questions and particular student work shared. Although one genre was the primary focus of each meeting, others were discussed when student work illustrated other genres. The goal of the professional development was to focus on *what* to teach, not *how* to teach. In the last two sessions, in response to teachers' frustration at not being able to make the connection between what was presented in the PD sessions and how to teach writing, the facilitator shifted the emphasis to instructional practices, providing a guiding list of steps for teachers to follow when teaching writing.

The facilitator realized that the PD needed to explicitly connect with the materials teachers were already using. Thus, in addition to the materials specially prepared for the PD, connections were made with the commercial programs the schools were using for writing and reading. Sensing that the teachers were struggling with all the new concepts, the facilitator decided to analyze student texts and published texts before each meeting to prepare for the discussion.

These adaptations had both positive and negative repercussions. Focus on genres and their organizational structure was attractive to teachers; this was accessible material that could be readily applied to lessons. However, spending so much time on genres left little time to emphasize language, which is central to SFL theory and much needed by the students. Helping teachers connect theory with practice with suggestions about how to teach and organize the units helped teachers gain confidence in implementing these new ideas, but this took time away from learning about the theory and understanding language and its function, which should have been the priority so teachers would have the theoretical understanding to help children create the meanings they want to convey. The facilitator's analysis of published texts helped the teachers talk about the readings in new ways, and her analysis of students' writing helped the teachers recognize their students' capabilities. Much greater impact could have been achieved, however, if teachers had done the analysis themselves with the support of the facilitator.

Teachers' Perceptions of the Impact of the Professional Development

In the interviews and occasionally during classroom visits, teachers expressed their opinions about the impact of the PD on their teaching and students' learning. The majority of the teachers interviewed stated that the one-to-one coaching during classroom visits provided by the researchers had the most direct impact on their teaching and on student learning. They said they enjoyed these sessions and found the support helpful for incorporating features of text organization and language into existing writing lessons. They were able to plan, enact, and revise writing lessons with specific text organization and language features in mind, and receive immediate feedback that impacted their pedagogical approaches. They also liked the feedback on specific students' performance.

Teachers remarked that the PD had heightened their awareness of the need to teach writing. For example, one commented, "Now I feel I teach writing; before I was unsure what to do, so I didn't do much" (teacher interview, February 12, 2007). Although all teachers tried new ways of teaching writing, about two-thirds of them carried out well-planned writing units integrated with their literacy and content area lessons. They considered what they learned a good complement to the curricula they had been using. Writers'

Workshop helped them structure their classes, while organizing their teaching around the various genres generated ideas of what to teach. They found it useful to move the students from writing in their journals just for themselves to writing for an audience and with a purpose in mind. They found the binder with materials useful for planning their classes.

Some teachers commented on how they felt the changes they had made in their approach to teaching writing had impacted their students. Teachers felt that the students' writing improved because students had been "let in on the secret" of how, in the context of American culture, text is created. Students had previously been encouraged to write personal recounts or narratives. With this new approach, which focused on the whole text rather than small and unrelated sections, students ventured into other genres and through them into a greater range of themes. One teacher reported that what she learned in the professional development gave her direction on what to teach. She felt she had increased confidence in her own abilities to teach writing with direct impact on her students' work. Another teacher felt she was giving the students better directions and coaching them better while working on their individual pieces. She was particularly satisfied with the progress of one of her lowest performing bilingual students. He moved from reluctantly writing personal narratives all about playing soccer to writing longer, more coherent pieces about a variety of topics within the various genres taught, while gaining enthusiasm for writing.

Zooming In: A Closer Look at One Kindergarten Teacher's Implementation

The purpose of looking closely at one classroom is to provide a detailed examination of how one teacher implemented what she learned from the professional development in her classroom. Ms. Rallis (a pseudonym), the kindergarten teacher, was selected because of her enthusiasm for implementing the approach and her desire to continue the project despite having to change grade levels from a fourth-grade to a kindergarten classroom. Ms. Rallis introduced fictional narrative (FN) over a three week period. The FN unit was divided into three phases, corresponding to the weeks of the unit. During each phase, distinct elements of FN, including purpose and audience, were introduced. The decision to carry out the instruction in these phases was a result of collaboration between the teacher and the second author. These decisions also reflected the model provided by the facilitator encouraging teachers to do un-coached writing at the beginning and end of each unit. Writing instruction occurred during the Writers' Workshop time, which was conducted two to three times per week.

Teaching Fictional Narrative

Phase One. In the first week of instruction on FN, the teacher used a stimulus and then collected an un-coached writing sample. Ms. Rallis modeled drawing and telling a FN about a past event that included a description of the characters, setting, problem, and solution through a realistic fictional recount. Because she wanted to be sure to include all the structural elements, her modeled story was personal and was presented as a past event that had actually occurred rather than an imaginative story. The teacher intentionally did not introduce the elements explicitly nor did she instruct students in following an explicit structure because she wanted to get a sense of what students would produce after listening to the stimulus. Ms. Rallis asked the students to "write" their own narratives using blank sheets of paper and to add any letters or words if they wanted. This served as the students' un-coached sample.

Phase Two. During the second week, Ms. Rallis introduced the structural elements of FN, namely orientation (using the terms "character" and "setting"), complication (referred to as "problem"), resolution (referred to as "solution"), and ending (referred to as the "lesson of the story"). To introduce these terms, the teacher combined reading and writing instruction. This reflected the PD sessions, which encouraged the use of published texts as mentor texts to scaffold writing instruction. She read *Chrysanthemum*, by Peter Henkes, aloud in order to give the students a model of a narrative. The teacher modeled using puppets to retell the story with all the narrative structural elements and prompted the students to recall and state the elements of the story. Students later worked in pairs to retell the story using the puppets.

Later that same morning, the teacher began Writers' Workshop asking students to recall the structural elements included in narratives. Ms. Rallis modeled drawing and retelling her own FN. As she drew pictures, she gave the details of her story. The teacher indicated that she was planning on adding details to provide a model of all the structural elements, but felt that the students' attention was waning, and they would not be able to sit that long. However, in essence, what she modeled was another personal recount with some FN features, rather than a traditional FN. She then instructed the children to work on FN stories of their own. The facilitator recognized the mixture of genres and suggested modeling the genre with the more traditional elements in Phase Three in order to minimize confusion for the students.

Phase Three. In the third week, Ms. Rallis connected the reading and writing to introduce the concepts of purpose and audience. First she used a published text as an example. She read the story *We Share Everything* by Robert Munsch to demonstrate the notion of purpose and audience in FNs. She explained that the author wrote the story to teach kindergarteners the importance of sharing. Ms. Rallis asked the students to think about lessons they thought kindergarteners should learn. Each student participated by describing a lesson he or she felt was important to learn.

Once again, Ms. Rallis modeled a FN, this time using animals as characters with names of the students in the class. In this phase she elicited the structural elements from the students. Ms. Rallis reviewed the notion of purpose by asking the students why she had written the story. The teacher reminded the students of the narrative structural elements and the FN story they had just constructed together. She then asked them to write their own FNs with the purpose of sharing a lesson they felt would be important for other kindergarteners to learn. The writing samples of the students were collected to see how their drafts compared to their initial un-coached samples and to get a sense for which elements of FN and what types of language choices the students were making when writing their own FNs. By following the instructional practice guideline distributed and discussed in the PD sessions, the teacher and second author could examine the impact the instruction had on the students' writing development.

Impact on Kindergarten Writers

Ms. Rallis selected three bilingual students as the focus for the project. Ms. Rallis and the researcher discussed the students and selected students that reflected a range of proficiency levels to see how an SFL-based approach would impact the students' writing development. The three students, Hassan, Lorena, and Clarisa (all pseudonyms), were five years old at the time of the study. Hassan is from Somalia; he also lived in Kenya with his family before immigrating to the United States in 2004. Hassan reported that Somali is spoken at home with his family, especially his uncle. Hassan's mother indicated that she reads to Hassan in both Somali and English. Lorena arrived from the Dominican Republic in October, 2006. Lorena spoke Spanish both at home and upon her first arrival at school. At the time of this observation, she was beginning to incorporate some English words, but primarily communicated in Spanish with the teacher, who is proficient in Spanish. Clarisa is Thai-American and speaks primarily English in school and at home with her mother; however, her parents also use Thai in the home. Clarisa's parents indicated that they read to Clarisa in English. Each week, the three students responded to requests to produce "stories." To demonstrate the variation from one week to the next, a summary of Phases One and Two, and a more in-depth focus on Phase Three are provided below.

Phase One. After being exposed to the stimulus, the teacher's modeled story, all three students put together more than two events and used chronological order as evidenced with the marker "then" in the pieces by Hassan and Clarisa. All three students' writing appeared to be more similar to what Martin and Rothery (1986) call a personal recount than a fictional narrative. Lorena was the only student who included an explicit complication and resolution in the first attempt at dictating an FN structure. None of the three students included an ending in their first draft. All three students' writing resembled the teacher's modeled text by including family members as characters in the story. Hassan and Clarisa also included animals in their stories, as they attempted to emulate the teacher's text, which referred to her pet rabbit. Lorena might have had more difficulty emulating the teacher as she was still developing English as her second language. Instead, Lorena focused on the task which was described to her in her native language (Spanish) by the second author. The second author translated the teacher's text and asked the student to retell an event similar to the teacher's example, which included a problem and a solution. Whereas Lorena was the only one with an explicit complication and resolution, Hassan had an implicit complication and resolution. Clarisa focused on the orientation elements, including characters and setting.

Phase Two. All three students' texts imitated the teacher's text, which modeled a personal recount and did not get as far as including the problem and solution. The students drew pictures and labeled their pictures with strings of letters. Martin and Rothery (1986) refer to this as an observation, and note that observations developmentally precede personal recounts. Even though they did not have trouble identifying the FN structural elements in retelling *Chrysanthemum* that same morning, the students produced observations rather than FNs. The pictures the students drew carried different aspects of the structural elements of FN than those in the previous samples examined. For example, Hassan did not include any of the characters in his illustration but was more focused on the setting in this phase. Lorena included all her characters, but the setting was not clear, and Clarisa included animals as characters that were her "friends" but did not explicitly state this when retelling her "story." Through the drawing, Clarisa demonstrated that she understood that fictional narratives include imaginative characters, while it was unclear whether Hassan and Lorena understood this feature from their illustrations. The students' perception of the teacher's text as the model as opposed to her oral instructions influenced what children produced and the structural elements of FN that were included in children's texts.

Phase Three. The students' FN texts in phase three show how influential the teacher's modeled text was in their creation of a FN. Students were perceptive and able to imitate what the teacher had done and to include the elements modeled and discussed in Phase Three. The drawings for this third attempt at FN spanned three pages to reflect the distinct sections of the narrative. In the first page, all three students included the orientation. On the second page, they included the complication, and finally on the last page the students included the resolution. In addition to the fact that the text approached more adult-like FNs that include all the structural elements, the illustrations also incorporated more details than Phase One and Phase Two writing. All three students wrote a FN that dealt with behaving appropriately. The students' third FNs are presented in Table 7.1 with an analysis of structural elements.

From the results of Phase Three as shown in Table 7.1, it is clear that Hassan continued to focus on personal events while incorporating the structural elements. His sample seemed to be a personal recount building toward a FN. Lorena and Clarisa appeared to have used the teacher's text as a guide for what they perceived was expected of them. Both girls were able to use imagi-

Table 7.1 Students' Phase 3 Fictional Narrative Samples (With Student-Dictated FNs in Italics)

Structural Elements	Hassan	Lorena (Translated text)	Clarisa
Title/Orientation Note: Drawings provided most of the orientation features such as characters and setting (unless they specified these elements in their dictation, which is indicated in italics).	No title given Characters: *Me and my uncle* Setting: Outside the house *1. When me and my uncle were playing soccer.*	No title given Characters: Boy, the class, the teacher, the pet rabbit Setting: Classroom	No title given Characters: Somebody (stranger), boys and girls, and teacher Setting: School
Events and Complication	*2. I kicked the ball up high into the house.* *3. He was so mad because I was not listening to him.*	*1. He (in purple) was screaming, "AHHH!"* *2. No one inside the class wanted to play with him.* *3. They tired of hearing him scream.* *4. He was very sad. They were playing. He wasn't allowed to because he would scream.* *5. The rabbit had to go to the bathroom.*	*1. Somebody went to school and saw fighting* *2. and the teacher was mad and made the girls and boys clean up.*
Resolution	*4. I said "sorry" and he hugged me.*	*6. He stopped screaming and played with the others.*	*3. The people fighting get in trouble so they go to jail.*
Ending	*Then we go back to play.* *Then we go home.* *Then a little while we play soccer and I listen.*	*7. The teacher was tall and happy.*	*4. The teacher takes somebody else to play with the old kids.* *Everyone plays nicely.*

native elements to entertain the listener/reader while teaching the ways of behaving valued in most American classrooms, something closely associated with FN structures (Butt et al. 2000; Martin & Rothery, 1986; Schleppegrell, 2004).

Not all students responded to these demands with equal success, but they were all given the opportunity and the support, and each showed some development without being made to feel different or inferior. For example, Hassan's stories blended the structural components of FNs with features of personal recounts, while Clarisa and Lorena were further along in their development by creating stories with fictional characters (see Table 7.1). All three students were very attentive and sensitive to the teacher's explicit directions. The close resemblance to the teacher's modeled text appears to have influenced some of the cultural contextual features for students' writing.

Lessons Learned

While this chapter describes some of the accomplishments of this PD project, we want to acknowledge that the work is still far from over. It will take time for schools to adopt this framework as an approach to language and writing that would benefit bilingual students. The following recommendations for teacher educators, derived from the experience of the PD, address content and process.

First, professional development for teachers on SFL should give attention to instructional strategies that reflect this theory. SFL is a theory of language that provides specific notions for the content of literacy instruction. Presenting this theoretical content was an essential foundation for successful implementation. However, teachers also needed specific suggestions for connecting SFL to practice.

Teachers are drawn to the idea of genres; it makes sense within their curricular demands. However, our second recommendation is to constantly remind teachers that genres cannot be presented as a set of fixed rules. Context matters and it influences the language choices students make. The context of culture defines the features of genres and the context of situation defines the choices to be made around a specific text. The value of SFL with bilingual learners (including children who speak varieties of English) is that their languages and dialects have a legitimate place in the literacy practices of these students. Thus, it is perfectly acceptable for students to write in a language other than English or in a dialect other than Standard English if their audience is proficient in that language. Children have to be exposed to the cultural norms for language use of the academic English context. They must also be taught that they can make different choices if they have a reason for them (Gebhard, Harman, & Seger, 2007).

We also learned that the analysis of genre and discussion of language in PD initiatives should be constantly connected to all content areas. When writing is presented as integral to all content areas, the teaching of writing becomes more integral to instruction across the curriculum, which means student writing improves as more time is devoted to teaching and learning writing skills. In the SFL PD discussed in this chapter, the schools were teaching writing using Writers' Workshop as part of the English Language Arts curriculum, rather than throughout the content areas. For SFL, the unit of study is the text present in all content areas and language use in the school day. We found that we had to make an explicit connection to writing and the content areas since the writing curriculum in the schools did not always do so.

Our experience with introducing SFL theory to teachers, while fruitful, was difficult for all because the teachers were not familiar with this theory and we were observing implementation of this theory for the first time. It was, therefore, useful to have a collegial attitude in which the teachers learned from us but we also made it clear that we were learning from their experience and sharing it across schools (Lieberman & Wood, 2002). We recommend consciously cultivating such a collegial approach in similar PD efforts. As part of such an approach, it would be useful to bring together all teachers at the end to share their experiences implementing these new ideas.

Our fifth recommendation is to devote as much time as possible to help the teachers learn SFL theory and to apply it to their teaching. Although a focus on language is essential in the instruction of second language learners, because of the amount of time it took to address the concept of genres and their structural organization, little time was left to focus on language. Because of the newness of the content, teachers needed more time to go deeper into an exploration of language. Issues of language should have been central to the syllabus to have a greater impact on classroom practices. With more time, we could have had the teachers produce texts for different purposes and audiences and analyze text to raise the awareness of how authors use language and what children can do with language and what support they need while writing.

Whole group PD sessions were not enough to convert this new theory to classroom practice. Thus, we also recommend building time into the PD for classroom visits and short meetings with teachers. Teachers found the one-on-one coaching sessions with the facilitator the most beneficial aspect of the process. They were able to plan, enact and revise writing lessons with specific text organization and language features in mind, and receive immediate feedback that impacted their pedagogical approaches to teaching.

Finally, in planning the project we should have been more conscious from the start about the approach to writing used in the schools. Although we were familiar with these teachers' practices, connecting their practices with the new theory was only done informally during the sessions. Either at the beginning or at the end, we recommend making structural connections with participants' practices. This would soften some of the resistance of some teachers who did not always see the coherence between the new content knowledge and the district and school approaches to teaching writing.

Adapting SFL theory is a promising approach to the teaching of writing, especially in schools with children who are not socialized to the language of schooling in other environments. SFL brings the connection of language and culture to the surface rather than leaving it tacit in writing instruction. The focus on language in literacy instruction offers much needed content for second language learners (including speakers of different English dialects). Emphasizing that language choices derive from context provides an opportunity to include multiple languages and dialects in the classroom discourse.

Some of the recommendations above are more easily implemented than others. They require considerable preparation on the part of the teacher educators—for example, to learn about the approaches to teaching writing in the schools, and to understand the sometimes subtle connections between language and different school content areas. They also require devoting time to visiting schools and giving feedback to teachers. Probably the greatest challenge is the need for more time—which is always at a premium. We encourage other teacher educators to take up the challenge, applying what we have learned as appropriate.

References

Bernhardt, E.B. (1991). A psycholinguistic perspective on second language literacy. *AILA Review, 8*, 31–44.

Butt, D., Fahey, R., Feez, S., Spinks, S., & Yallop, C. (2000). *Using functional grammar: An explorer's guide*. Sydney: National Centre for English Language Teaching and Research, Macquarie University.

Christie, F. (1998). Learning the literacies of primary and secondary schooling. In F. Christie & R. Mission (Eds.), *Literacy and schooling* (pp. 47–73). London: Routledge.

Cope, B., & Kalantzis, M. (1993). Introduction: How a genre approach to literacy can transform the way writing is taught. In B. Cope & M. Kalantzis (Eds.), *The powers of literacy: A genre approach to teaching writing* (pp. 1–21). Pittsburgh, PA: University of Pittsburgh Press.

Dewsbury, A. (1994). *Writing Resource Book*. Portsmouth, NH: Heinemann.

Fillmore, L.W., & Snow, C.E. (2000). *What teachers need to know about language*. Washington, D.C.: Center for Applied Linguistics.

Fitzgerald, J. (2006). Multilingual writing in preschool through 12th grade: The last 15 years. In C.A. MacArthur, S. Graham, & J. Fitzgerald (Eds.), *Handbook of writing research* (pp. 337–354). New York, NY: Guilford Press.

Gebhard, M., Harman, R., & Seger, W. (2007). Reclaiming recess: Learning the language of persuasion. *Language Arts, 84*(5), 419–430.

Halliday, M.A.K. (1985). *An introduction to functional grammar*. London: Edward Arnold.

Halliday, M.A.K., & Hasan, R. (1989). *Language, context, and text: Aspects of a language in a social-semiotic perspective* (2nd ed.). Oxford: Oxford University Press.

Harper, C., & de Jong, E. (2005). Working with English language learners: What's the difference? In A.G. Huerta-Macías (Ed.), *Working with English language learners: Perspectives and practice* (pp. 55–68). Dubuque, IO: Kendall Hunt Publishing Co.

Henkes, K. (1991). *Chrysanthemum.* New York, NY: Greenwillow Books.

Lieberman, A., & Wood, D.R. (2002). From network learning to classroom teaching. *Journal of Educational Change, 3,* 315–337.

Martin, J., & Rothery, J. (1986). What a functional approach to the writing task can show teachers about "good writing." In B. Couture (Ed.), *Functional approaches to writing: Research perspectives.* Norwood, NJ: Ablex.

Munsch, R. (1999). *We share everything.* New York, NY: Scholastic.

National Clearinghouse for English Language Acquisition. (2006). *ELL demographics by state.* Retrieved from www.ncela.gwu.edu/stats/3_bystate.htm.

Schleppegrell, M. (2004). *The language of schooling: A functional perspective.* Mahwah, NJ: Lawrence Erlbaum.

Smith, M., Cheville, J., & Hillocks Jr., G. (2006). "I guess I'd better watch my English": Grammars and the teaching of the English language arts. In C.A. MacArthur, S. Graham, & J. Fitzgerald (Eds.), *Handbook of writing research* (pp. 263–274). New York, NY: Guilford Press.

Thompson, G. (2004). *Introducing functional grammar* (2nd ed.). London: Arnold.

Chapter 8

Preparing Teachers to Reach English Language Learners
Pre-Service and In-Service Initiatives

Constance L. Walker and Karla Stone

Two realities in American education in the last decade have combined to dramatically affect the professional lives of teachers—a school population that is increasingly more diverse in its makeup, and a national agenda for accountability that requires attention to the achievement of all students. The changing demographics of American schools, particularly an increase in the number of students for whom English is a new language, is part of the national conversation in education. Growth in the number of linguistically diverse learners has increased rapidly across the nation, particularly in the Southeast and Midwest. During the period between 1995 and 2005 the national growth rate of the K-12 English language learner (ELL) population was 61% while the overall growth rate for all students enrolled in public schools was 2.6% (National Clearinghouse for English Language Acquisition, Language Enhancement, and Academic Achievement for Limited English Proficient Students (NCELA), 2006).

During the same period in Minnesota, the location of programs discussed in this chapter, ELL growth was over 161%, outpacing the national growth trend significantly, while the state total K-12 enrollment *decreased* by 6.5% (NCELA, 2006). The number of foreign-born immigrants doubled in the 1990s, from 2.6% of the state population to 5.8%. Minnesota has long been a state that welcomes refugees, and the refugee population has always been a significant portion of Minnesota immigrants. Between 2000 and 2005, the state resettled 21,743 refugees. Minnesota ranked second among states in refugee immigrant arrivals in 2004–2006. The Hmong population in Minnesota (estimated at 60,000) is second in size only to the California Hmong population, and the state is now home to 30,000 Somali residents—the largest community of Somalis in the United States. More than 60,000 ELL students are currently enrolled in Minnesota schools, representing more than 110 different language groups. Minnesota's growing numbers of ELL and refugee students present educators with new challenges. The increase in refugee students and the fact that many of them have little formal education before arriving in Minnesota coincided with the full introduction of Minnesota's accountability system, developed under Title I, and the new accountability provisions in Title III, the federal education program for ELL students. Sadly, as suggested by Ruiz-de-Velasco and Fix (2000), the needs of immigrants with "significant education gaps" are simply overlooked—and correspondingly, drop-out rates are very high. The growth of second language learners statewide has led to a gap in achievement between these learners and other students that is of concern to both educators and policy-makers. Are teachers prepared for these challenges?

The impact of increasing numbers of second language learners on teachers ill-prepared to meet their needs is substantial in many communities (Walker, Shafer, & Iiams, 2004). The pressure to meet achievement goals for all sub-groups of learners requires that individual teachers as well as schools take responsibility for learning outcomes demonstrated by English language learners—a direct contrast to the historical practice of leaving this work exclusively to ESL and bilingual specialists. The task has fallen to in-service education to provide opportunities for practicing content and grade-level teachers to develop the expertise to successfully teach ELLs. At the same time, colleges and universities are faced with the daunting task of preparing pre-service teachers to attend to these language learners in their future classrooms.

What is required for effective teacher development in both pre-service and in-service settings? In this chapter we examine the challenges inherent in preparing both groups to meet the complex linguistic and academic needs of second language learners by describing two very specific models of engagement with educators. We first describe the structure and content of a course module on English language learners at the University of Minnesota designed specifically for different K-12 pre-service content area programs. Data from a cohort in science education provide a sense of the challenges and outcomes of this approach. We then describe a professional development initiative designed for elementary school staff that was site-based, collaborative, and long-term (two years). Finally, as teacher educators, we offer thoughts on what other teacher development programs can do to maximize efforts to improve teacher learning regarding the education of English language learners.

Elements of Effective Teacher Development

The complexity of teaching and learning processes is clearly reflected in teacher development: as teacher educators, we teach (and, we hope, individuals learn) how one can implement teaching practices that will result in learning in the classroom. At the University of Minnesota, our teacher education pedagogies emphasize three knowledge domains—knowledge of learners, knowledge of self, and knowledge of how to continue to learn in teaching (Banks et al., 2005). Drawing especially on the work of Darling-Hammond and Bransford (2005) as well as our own experiences with both pre- and in-service teacher development, we have designed our teacher preparation curricula to incorporate research on how teachers learn. Teacher learning can be optimized in a way we believe best addresses their preparation for the language and content learning needs of English language learners. Four fundamental elements for effective teacher preparation and teacher development focusing on English language learners serve as the foundation upon which we structure our programs, and the lens through which we examine and describe them here.

- Respect for learners as individuals guides the structure and content of teacher development efforts, which are differentiated according to teachers' needs, blending theory and practice as appropriate with opportunities for personalized active learning (Ballantyne, Sanderman, & Levy, 2008; Darling-Hammond & Bransford, 2005; Garet, Porter, Desimone, Birman, & Yoon, 2001).
- Opportunities exist to build collaborative relationships. The importance of working in community rather than as isolated individuals cannot be overestimated. Growth within community structures benefits both beginning and experienced teachers (Ballantyne et al., 2008; Cochran-Smith & Lytle, 1999). Practicing their craft in a purposefully constructed learning community as members of a group (school, grade level, or department) can have cumulative effects on changing teacher practice (Desimone, Porter, Garet, Yoon, & Birman, 2002).
- Successful professional development provides time for building relationships with colleagues, addressing real issues within the classroom, and exploring the rewards and challenges of teaching English language learners. Time is a critical dimension of successful teacher development (DuFour, Eaker, & DuFour, 2005; Fullan, 2001; Improving America's Schools Act, 1994; Sparks & Hirsch, 1997).
- Professional development is contextualized, connecting with real students in actual classroom settings, and is thus firmly situated in and framed by the day-to-day happenings of school (Molnar, 2002). Like students, teachers and future teachers learn better when what they are learning is embedded in and related to their own contexts and situations (Echevarria, Vogt, & Short, 2007; Gibbons, 2002).

These core elements are foundational to two initiatives at the University of Minnesota that seek to improve teacher preparation to address English language learners' language and academic content learning needs—a one-credit course for pre-service teachers and a Title III grant-funded project for a limited number of in-service teachers. Below, we discuss how these two programs value teachers as learners, and the extent to which they encourage collaborative relationships, provide time for growth and learning, and contextualize the learning experiences in ways that connect them to actual learners and classrooms.

Pre-Service Preparation: Benefits and Challenges of a One-Credit Content-Specific Course

In this section, we discuss our efforts to prepare pre-service elementary and secondary teachers to teach ELLs through a required one-credit course module. We describe the development, conceptual framework, and content of the course; present findings from a case study of science teachers who took the course in 2005; and conclude with a consideration of what we learned from these science teachers that can inform teacher preparation to serve ELLs. We also address the extent to which the course reflects the fundamental elements of teacher preparation discussed earlier.

At the University of Minnesota, preparing all future teachers to work with ELLs has required a paradigm shift, as it has on a national level. There is some indication that colleges and universities have begun to address the need to prepare teachers to work with culturally and linguistically diverse populations (Lucas & Grinberg, 2008; Téllez & Waxman, 2006; Villegas & Lucas, 2002; Zeichner, 2005), but there is no national teacher development policy that guides both the content and structure of how this should take place, and most pre-service teacher preparation programs provide minimal attention to the needs of English language learners. Convincing faculty that these efforts are necessary can be one of the great challenges in developing such programs within institutions. Teacher educators may be either unaware of the growth and impact of ELL populations or unwilling to accept that this is as important an issue as others—e.g., special education and the impact of poverty on learning. Historically, ESL and Bilingual Education (BE) teacher development has taken place within particular institutions in states and regions with large numbers of immigrants, refugees, and/or language minority populations. Licensure programs for ESL and BE have been isolated, attracting individuals who want to work specifically with English language learners. Only recently, at institutions whose teachers are asked to serve increasingly diverse populations, has the focus for preparation on these issues shifted to *all* teachers.

Modules for Pre-Service Teachers at the University of Minnesota

Teacher education at the University of Minnesota is a post-baccalaureate program that requires full-time study over 15 months. Teachers are prepared through department programs in cohorts: elementary education and several secondary content areas (art, English literature/language arts, math, science, second languages (world languages/ESL), and social studies). Beginning in the 1980s, faculty in the area of bilingual education and ESL were occasionally asked to make guest presentations in elementary education methods courses, but no formal mechanism existed for preparing teachers to consider English language learners in their future classes. In 1996, the college committee charged with managing teacher education tried but failed to agree on a required course for all pre-service teacher preparation programs that would specifically address language minority students as learners. The Department of Curriculum and Instruction, the unit housing elementary and secondary teacher development programs (but not including other areas such as physical education, special education, music, agricultural education), agreed to include a one-credit course module that would be a requirement for licensure in each program area.

Charged with the development of the modules, the faculty and staff in the Second Languages and Cultures (SLC) Education program area (including the first author of this chapter) considered (and still considers) such an option to be the minimum that should be available for prospective teachers. The objectives for students in the module were: (1) to explore the benefits and challenges of working with non-native English speaking students, (2) to explore the linguistic features of particular content areas, and (3) to examine instructional strategies and approaches that help to integrate language learners into the mainstream classroom. Rather than develop a course generic to all content areas for pre-service teachers to take together, SLC staff have held to their belief that content-based modules would at least provide a more focused venue in which to address learner needs and integrate language and content. We recognized that we could not fully prepare teachers to teach ELLs in a one-credit course; instead, our objectives were to ensure that pre-service teachers understood that becoming a content teacher requires the ability to facilitate their students' development of English proficiency so they can navigate and manipulate academic content and to introduce them to language-sensitive instructional practices for English language learners in their teaching context.

The one-credit modules, entitled Working with Culturally and Linguistically Diverse Students in the Mainstream Classroom, address very broad fundamental concepts in second language education, in addition to grade-level or content-specific information. The concepts and activities that cross levels and content areas include:

- Demographic and cultural information about English language learners in the U.S. and locally.
- The key theoretical principles related to the instruction of English language learners.
- The content-specific nature of academic language and ways in which content and language development can be integrated.
- An in-school experience tutoring an English language learner.

In addition, each course includes examples from practice and texts that are specific to the content area. Because each content area requires specific course module development, instructors are hired with a background in either elementary or secondary education, and, most importantly, a strong background in second language education. All instructors have experience as classroom teachers. Evaluations of the course modules have been very positive, indicating that pre-service teachers understand the need to attend to English language learner issues as they begin their teaching careers and recognize the importance of preparing themselves for this population. While some students report feeling put-upon by this addition to their workload, the most common complaint regarding the modules is that they are too short.

A Case Study of Pre-Service Science Teachers

In order to gain insight into our efforts with pre-service teachers, we examined one particular content cohort more closely. In 2005 we conducted an exploratory study of pre-service science teachers enrolled in the module (which was taught by the second author). We wanted to examine the initial and developing perceptions and understandings of this cohort of pre-service teachers at different phases in their development and to determine the impact of the module on that development. We collected data at four points in time: when students entered the module (through surveys and feedback on the first class session), after a tutoring experience with an English language learner (through their written reflections), when they were completing the module (through an evaluation questionnaire), and two months into their first year of teaching (through a focus group). Participants were 26 pre-service teachers; 11 of those participated in the focus group.

The initial survey indicated that participants were not aware of the large numbers of ELLs in many Minnesota school districts and underestimated the probability of having such students in their future classes. Their estimates of the proportion of English language learners in Minnesota schools ranged from 3–4% to 60%. As the extreme range of the estimates shows, these future teachers were completing their teacher preparation with very little sense of who their students would be. The survey also revealed that these pre-service teachers were concerned about and frustrated by the need to adapt their instruction for yet another learner group with unique educational needs. Questions they included in their feedback on the first session of the course indicate some of their concerns: How can teachers accommodate students with a variety of language backgrounds? How do we strike a balance between the needs of ELLs and those of native speakers? How do you modify assessment? How do ELLs learn biology and chemistry best?

While many concerns and apprehensions remained at the end of the course, there were also indications that the students had developed greater awareness of the needs of ELLs and were better prepared to adapt their instruction to meet those needs. In the evaluation at the end of the module, students reported that they had learned more than expected, in particular that they had learned new strategies and techniques for working with English language learners. One of the most positive aspects of the course for participants was the instructor's modeling of a variety of activities and strategies using examples from science that could easily be applied in student teaching or first-year teaching. Many students also indicated surprise at the numbers of ELLs in Minnesota as well as the diversity within the ELL population. Participants reported that they would have liked more information regarding the particular ethno-linguistic groups prevalent in Minnesota schools (primary students with Hmong, Somali, or Spanish language backgrounds) and more time devoted to culture-specific information.

In a focus group held after their first two months of teaching, one participant described a practicum placement where the teacher would not attempt to pronounce the names of the students correctly, even though the student teacher had knowledge of the language and offered to assist. The same teacher generally did not attend to the needs of ELLs at all, causing the future teacher to wonder, "What are we obligated to do as teachers? What are the legal ramifications?" Some individuals felt ill-prepared in such situations, wanting to call teachers on ineffective practice, yet not feeling empowered to do so. Some reported observing institutional resistance to addressing the needs of English language learners in the schooling process. Such resistance is consistent with an "underlying cultural predisposition to argue for assimilation for ethnic and linguistically diverse groups [that] often produces the following question, 'Is this really necessary?'" (Walker, Ranney, & Fortune, 2005, p. 326).

Another new teacher commented on the constant challenge of discerning where, in fact, the primary learning obstacles for a student lie. She said, "The thing that's causing me the most grief … is trying to grade lab reports. I'm having trouble figuring out what is the ELL barrier, what's the content barrier, what's the writing ability barrier?" This comment captures a central question facing content teachers of English language learners: when is the problem one of learning as opposed to one of language?

Consistently, the most valuable experience of the course is tutoring an English language learner. We have found this over multiple offerings of this content-based module across elementary and secondary programs. The overall consensus is that this assignment allows pre-service teachers to put theory into practice while opening their eyes to the nature and the range of experiences ELLs bring to their classrooms. This science cohort was no exception. While there was admitted skepticism and initially even some anxiety regarding the tutoring assignment, the experience ultimately proved rewarding, with lasting outcomes. In a reflection paper, a pre-service science teacher wrote:

> I was surprised by how much I learned during this tutoring experience. I was quite hesitant at first—I had never worked with an ELL child before, so I was unsure of how much help I could offer. I was afraid of making

mistakes, and I was also concerned about how well I would be able to communicate with [her]. By the middle of our second session, all those fears had subsided.... All in all, I believe this tutoring experience made me a better teacher. I am now able to appreciate the difficulties ELL students face when learning new material in a foreign language. I also realize that these students may need extra time, patience, and several different approaches to fully understand the novel topics presented in class. While ELL students may move at a slower pace than native speakers, ELL students bring in a wealth of diversity and experiences that enrich the classroom culture.

Comments like this reveal the importance of providing pre-service teachers with an opportunity for direct contact with an English language learner. Without such contact, apprehension and fears may prevent a novice teacher from teaching these students with confidence and compassion. The experience of working closely with a language learner also helped teachers see the wide variety of knowledge, skills, and experiences that English language learners can contribute to the classroom, rather than viewing them only as a challenge. Most importantly, the luxury of working with one ESL learner very closely (albeit for a limited period of time) helped these future teachers gain insight they might never have attained once they were facing 150 students per day. Tutoring also allowed pre-service teachers to reflect on their pedagogy in light of the needs of English language learners. As one individual wrote:

Before I began tutoring [her], I always thought I was doing a fair job with the vocabulary I use in lectures and on assignments. Because I teach Meteorology, I use a number of maps and make several references to different geographical locations in the United States. However, [my tutee] pointed out to me that she was not familiar with all of the states and geographical regions in the United States. Since she brought this to my attention, I have provided maps for her (and anyone else who needs a refresher) to use on assignments and quizzes.

This teacher also noted that she had become much more aware of her word choice during class, which had spurred her to define complicated terms on the board for all kids, even during quizzes. Like many others, this teacher continued tutoring her English language learner well beyond the required five hours.

The tutoring experience helped many of the teachers to recognize the need to make real-world connections to assignments and to be careful about assumptions regarding students' facility with school-based tasks such as notetaking or even general organizational strategies. Teachers also commented on the importance of understanding a student's background knowledge and literacy skills, the benefits of encouraging students to use their first languages when appropriate, and the social stigma that some ELLs fear—not wanting to produce the wrong word or to be viewed as someone in need of additional help.

We have described at length in another venue (Walker et al., 2005) the complexity of developing and carrying out a rigorous, yet compact, introduction to English language learners for pre-service teachers across grade levels and content areas within a university teacher development framework. Instructing multiple sections each year at both elementary and secondary levels, we continue to learn a great deal about the idiosyncrasies of particular content areas (in terms of both the content and the pre-service teachers) as well as those issues of learning content and language which are common to pre-service teacher education regardless of grade level.

As we have discussed, the one-credit module is not an ideal approach to preparing pre-service teachers to teach ELLs. The content is offered in an add-on module, predictable in its format and execution. Both faculty and pre-service teachers agree that the student credit-hour restrictions severely limit the scope of what can be accomplished with regard to the elements of effective teacher development. However, attention to learner needs *is* emphasized, especially regarding pre-service teachers' desire to explore new content while simultaneously experiencing teaching strategies they could implement in practicum. With regard to time, some of the case study students noted how the course felt rushed. While every attempt was made to model effective pedagogy, particularly through the development of a content-specific focus for each cohort, there was no opportunity for collaborative interaction related to ELL issues. While module course meetings provided opportunities for small group discussion, optimal exploration through collaborative problem solving was not possible. Finally, through the tutoring assignment, the pre-service teachers' exposure to an individual English language learner provided a situational context for examining the challenges of learning in a specific content area. This last aspect of the module is its greatest strength. The pre-service modules offer exposure—albeit cursory—to the reality of ELLs in the mainstream classroom. Given the constraints of the pre-service teacher education program, our inquiry into this cohort of pre-service science teachers suggests that, despite its limitations, this one-credit ELL module offers benefits for pre-service teachers they otherwise would not have.

A Collaborative In-Service Model for Teacher Development

Just as issues of English language learners need to be fully integrated into pre-service programs, they also must be at the forefront of in-service education. Many teachers received their preparation before the rapid growth in the number of English language learners in Minnesota. Others have taught in schools where ESL is peripheral to the school, pulling students from the regular classroom and allowing for wholesale abrogation of school and main-stream teacher responsibility for their achievement. ESL teachers themselves are not exempt from a need for professional development. Many were pre-pared to be *language* teachers and have been allowed to offer their own cur-riculum without consideration of the academic needs of their students. The largest challenge of all, however, is overcoming the tendency of school dis-tricts to want to address the issue of English language learners with "quick fixes" and short term professional development responses. Structurally, dis-tricts are complex entities—some with ELL students distributed throughout the district, others with children concentrated at particular schools. Schools themselves are fragmented—by grade levels at the elementary level, by content area at the secondary level. How can ELL issues be more than a "hot topic" elective on the professional development calendar? How can professional development be structured to respond to individual school needs as well as individual teacher needs?

Beginning in 2002, with receipt of a Title III Teacher Development Grant from the U.S. Department of Education, the authors and others in Second Languages and Cultures Education at the University of Minnesota began to work closely with practicing elementary teachers in a small in-service effort to enhance teaching capabilities for educating English language learners. As mentioned previously, a vision of professional development that is collabora-tive, teacher-driven (focusing on the needs of individual teachers and school sites), and long-term (DuFour et al., 2005; Improving America's Schools Act, 1994) informed the development of the TEAM UP project—Teaching English-Language-Learners Action Model to Unite Professionals. TEAM UP developed out of a desire to attend to staff development in a more focused way, with small numbers of teachers collaborating within their schools and across schools and districts, to inform their teaching of English language learners. As experienced teachers/teacher educators, staff aimed to offer sus-tained and meaningful in-service staff development that built on relationships between educators as they worked to explore attitudes, behaviors, and prac-tices in the classroom. Beyond improving the education of ELLs, we wanted to develop a model of staff development based on collaborative efforts focused on teachers' specific professional and instructional needs, and emphasizing value and reward for teacher time and effort.

We identified prospective schools based on the population of ELLs, changes in the ELL population within recent years, and state assessment data results in reading and mathematics. University staff examined district demo-graphics to ensure representation from urban, suburban, semi-rural, and rural communities. The project information was given to all school staff at the sites we visited, and discussions with the principal determined whether the school would participate. Our instructions to the principal in the formation of the team was that individuals should be interested in improving the efforts of staff in working with ELLs, and be seen as positive individuals within their buildings. We selected four schools (28 teachers in total) for our first cohort, and two years later repeated the process in order to select the same number for the second two-year cohort.

Each school was asked to form a team of seven members comprising ESL teacher(s), grade-level classroom teachers, and paraprofessional(s). The final composition of each team varied—some had only one ESL teacher (as do many schools), others had more. Our goal was representation from each role group within the building. Participants enrolled in a three-credit graduate course each year in the project, specifically designed for the time span and characteristics of the TEAM UP project. The curriculum addressed multiple content areas, with topics including instruction, assessment, cultural/family issues, literacy development, co-teaching and collaboration, and curriculum planning for language and content.

All four teams worked together as a large group during two-week summer institutes in two consecutive summers and three two-day sessions during each academic year, and worked as individual teams during monthly on-site meetings at their schools. Each team developed a School Action Plan that would drive their efforts at improving student achievement. While university staff gave input in the process, the Action Plans were very much the vision of each school team. The plans became their "working document." Additionally, as part of the graduate course(s) in which they were enrolled, participants wrote extensively in journals and reader response logs, and were observed in classrooms by a university staff member on an informal basis. University staff sat in on their monthly meetings at least twice during the academic year and communicated with them via email. Each team member developed a Personal Professional Action Plan at the beginning of the process to map a course for professional development. Personal Professional Action Plans provided an opportunity for each teacher to set individual goals for enhancing understanding and improving practice. Each individual plan was unique and provided a map for the upcoming two-year experience. Federal grant funding provided resources for buying teacher time, compensating teachers for their work, paying for university tuition for graduate course credit, providing extensive print and online resources, and facilitating attendance at professional conferences and meetings.

Through reading, writing, and reflection as a team, participants engaged in serious work. Equally important, new information was filtered through participants' own experiences and daily work as teachers and their interactions with ELL students. Because TEAM UP gave teachers time and professional recognition and allowed participants to address both their individual and school-specific needs, it contextualized teacher development (Shulman, 2005) and led to changes in teachers' knowledge, awareness, attitude, and practice. For some, their participation in the program required an entry into the worlds of learners they had not been prepared to teach and were surprised to find in their classrooms. Mainstream teachers were asked to do things in very different ways, trying out new approaches within their classrooms. Co-teaching with

ESL teachers in their classrooms, where they still "owned" the space, now required that they "own" English language learners as well. After their second year of effort, teachers reported further success in engaging in these new forms of instruction. Yet, in contrast with ESL teachers, their overall role changed very little. ESL teachers, however, claimed a greater sense of status among their peers and a more active involvement in the school itself. They reported a sense of ownership, shared responsibility, and increased professionalism. The complexity of learning a second language while learning grade-level content took on new meaning for practicing ESL teachers, as reflected in the comments of one participant:

> Having once been the only ESL teacher in my building with a small little room and 40 pull-out students, I am amazed at how far we have come. Some days I miss the autonomy and solitude of closing my door, doing my own thing and letting the classroom teachers worry about content curriculum. I do not, however, miss the limited progress my students made, or the disconnect between myself and the rest of the staff.... I feel that my students are making greater progress in an inclusion setting.

As we worked with eight teams (over four years), our observations, conversations with teachers, and their written work expanded our knowledge of the daily lives of teachers serving ELLs, and has helped us to construct experiences that encourage development of a knowledge of self, knowledge of learners, and an appreciation for continual professional learning. Several small studies have been completed that resulted in multiple presentations in a variety of education venues (Walker, Edstam, & Stone, 2007a, 2007b, 2008). Examination of teachers' Personal Professional Action Plans, school Action Plans, journal entries, reader responses, and end-of-program written reflections allowed for insight into both processes and outcomes of the TEAM UP project. We examined school contexts, staff roles, the kinds of instructional changes made, and teachers' perceived growth in professional development. With each study, micro- and macro-level themes were catalogued and analyzed by three university staff members. We examined written texts for salient patterns that appeared across and within individuals and programs. Drawing from these sources, we have identified several general directions for teacher educators, congruent with the four essential elements that optimize effectiveness for preparing teachers for work with English language learners:

- Emphasizing a small team structure and a limited number of participants supports a learner-centered approach to in-service education that is voluntary and builds on individual strengths.
- Collaborative relationships are at the core of the program, as teachers work in teams and with other teams to process what they learn. Teachers do not learn in isolation.

- Extended time is needed for collegial relationships to form, change to be implemented, and results to be manifested.
- Specific communities of ELL learners, their parents, and the school community are the context of this in-service professional development effort. Changes take place in different ways at each school site, dependent upon school culture and leadership. Teachers working within a school can best navigate the barriers to effective instructional practice.

As other work with large numbers of teachers has shown (Garet et al., 2001; Penuel, Fishman, Yamaguchi, & Gallagher, 2007), particular structural features of in-service offerings significantly affect teacher learning: (a) the form of the activity (traditional workshops as opposed to professional learning groups); (b) collective participation of teachers from the same site (school, grade, or subject); and (c) the duration of the activity. The primary challenge of in-service education for teachers has traditionally been a reliance on "one-shot" efforts that are unrelated to the contexts of actual daily life in classrooms (Knight & Wiseman, 2006). We have found that in-service work that "thinks small," is long-term, collaborative, and directed to the work teachers do within their own classrooms and schools is rewarding to both teachers and teacher educators alike.

Conclusion

We have learned from our work with both content area pre-service teachers and practicing teachers in an in-service program that teacher development requires attention to some fundamental elements that can foster personal and professional growth. One of the most salient of these is that, to be successful, teacher development needs to take place in relation to and concurrent with actual relationships and responsibilities of the classroom. The learning of the pre-service science teachers in the one-credit module was contextualized through their tutoring of an ELL in the academic subjects of their licensure. The tutoring experience showed soon-to-be teachers that these learners face a mighty task—mastering English while navigating the subject matter content at school. The TEAM UP model required small teams of teachers within a school to address student needs within the contexts of actual classrooms and schools.

For these pre-service and in-service teachers in Minnesota, preparation to teach ELLs required a realization that working with English language learners is more than "just good teaching" (de Jong & Harper, 2005). The future science teachers learned through both the course and their student teaching experiences that all was not well with the status quo offered to students learning science through English. Veteran teachers learned through their work with their school teams that their individual and collective efforts were not always the best choices for their ELL students. Where the struggles of ELLs are concerned, both groups learned that teachers are a major part of the equation.

For both pre- and in-service teachers, these initiatives are a beginning. In the same way that the "taste" of experience with ELL issues was a first step for pre-service teachers, participation in a two-year collaborative effort by experienced teachers was a launching point for what we can only hope are years of future productive work as colleagues. We have distilled some of the key insights we have gained from our experiences with both programs and present them here as suggestions for other teacher educators:

- Focus courses and professional development on teaching ELLs in specific content areas. Avoid generic recommendations.
- Provide examples of language demands specific to particular content areas and model the use of scaffolds and strategies.
- Identify teachers' needs and differentiate accordingly. Build on effective practices where they exist, and critically examine what is not working.
- Provide opportunities to observe examples of effective teaching and collaboration in practice, either through observation or through video, with ample time for reflection.
- Provide ongoing, structured opportunities for reading and discussions around proven practices for ELLs in both pre-service and in-service contexts.

Attention to providing more effective professional development at both pre-service and in-service levels is an ongoing process. While our institution has a history of preparing second language (ESL, world language, immersion) teachers for diverse student populations (González & Darling-Hammond, 1997; Mellgren, Walker, & Lange, 1988; Walker & Tedick, 1994), we are not immune to the struggles to fully integrate the needs of English language learners into the teacher development curriculum. The two initiatives we have described illustrate ways we are attempting to address these challenges.

References

Ballantyne, K.G., Sanderman, A.R., & Levy, J. (2008). *Educating English language learners: Building teacher capacity.* Washington, D.C.: National Clearinghouse for English Language Acquisition. Retrieved from www.ncela.gwu.edu/practice/mainstream_teachers.htm.

Banks, J., Cochran-Smith, M., Moll, L., Richert, A., Zeichner, K., LePage, P., Darling-Hammond, L., & Duffy, H. (2005). Teaching diverse learners. In L. Darling-Hammond & J. Bransford (Eds.), *Preparing teachers for a changing world: What teachers should learn and be able to do* (pp. 232–274). San Francisco, CA: Jossey-Bass.

Cochran-Smith, M., & Lytle, S.L. (1999). Relationships of knowledge and practice: Teacher learning in communities. *Review of Research in Education, 24,* 249–306.

Darling-Hammond, L., & Bransford, J. (Eds.). (2005). *Preparing teachers for a changing world: What teachers should learn and be able to do.* San Francisco, CA: Jossey-Bass.

de Jong, E.J., & Harper, C.A. (2005). Preparing mainstream teachers for English language learners: Is being a good teacher good enough? *Teacher Education Quarterly, 32*(2), 101–124.

Desimone, L.M., Porter, A.C., Garet, M.S., Yoon, K.S., & Birman, B.F. (2002). Effects of professional development on teachers' instruction: Results from a three year longitudinal study. *Educational Evaluation and Policy Analysis, 24*(2), 81–112.

DuFour, R., Eaker, R., & DuFour, R. (2005). *On common ground: The power of professional learning communities.* Bloomington, IN: Solution Tree.

Echevarria, J., Vogt, M., & Short, D. (2007). *Making content comprehensible for English learners: The SIOP® model* (3rd ed.). Columbus, OH: Allyn and Bacon/Merrill Education.

Fullan, M. (2001). *Leading in a culture of change.* San Francisco, CA: Jossey-Bass.

Garet, M.S., Porter, A.C., Desimone, L., Birman, B.F., & Yoon, K.S. (2001). What makes professional development effective? Results from a national sample of teachers. *American Educational Research Journal, 38*(4), 915–945.

Gibbons, P. (2002). *Scaffolding language, scaffolding learning: Teaching second language learners in the mainstream classroom.* Portsmouth, NH: Heinemann.

González, J.M., & Darling-Hammond, L. (1997). *New concepts for new challenges: Professional development for teachers of immigrant youth.* Washington, D.C.: Center for Applied Linguistics.

Improving America's Schools Act, Pub. L. 103–382. (1994).

Knight, S.L., & Wiseman, D.L. (2006). Lessons learned from a research synthesis on the effects of teachers' professional development on culturally diverse students. In K. Téllez & H. Waxman (Eds.), *Preparing quality educators for English language learners: Research, policy, and practice* (pp. 71–98). Mahwah, NJ: Lawrence Erlbaum.

Lucas, T., & Grinberg, J. (2008). Responding to the linguistic reality of mainstream classrooms: Preparing all teachers to teach English language learners. In M. Cochran-Smith, S. Feiman-Nemser, & D.J. McIntyre (Eds.), *Handbook of research on teacher education: Enduring issues in changing contexts* (3rd ed., pp. 606–636). New York, NY: Lawrence Erlbaum.

Mellgren, M., Walker, C., & Lange, D. (1988). The preparation of second language teachers through post-baccalaureate education. *Foreign Language Annals, 21*(2), 121–129.

Molnar, A. (Ed.). (2002). *School reform proposals: The research evidence.* Tempe, AZ: Educational Policy Research Unit, Arizona State University.

National Clearinghouse for English Language Acquisition, Language Enhancement, and Academic Achievement for Limited English Proficient Students. (2006). *The growing numbers of limited English proficient students, 1994–95–2004–05.* Office of English Language Acquisition, Language Enhancement and Academic Achievement for Limited English Proficient Students, U.S. Department of Education. Retrieved from: www.ncela.gwu.edu/policy/states/reports/statedata/2004LEP/GrowingLEP_0405_Nov06.pdf.

Penuel, W.R., Fishman, B.J., Yamaguchi, R., & Gallagher, L.P. (2007). What makes professional development effective? Strategies that foster curriculum implementation. *American Educational Research Journal, 44*(4), 921–958.

Ruiz-de-Velasco, J., & Fix, M. (2000). *Overlooked and underserved: Immigrant students in U.S. secondary schools.* Washington, D.C.: Urban Institute.

Shulman, L. (2005). *The signature pedagogies of the professions of law, medicine, engineering, and the clergy: Potential lessons for the education of teachers.* Presentation to National Research Council's Center for Education, February 6–8, Irvine, CA.

Sparks, D., & Hirsch, S. (1997). *A new vision for staff development.* Arlington, VA: Association for Supervision and Curriculum Development.

Téllez, K., & Waxman, H.C. (2006). *Preparing quality educators for English language learners: Research, policy, and practice.* Mahwah, NJ: Lawrence Erlbaum.

Villegas, A.M., & Lucas, T. (2002). *Educating culturally responsive teachers: A coherent approach.* Albany, NY: SUNY Press.

Walker, A., Shafer, J., & Iams, M. (2004). "Not in my classroom": Teacher attitudes towards English language learners in the mainstream classroom. *NABE Journal of Research and Practice, 21*(1), 130–160.

Walker, C., Edstam, T., & Stone, K. (2007a). *Two years, three kinds of educators, and four schools: Improving education for English language learners.* Paper presented at the Annual Meeting of the American Educational Research Association, Chicago, IL, April.

Walker, C., Edstam, T., & Stone, K. (2007b). *Schools as a locus of change: Toward purposeful professional development.* Paper presented at the Fifth International Conference on Language Teacher Education, Minneapolis, MN, May.

Walker, C., Edstam, T., & Stone, K. (2008). *Less is more: Using one professional learning community to address English language learner needs.* Paper presented at the Minnesota Elementary School Principals' Association, 53rd Annual Institute, Bloomington, MN, February.

Walker, C.L., & Tedick, D.J. (1994). Creating a culture of reform and reflection: Making change in teacher education. *Teaching Education, 6*(2), 81–95.

Walker, C.L., Ranney, S., & Fortune, T.W. (2005). Preparing preservice classroom teachers for students learning through a second language: A content-based approach. In D. Tedick (Ed.), *Second language teacher education: International perspectives* (pp. 313–333). Mahwah, NJ: Erlbaum.

Zeichner, K. (2005). A research agenda for teacher education. In M. Cochran-Smith & K. Zeichner (Eds.), *Studying teacher education: The report of the AERA panel on research and teacher education.* Mahway, NJ: Lawrence Erlbaum.

Chapter 9

Fostering Collaboration Between Mainstream and Bilingual Teachers and Teacher Candidates

Karen Sakash and Flora Rodriguez-Brown

Greater numbers of English language learners (ELLs) are being taught in mainstream classrooms by teachers who have received no special preparation (Menken & Antunez, 2001; Strizek, Pittsonberger, Riordan, Lyter, & Orlofsky, 2006), yet pedagogical content related to teaching ELLs is too often absent from the teacher preparation curricula for early childhood, elementary, and secondary teachers. In many teacher preparation programs, second language learning issues are blended into an unwieldy multicultural course, taught by an instructor versed in the broadly conceived area of multicultural education, but not familiar with specific knowledge related to ELLs. Teacher candidates in such programs often have no access to substantive content involving language acquisition, and issues surrounding ELLs are submerged in a host of competing "diversity" themes. Too few teacher candidates are provided with direct experience of working with ELLs and sometimes when they do encounter ELLs in their pre-service field experiences they do not have the skills to differentiate instruction for them. Fortunately, in recent years, federal funding focusing on programs that target *all* teachers has enabled more teacher candidates to take coursework leading to bilingual and ESL endorsements and credentials. But the challenge of preparing teachers to serve ELLs is still great and it encompasses both pre-service (teacher candidates) and in-service (already certified practicing teachers) domains.

Since their inception, bilingual programs within elementary schools have typically been isolated from the mainstream (Griego-Jones, 1995; Sakash & Rodriguez-Brown, 1995). The need for collaboration between ESL and mainstream teachers was highlighted over 20 years ago (Penfield, 1987). Bilingual/ESL teachers[1] and mainstream teachers, isolated from each other, often create different language learning environments for ELLs based on their perceptions of how best to serve the students. They sometimes fault each other for what ELLs have not yet learned. One of the keys to bridging the instructional gap at the in-service level is to break down communication barriers and facilitate conversation between mainstream and bilingual/ESL teachers. Collaboration that encourages teachers to share goals, experiences and responsibilities is central to the establishment of an optimal learning environment (Smylie, 1995).

Wagner (2001) examined the characteristics and behaviors of collaboration between bilingual/ESL and mainstream teachers. Data collected through interviews and classroom observations in four elementary schools with 10 teachers and four principals revealed that transitioning into all-English instruction was a gradual process for ELLs when teachers collaborated. Teachers' self-reported collaboration behaviors included trusting and supporting each other; identifying and solving problems together; sharing leadership and making joint decisions; and examining and analyzing practices, beliefs, and assumptions together. Collaboration led to less isolation among ELLs and more opportunities for them to use English for social and academic purposes. Mainstream teachers who taught ELLs before the official exit from the bilingual program had more positive perceptions of ELLs once they were transitioned. In another study, four high schools—two in California, one in New York, and one in Iowa—were studied to identify promising practices for serving immigrant students (Walqui, 2000). Findings revealed that flexible forms of teacher collaboration, responsive to complex contextual settings, were key to program effectiveness.

Teachers who interact with each other have achieved success in making school-based changes (Mosca, 2006; Sakash & Rodriguez-Brown, 1995; Wagner, 2001). Both mainstream and bilingual teachers benefit from collaborative relationships, and when students are mixed for instruction, under the focused guidance of bilingual teachers, everyone learns more about language and culture (Whitmore & Crowell, 2005). Wagner (2001) found that co-planning and co-teaching resulted in classroom structures that helped ELLs to develop cross-cultural working groups and friendships.

Over the past 16 years, the Bilingual Teacher Training Program at the University of Illinois at Chicago (UIC) has focused on preparing mainstream classroom teachers and teacher candidates to better serve ELLs. We have found that having a critical mass of bilingual teachers/teacher candidates enrolled in our mainstream teacher preparation programs can add significantly to the conversation surrounding ELLs, even when the instructors do not possess a background in bilingual/ESL education. Outcomes from a program evaluation also led us to this conclusion (Li, 2005). Typically, at UIC, about one third of the teacher candidates are preparing to become bilingual or ESL teachers in undergraduate and graduate mainstream elementary teacher education programs. Candidates seeking Bilingual and/or ESL Approval by the state of Illinois must take five additional courses. Given what we have observed over the years regarding their impact, we realized that we should be strategic about utilizing these teacher candidates as a resource. Additionally, we saw the opportunity to increase collaboration among practicing Chicago Public Schools (CPS) mainstream and state-approved bilingual/ESL teachers in school settings, extending our pre-service strategies to the in-service context. As part of a needs assessment conducted prior to implementing a federal grant, we asked 200 CPS bilingual/ESL and mainstream teachers what they thought would further their ability to serve ELLs in their schools. Because they reported that they needed more time to talk to each other, we structured opportunities for mainstream teachers and bilingual/ESL teachers to learn from each other within courses and within schools.

In this chapter we first describe structures we have created in our pre-service programs to infuse attention to educating ELLs into our urban university's teacher preparation programs. We then discuss what we have done to foster collaboration between in-service bilingual/ESL and mainstream teachers in their school settings, using two specific programs as examples. *Project 29* is a Master's degree and certification program for provisionally certified elementary bilingual teachers in CPS. *Project TATAT: Teaching All Teachers About Transitioning* is an in-service model that focuses teacher collaboration around the services that students receive as they move from native language instruction to all-English instruction, sometimes referred to as "transitioning." For each program, we highlight a case that exemplifies our use of program structures to foster collaboration between mainstream and bilingual/ESL teachers.

Strategies and Structures for Supporting Communication Between Mainstream and Bilingual/ESL Pre-Service Teacher Candidates

Mainstream teacher candidates enhance their understanding of ELLs when they directly encounter persons with expertise in serving ELLs and when they work directly with ELLs in educational settings. Teacher educators must make a conscious effort to focus pre-service preparation on ELLs and to place teacher candidates in programs, schools, and initiatives that serve ELLs. Following are descriptions of strategies we have found successful at UIC.

Proactively Advising Students to Seek ESL and/or Bilingual Approval

When students are admitted to the degree/certification programs at UIC, they often do not know that they will likely encounter ELLs in their future classrooms, that they might increase their chances of being hired if they obtain Illinois ESL/Bilingual Education Approval, or that UIC offers all the required courses, some of which double as required certification courses. Proactive and accurate advising in these matters is important. Advisors reach out to newly admitted students to make sure they know that they do not have to be bilingual to take the state-approval courses and that they will become better prepared to teach the recently transitioned K-8 students they will find in CPS once they are fully certified, particularly in an era of mandated state testing of ELLs in English.

Because our college mission includes preparing teacher candidates to teach in CPS, where 52,425 ELLs were reported in 2008 (Office of Language and Culture Education, 2008), we have created programs that merge and overlap courses that address the needs of ELLs. Through advising, we have increased the number of teacher candidates taking these courses in addition to their degree/certification courses. By taking five courses, all teacher candidates can earn a state-issued ESL Approval, and if they are bilingual and pass a state language proficiency test, they earn an additional Bilingual Approval in a particular targeted language. Two of these courses within the graduate elementary education program and one at the undergraduate level are already included in their "regular" program. In the graduate program, students may substitute "Foundations and Current Issues in Educating English Language Learners" for a course that addresses the Illinois standards for diversity. Students may also elect to take "Bilingualism and Literacy in a Second Language" to fulfill their second reading course requirement. In the undergraduate program, all students take "Multiculturalism, Bilingualism, and Diversity in Elementary School," which addresses the standards for foundations of ESL/Bilingual Education. By ensuring that students understand the program and the benefits of seeking Bilingual/ESL Approval, we have been able to include more discussions surrounding the needs of ELLs throughout the program.

Hiring Monolingual Graduate Assistants for ELL Initiatives

The six full-time bilingual education program faculty at UIC conduct research and implement programs that are often resourced through federal grants or foundations. One strategy we have used to increase attention to ELLs across all the teacher education programs is to hire some non-bilingual graduate assistants to work in these programs. For example, Project Total School Change (1998–2003), which targeted school reform in one CPS, was coordinated by a non-bilingual graduate assistant. Project Success (1997–2003), a UIC partnership with another CPS, employed non-bilingual mentors. Project FLAME, a research-based family literacy program that has existed for 19 years (Rodriguez-Brown, 2004), fills its continual need for teaching assistants to work in the Chicago Latino community partly by hiring graduate students not in the bilingual or ESL program. Thus, we recruit new teacher candidates (not always bilingual) as graduate assistants who receive specialized preparation to become family literacy teachers in programs serving CPS. The program coordinator of the M.Ed. in Instructional Leadership—Elementary recommends newly admitted candidates who express an interest in ESL on their applications to the director of Project FLAME. While working in the program, they increase their own awareness and knowledge of ELL education, and they bring their experiences and input to mainstream graduate elementary education courses, helping to focus discussions of teaching and learning on ELLs. Students who would not otherwise take as keen an interest in issues related to ELLs because of a lack of experience are thrust into leadership positions, and most eagerly embrace their responsibilities. Their work in the FLAME program gives them tuition waivers and enhances their resumes; we have noted that most of them also become staunch advocates for ELLs and their families, and they influence similar non-bilingual classmates to recognize the issues surrounding ELLs and to advocate for them.

Placing Teacher Candidates in Schools and Classrooms with ELLs for Field Experience

For field experience we have purposefully placed non-bilingual teacher candidates to learn side-by-side with bilingual teacher candidates in the graduate elementary education program. Evaluation data indicate that this has helped both groups develop new understandings related to language and culture (Li, 2005). For example, placing non-bilingual teacher candidates in bilingual/ESL classrooms for at least a portion of their field experiences has challenged our teacher candidates to develop lessons, assessment strategies, and learning environments for ELLs in K-8 classrooms. Also, pairing bilingual and non-bilingual pre-service teachers to work together in field experiences has facilitated rich conversations about appropriate instruction for ELL students (Li, 2003). In our undergraduate and graduate elementary education programs, almost all pre-service students experience a placement in a school with ELLs and have opportunities to gather information about the bilingual and ESL programs that serve them. Sometimes a teacher candidate is placed in the classroom of a currently enrolled provisionally certified bilingual/ESL teacher and together they create curriculum and complete lesson plans and other class assignments. The program evaluation indicated that one outcome of increased exposure to observing and working with ELLs in their school environments, within a variety of program models, is that non-bilingual pre-service teachers have identified and embraced their role in teaching ELLs (Li, 2005).

Appointing Bilingual Faculty to Coordinate and Teach in General Professional Education Programs

We use several strategies to ensure that teacher candidates in mainstream programs have the opportunity to learn from faculty members with expertise in the education of ELLs. Whether a teacher educator is bilingual may matter less than the individual's informed understanding of current assessment and instruction policies at local, state, and national levels. All teacher educators need to know current policies regarding the education of ELLs. Some grants we have received, such as Project TAT (Teaching All Teachers, 1999–2004), have targeted mainstream faculty development.

One strategy for ensuring that ELLs are addressed within courses is to have a bilingual faculty member coordinate the regular graduate elementary program. This allows her to select bilingual adjuncts for "regular" methods and foundations courses, thus giving future mainstream teachers exposure to bilingual individuals and to their knowledge of ELL education. Currently, bilingual instructors teach two different reading methods courses, two different math methods courses, and the social studies methods course that all students take. A second strategy we use is to intentionally organize our course loads so that bilingual/ESL faculty members teach in the "regular" program as well as in the Bilingual/ESL program. This ensures that issues of relevance to teaching ELLs are included in the curriculum. Other strategies we have begun pursuing at UIC are hiring bilingual/ESL faculty into general teacher education positions and having them teach general foundations and methods courses. For example, the graduate elementary social studies methods instructor in the Department of Curriculum and Instruction happens to also be state-certified as a bilingual teacher. Also, at the time of publication of this chapter, we are preparing to conduct a search for a clinical faculty member in elementary education. This will not be a bilingual faculty position, but among the job qualifications we seek will be bilingual proficiency and experience as a bilingual/ESL teacher. If more faculty with knowledge of ELL education were used in these ways in mainstream teacher education programs, regular teachers' knowledge regarding English language learners would grow.

In-Service Initiatives to Foster Collaboration Between Mainstream and Bilingual/ESL Teachers

At UIC, we have had several externally funded initiatives over the past 16 years that have promoted collaboration between practicing mainstream and bilingual/ESL teachers. Some of these programs have continued after funding ended, and others have evolved or been adapted to extend the work begun in the funded project. These projects have allowed us to create structures that involve mainstream teachers and bilingual/ESL teachers working together on projects and collaborating to solve problems and to make changes to better serve ELLs in CPS. In this section, we describe two of these projects—one that joined provisionally certified bilingual teachers and mainstream teachers to work together on a curricular initiative, and one that brought together teams of teachers from one school to work together to improve their program for ELLs.

Project 29

The impetus for Project 29 stemmed in part from Project TeamWorks, a three-year federally funded program designed to improve the coordination between bilingual programs and mainstream programs in CPS (Sakash &

Rodriguez-Brown, 1995). Pairs of bilingual and general program teachers from 30 schools were nominated by their principals to work together to solve problems and improve programs and curricula for ELLs at their schools. Inspired by Project TeamWorks and drawing on Wagner's (2001) dissertation research, we used the concept of collaboration among bilingual/ESL and mainstream teachers in our development of an in-service professional development model centered on the services provided to ELLs in schools, which also doubled as a course assignment for provisionally certified bilingual teachers.

Project 29 began as an externally funded teacher education program for non-certified CPS bilingual teachers. Originally funded by the DeWitt Wallace Reader's Digest Fund and later through federal grants, it included targeted recruitment and advising, curriculum adaptations, and developing teacher leadership. An especially innovative aspect of the program was that participants were allowed to "student teach" in their own classrooms under the supervision of bilingual field instructors (Sakash & Chou, 2007). Between 1994 and 2008, Project 29 enrolled 203 provisionally certified bilingual teachers in the elementary Master's program, comprising 13 cohorts, with a program retention rate of 95%.

From the beginning, we actively sought ways to anchor the program within the mainstream graduate elementary program. Instead of creating a separate track with separate courses, we integrated participants into our mainstream teacher preparation program for pre-service Master's students. The appointments of one of the Project 29 co-directors as dean of the college and the other as graduate elementary program coordinator were instrumental in facilitating and accelerating institutionalization of the program because it assured that the College and program leadership was supportive (Clewell & Villegas, 2001). We found that situating Project 29 inside a mainstream College program, rather than appending it, greatly eased the process of institutionalization. Since the program was essentially the same as the mainstream program—except for the student teaching course, a special section of a foundations course, and a math methods course—we were able to continue it when funding ended, with structures in place to deepen the exposure of mainstream students to ELL matters. For example, the math methods course focusing on ELLs is now available to mainstream students as a course option that meets state standards for teaching math.

Institutionalizing the program has had a positive impact on UIC's mainstream faculty and students, leading to greater understanding of ELLs (Sakash & Chou, 2007). It has also provided a continual supply of provisionally certified bilingual/ESL teachers for our M.Ed. program in Elementary Education. We recognized that integrating a significant number of bilingual teachers into the existing graduate elementary program would positively influence non-bilingual teacher candidates, just by their presence. Project 29 "Scholars" were practicing teachers who not only knew more about K-8 teaching and learning than their non-teaching peers, but also knew much more about serving ELLs. Other students and our own faculty embraced the Scholars' participation, seeing them as a powerful resource to enhance teacher preparation. The program respected the vast, collective experience and knowledge the bilingual teachers brought and we intentionally used this in informing our general teacher education program about teaching ELLs. For example, when course assignments involved group projects, we placed bilingual/ESL teachers in groups with non-bilingual teacher candidates. When teacher leadership surfaced, we encouraged and supported it. We have found that the "power of their presence" is one foundation for transformation in our urban teacher education program (Quiocho & Rios, 2000).

Classroom practices and conceptions of teaching emerge through a dynamic process of interaction among teachers, students, and subject matter (Talbert & McLaughlin, 1994). One requirement of the Project 29 Scholars' "student teaching" experience influenced monolingual teachers in the schools. The Scholars were required to seek out a non-bilingual colleague in their school to conduct a peer-to-peer project in which they interacted in some way for a minimum of 15 hours. This project led to deeper understandings among the school-based colleagues, and their experiences show what can occur when teachers view each other's students as every teacher's responsibility (Li, 2005). Below, we present the story of two teachers, showing how coming together to discuss instruction led to positive changes for a group of special education students in one Chicago school with a Latino population over 95% (Sakash, 1995).

Luisa was a bilingual teacher in a second-grade special education class. Several of her students were more proficient in Spanish than English. In her daily activities she used Spanish to clarify and explain concepts to her ELL students. Across the hall from her, Valerie, a non-bilingual special education teacher, had a classroom of fifth-to-eighth-graders, many of whom were Spanish speakers. Realizing that with a different teaching structure they could better utilize Luisa's proficiency in Spanish, the two teachers teamed up to provide appropriate instruction to all their Spanish- and English-proficient children. In effect, they changed the program model so that it would better meet the needs of the children, taking into consideration the language capabilities of the teachers and their students. The teachers planned lessons using cooperative learning structures for team-teaching science, art, reading, writing, and social skills.

Important outcomes resulted from the collaboration for both teachers and their students, as the teachers' comments indicated. Valerie wrote a letter summarizing her experience with the project. She described several of the joint activities they engaged in and mentioned how much respect Luisa gained as a teacher from *other* mainstream teachers in the school. She described some of the instructional benefits to her students and to her own professional growth:

Some of the students had good ideas but had a hard time expressing them. In this opportunity that we had to team teach they had the opportunity to let me know all the ideas that maybe they always wanted to tell me but they couldn't. By talking with Ms. C they were able to complete all the activities and assignments without any difficulty.... She has brought many good ideas to my teaching career, especially on integrating students from different cultural backgrounds.

In her writings, Luisa also commented on the mutual benefit of the collaboration:

I have always known Valerie to be a smart, experienced, and talented teacher. Through this project, I have learned that even a teacher like Valerie can gain from our working together. She is now using current techniques that I have learned through my coursework; and I have learned many specific activities and ideas she has brought from her years of experience.... Valerie was always making sure that my ideas, related to social interaction and strategies to be used in social skills, were pedagogically and purposefully applied to curricular goals and objectives.

About the students, Luisa wrote:

Valerie and I believe that our enthusiasm and cooperation were ... reflected in the students. In general we saw the students more on task. Less class management was needed, and there was more cooperation and interaction among students. Children were more communicative with teachers. Since they were allowed to use the language they feel more comfortable with, they showed more excitement, enthusiasm and productivity.

Luisa and Valerie would have continued teaching in isolation had it not been for this course requirement, implemented during Luisa's "student teaching" semester, which required that she choose a monolingual teacher with whom to develop a collaborative project involving their students. With a slight variation, but holding onto the premise that collaboration results in learning (Wagner, 2001), teacher educators could require an assignment in which mainstream teacher candidates select (or are placed with) practicing bilingual or ESL teachers to collaboratively develop a project, or a lesson plan or a unit, that engages the teacher candidate in working with ELLs. As teacher educators, it is our role to help facilitate more direct exposure and communication between ELL specialists and those learning to teach. This can happen when teacher educators (mainstream or bilingual/ESL) seek field placement partnership schools with significant numbers of ELLs and programs to serve them, and when ELL specialists are included among the teacher mentors selected to receive mainstream teacher candidates.

Project TATAT (Teaching All Teachers About Transitioning)

As with Project 29, elements of Project TeamWorks were adapted in developing Project TATAT (Teaching All Teachers About Transitioning), funded from 2001 to 2006. The program paid participants' tuition for two required program courses. Most participants continued their professional development and transferred the credits for these courses into a degree program or met additional goals, such as state ESL Approval or Reading Endorsement. Project TATAT raised awareness among all participating teachers as to their role in the education of ELLs (Rodriguez-Brown, 2006). As the project ended, we were able to continue teacher collaborations through Project ATTACH (All Teachers Teaching All Children), funded from 2007 to 2012. In both of these projects, mainstream teachers are prepared alongside bilingual/ESL teachers in settings designed to foster collaboration between them, to focus them on seeing their shared responsibilities in the education of all children, and to enhance their understanding of how ELLs move from native language instruction into full participation in English. Transitioning was chosen as a centering concept because it is the juncture at which mainstream teachers and bilingual/ESL teachers connect in their services to ELLs (Shannon, 1990). Both TATAT and ATTACH facilitate and support workshops, working sessions, and teacher meetings to discuss issues related to ELLs and allow teachers to develop or restructure a plan for their school. One underlying purpose is to help teachers learn about transition as a *process* for ELLs (rather than an *event*). Program records, interviews of project leaders, products developed, and survey data were collected and analyzed for evaluation purposes for Project TATAT (Li, 2006). Over the five-year funding period, 163 bilingual and monolingual teachers from 17 schools participated. In total, 47% were bilingual and 53% were monolingual teachers (Li, 2006). Data collected included an examination of the characteristics and behaviors of collaboration between bilingual and mainstream teachers, drawing on Wagner's (2001) results. Findings indicated that teacher collaboration occurred informally, with teachers sharing experiences, opinions, and ideas in a supportive environment (Li, 2006).

Participants in the project were initially enrolled in a four-credit course entitled "Teaching All Teachers About Transitioning English Language Learners"—a seminar with several guest speakers addressing topics that participants identified as the course progressed. Sessions on teacher collaboration, state transition and exit policies, case studies of successful transition programs, language transfer from L1 to L2, and community/parent involvement, were among the identified topics. Each team of teachers developed a school-wide plan based on a needs assessment they conducted of all teachers at their schools. The project was designed according to the premise that, to have the most impact, change must come from teachers themselves (Barth, 1990; Evans, 1996; Maeroff, 1993).

During the first year of the project, all the participants were third- or fourth-grade teachers struggling with teaching writing. Each week they brought in student work to discuss as a group. Whole-group discussions of individual students' writing helped them gain an understanding of how ELLs move from native language into English and what instructional methods facilitate writing development. During that year and in subsequent years, every teacher in the project presented at least one successful teaching strategy with ELL students to others in the seminar. Teacher development was an expected outcome of Project TATAT, concurrent with whole-school change stemming from teachers working together to address concerns and influence others in their schools.

In a second course, biweekly seminar sessions addressing topics selected by the teachers were held along with biweekly school-based meetings in which teachers continued planning and implementing their restructured school change plans, using the collaboration principles embraced by the program design, applying the theories and strategies acquired through the coursework. The school-based meetings allowed teachers to improve school practices in relation to ELLs and influence other non-participating teachers and administrators about the needs of these students. Teachers discussed, reviewed, and brainstormed suggestions, gathered input, and proposed changes in instructional practices, curriculum alignment, and social integration—which improved the structures surrounding the education and transition of ELLs in their schools.

Over the grant period, 83 teachers participated in additional professional development at UIC. Among these, 44 took the series of bilingual/ESL courses, 35 completed Master's degrees in Reading or Instructional Leadership, and four pursued both goals. A total of 25 school change plans were completed by the teams over the five years of the grant. Below is a description of one of these and its outcomes. For complete descriptions of all schools' transition plans, see Li (2006) or contact the authors.

Harwood School, where over 50% of the students are ELLs, established an after-school intramural sports program in the upper grades to ease the transition for newcomers and encourage their interaction with English-proficient students. Six Harwood teachers participated as a team in Project TATAT. The monolingual PE teacher and the eighth-grade bilingual teacher together proposed a plan to encourage communication and socializing between sixth-to-eighth-grade newcomer ELLs and the Latino "monolingual" students, many of whom had formerly been classified as ELL. They planned a structured recreational environment that they hoped would facilitate relationships among these students, girls as well as boys, in order to lower anxiety among the transitioning ELLs and give them more acceptance within the school. The teachers of both groups of students would have opportunities to meet and communicate with all students, and see them work together in the context of educational games, sports, and drama activities.

As part of TATAT, each team conducted a school-based needs assessment prior to planning project activities. The Harwood team partially fulfilled this requirement by observing the students. They "noticed the separation of students in front of the school in the morning, in the classrooms, even in the extracurricular activities.... This was neither a black–white issue nor a black–Hispanic issue; this was Hispanics not talking to other Hispanics" (Carmona and McDermott, 2006). Based on these observations, the teachers saw a need for change. They asked all fifth-through-eighth-grade students to respond to a survey of their attitudes, beliefs, and behaviors towards each other. Questions included: What activities would you consider doing with the students from the bilingual classes? If you had a chance to play a sport at Harwood, what would that be? If a student from one of the bilingual classes chose the same sport as you, would you welcome him/her on your team? (Carmona and McDermott, 2006).

From the responses, they developed structural changes within existing school activities to support and improve the transition of ELLs into the school. They altered the students' lunch period so that all seventh- and eighth-graders ate at the same time. This provided them the opportunity to socialize, which led to the next structural change. Dances were held for all seventh- and eighth-graders to which the students brought their own music, alternating between ranchero and rap, reggaeton and rock, and salsa and soul. The third structural change resulted in the greatest impact on the students' abilities and desire to become integrated. Soccer became the uniting element. Instead of having intact classes compete against each other, the teachers identified all students interested in playing soccer and the PE teacher organized teams of students in all programs combined, "with good players on all teams ensuring close and competitive games," and with bilingual program students as captains (Carmona and McDermott, 2006).

As described by the teachers:

> An amazing thing happened in our school. All of a sudden all of the soccer players were willing to help each other out. Students were hanging around with their teammates regardless of being an English or Spanish speaker. Former bilingual program students reached out to help the newcomers and made it a little easier for them to fit in. The newcomers were feeling better about themselves, becoming more relaxed and comfortable. As captains of the teams they were forced to lead. They gained respect and self-confidence. English speakers started using Spanish words such as *pegale, dale, pasale*. They even started greeting their teammates in Spanish.
>
> (Carmona and McDermott, 2006)

The Harwood team made other changes, including more academic integration. They concluded that the school became "a different place," with much more integration among English-speaking and Spanish-speaking students. They noted that, even in the cafeteria, there were no longer the earlier divisions between groups.

In its fifth and final year, Project TATAT hosted a teacher conference for all schools where teachers shared their products and plans with each other and with other administrators and teacher educators. They created poster presentations in this culminating activity to communicate the importance of collaborating in support of ELL students in their schools. One teacher summed up the outcome of Project TATAT: "I now know that if we teachers cooperate and collaborate, we can facilitate a differentiated curriculum that will help ELLs as well as our student population as a whole."

Through Project TATAT, mainstream and bilingual/ESL teachers were recognized as school leaders and given the time necessary (within the structure of a course at first, and later at their schools) to collaborate to make real improvements in the learning environment for ELLs. Supports were in place or created for them to work together and make changes. For example, teacher teams were only recruited from schools where the principal welcomed and supported teacher-led change. In many cases the biggest change was not school-based program structures, but a willingness on the part of the mainstream and bilingual/ESL teachers to see each other as partners in serving ELLs, and to recognize the need for a whole-school focus on sharing accountability for ELLs' learning (Li, 2006). This work continues through Project ATTACH.

Lessons Learned

For the past 16 years, we have consciously sought to foster collaboration between mainstream and bilingual/ESL pre-service and in-service teachers in the Bilingual Teacher Training Program at UIC. Since 1992, beginning with Project TeamWorks, this work has been supported by external funding for several projects and initiatives. With the benefit of this funding, we have developed strategies that have proven especially successful and that other institutions can apply or adapt, even without external funding. In pre-service programs, we have created structures for drawing in our regular program teacher candidates and mainstream teachers to engage with our bilingual program faculty and bilingual teachers and students in several ways. We focus our work with mainstream students on the importance of becoming prepared to teach ELLs; we give them roles as teaching assistants in grants involving Latino families and school reform activities within CPS schools with large Latino populations; we provide them with opportunities to become state-approved ELL teachers; we partner them with bilingual teachers and teacher candidates for course projects; we include courses that focus on ELLs in their regular certification programs; we place them in schools with programs for ELLs for field experiences; and we expose them to bilingual program faculty in regular program courses and to mainstream program faculty who have expertise as bilingual/ESL specialists. We have learned that direct encounters with individuals and initiatives serving ELLs result in deepening understandings of the needs of second language learners.

We have used many of the above strategies as well as others in promoting collaboration between bilingual/ESL teachers and mainstream teachers at the inservice level, including requiring candidates in bilingual and ESL programs to work with mainstream teachers in their schools on projects to benefit ELLs; offering (and providing tuition support for) courses focused on transitioning ELLs from special programs into the mainstream; and grounding courses and programs in the contexts and needs of particular schools and teachers. While some of these pre-service and in-service strategies may not be as successful in other contexts, we believe many of them could be applied in other settings, with the details determined by the context within and surrounding each institution.

In the remainder of the chapter, we draw on what we have learned to offer some advice for teacher educators in other institutions. First, while external support is not essential, it does allow changes to be made more quickly and can prevent objections to innovations if the funding requires them. Therefore, we recommend that teacher educators seek funding to get some projects off the ground—from federal sources such as Title II and Title III grants as well as from local and national foundations. As part of the development and implementation of these programs, it is important to build in plans for institutionalizing their key elements after external funding ends.

Second, undertaking the kinds of initiatives we have described requires human resources. Success depends on having faculty with the expertise and commitment to take the lead on developing programs, seeking funding, coordinating the programs, and reaching out to colleagues for their involvement and input. If a teacher education program does not already have faculty with this background, then priority should be given to hiring them. Expertise and experience with ELL education can be among the required or highly desired qualifications of "regular" faculty positions in teacher education, even if there is no support for hiring someone whose primary responsibility is preparing teachers to teach ELLs. Even though we have bilingual education faculty at UIC, we have learned to become strategic about how we use our human resources. For example, most of our search committees include at least one bilingual education faculty member who can tap into wider networks of bilingual scholars in fields such as literacy, math, science, and educational foundations. Because many of those in bilingual/ESL education also specialize in a discipline, if we are searching for an assistant professor of literacy, for example, we target our recruitment at literacy scholars who are bilingual as well as bilingual/ESL scholars whose research focuses on literacy.

A third lesson we have learned is that it is important to work with local school districts, school leaders, and teachers to build the support and structures to promote collaboration. We recognize that our success is partly due to our context: we are situated in a large school district with many public schools that provide bilingual education and ESL programs for ELLs, mandated by the state, and our college mission focuses on serving schools in the district. We have used funding to initially recruit experienced, provisionally certified bilingual teachers into our Master's program in elementary certification, and eventually, through their presence and our faculty's respect for their knowledge and expertise in matters pertaining to ELLs, we began to change the conversations in regular program courses to focus on ELLs. While most school districts do not have the commitment or the urgent need to devote as much attention to the education of ELLs as CPS, the number of ELLs in school districts and, in particular, in mainstream classrooms is rapidly increasing across the country, including in many school districts that have little experience with ELL education. Teacher educators can draw on the interest in improving the education of ELLs in those districts to forge collaborations like those we have with CPS. Regardless of the type of school district, success of collaborative projects is greatly enhanced when they are built around the perceived needs and strengths of the teachers in the schools—rather than predetermined by university faculty. Therefore, we recommend that the content and processes of joint projects be determined collaboratively.

Finally, leadership support is also crucial to initiating and maintaining the kinds of strategies and initiatives we have described. Teacher educators who are knowledgeable and supportive of ELL education should become leaders who volunteer to take on administrative positions in mainstream programs and initiatives, both at district and university levels. Such leaders can facilitate the integration and foregrounding of attention to ELLs in mainstream programs so that all teachers are more likely to complete the programs prepared to teach ELLs.

Intentional structures must be created so that pre-service and in-service teachers within K-12 schools and within teacher preparation programs can collaborate and learn from each other. Interaction among bilingual and mainstream teachers or pre-service teachers will occur when a critical mass of bilingual/ESL teachers and bilingual teacher candidates is present in teacher preparation programs, and bilingual/ESL and mainstream teachers have opportunities to collaborate toward a common goal: to teach all children. While it is true that *all* teachers need to recognize their responsibility for meeting ELLs' needs, and mainstream teachers are in great need of additional preparation, we believe this can be more easily accomplished when bilingual individuals join the conversation.

Note

1. In this chapter we use the term "bilingual/ESL teacher" to refer to teachers who are in possession of, or are working toward, a state approval to teach ELLs and are teaching ELLs in bilingual and ESL classrooms. Although a few may be English-proficient only, the Illinois state mandate for serving ELLs through bilingual instruction means that mostly the teachers we refer to are proficient in two languages.

References

Barth, R.S. (1990). *Improving schools from within: Teachers, parents, and principals can make a difference.* San Francisco, CA: Jossey-Bass.

Carmona, A., & McDermott, M. (2006). *Increasing social interaction among bilingual and mainstream students.* Paper presented at the 30th Annual Statewide Conference for Teachers Serving Linguistically and Culturally Diverse Students, Oakbrook, IL, December.

Clewell, B.C., & Villegas, A.M. (2001). *Evaluation of the DeWitt Wallace Reader's Digest Fund's Pathways to Teaching Careers Program.* Washington, D.C.: The Urban Institute.

Evans, R. (1996). *The human side of school change: Reform, resistance, and the real-life problems of innovations.* San Francisco, CA: Jossey-Bass.

Griego-Jones, T. (1995). *Implementing bilingual programs is everybody's business.* NCBE Focus Paper No. 11. Washington, D.C.: National Clearinghouse for Bilingual Education.

Li, R. (2003). *Biennial evaluation report: Project 29* (CFDA Program 84.195A Award #T195A010036). Washington, D.C.: Office of Bilingual Education and Minority Languages Affairs.

Li, R. (2005). *Summative evaluation report: Project 29* (CFDA Program 84.195A Award #T195A010036). Washington, D.C.: Office of Bilingual Education and Minority Languages Affairs.

Li, R. (2006). *Summative evaluation report: Project Teaching All Teachers About Transitioning* (CFDA Program 84.195A Award #T195B010064). Washington, D.C.: Office of Bilingual Education and Minority Languages Affairs.

Maeroff, G. (1993). *Team building for school change: Equipping teachers for new roles.* New York, NY: Teachers College Press.

Menken, K., & Antunez, B. (2001). *An overview of the preparation and certification of teachers working with limited English proficient (LEP) students.* Washington, D.C.: National Clearinghouse for Bilingual Education.

Mosca, C. (2006). How do you ensure that everyone in the school shares the responsibilities for educating English language learners, not just those who are specialists in the field? In E. Hamayan & R. Freeman (Eds.), *English language learners at school: A guide for administrators* (pp. 109–110). Philadelphia, PA: Caslon Publishing.

Office of Language and Culture Education. (2008). *At a Glance.* Chicago Public Schools. Retrieved from www.olce.org/pdfs/OLCE%20At%20A%20Glance%20-%20February%202002008.pdf.

Penfield, J. (1987). ESL: The regular classroom teacher's perspective. *TESOL Quarterly, 21*(1), 21–39.

Quiocho, A., & Rios, F. (2000). The power of their presence: Minority group teachers and schooling. *Review of Educational Research, 70,* 485–528.

Rodriguez-Brown, F.V. (2004). Project FLAME: A parent support family literacy model. In B. Wasik (Ed.), *Handbook of family literacy* (pp. 213–229). Mahwah, NJ: Erlbaum.

Rodriguez-Brown, F.V. (2006). *Teacher collaboration and school improvement: Teaching all children.* Paper presented at the California Association for Bilingual Education, San Jose, CA, March.

Sakash, K. (1995). Teacher collaboration in culturally and linguistically diverse school settings: It can change teachers, students, and schools. Unpublished manuscript, University of Illinois at Chicago, Chicago, IL.

Sakash, K., & Chou, V. (2007). Increasing the supply of Latino bilingual teachers for the Chicago Public Schools. *Teacher Education Quarterly, 34*(4), 41–52.

Sakash, K., & Rodriguez-Brown, F.V. (1995). *TeamWorks: Mainstream and bilingual/ ESL teacher collaboration.* NCBE Program Information Guide No. 24. Washington, D.C.: National Clearinghouse for Bilingual Education.

Shannon, S.M. (1990). Transition from bilingual programs to all-English programs: Issues about and beyond language. *Linguistics and Education, 2,* 323–343.

Smylie, M.A. (1995). Teacher learning in the workplace. In T.R. Guskey & M. Huberman (Eds.), *Professional development in education: New paradigms and practices* (pp. 92–113). New York, NY: Teachers College Press.

Strizek, G.A., Pittsonberger, J.L., Riordan, K.E., Lyter, D.M., & Orlofsky, G.F. (2006). *Characteristics of schools, districts, teachers, principals, and school libraries in the United States: 2003-04 Schools and Staffing Survey* (NCES 2006–313 Revised). U.S. Department of Education, National Center for Education Statistics. Washington, D.C.: U.S. Government Printing Office.

Talbert, J.E., & McLaughlin, M.W. (1994). Teacher professionalism in local school contexts. *American Journal of Education, 102,* 123–153.

Wagner, S. (2001). Crossing classroom borders: Pathways to the mainstream via teacher collaboration. Unpublished doctoral dissertation, University of Illinois at Chicago.

Walqui, A. (2000). *Access and engagement: Program design and instructional approaches for immigrant students in secondary school.* Washington, D.C.: Center for Applied Linguistics.

Whitmore, K.F., & Crowell, C.G. (2005). Bilingual education students reflect on their language education: Reinventing a classroom 10 years later. *Journal of Adolescent & Adult Literacy, 49,* 270–285.

Chapter 10

The Growth of Teacher Expertise for Teaching English Language Learners

A Socio-Culturally Based Professional Development Model

Aída Walqui

Accomplished teachers are key to their students' success. Teacher expertise develops over time, through multiple, coherent opportunities to experience, understand, act, and reflect, many times with colleagues, sometimes alone, sometimes spontaneously, and at other times through structured professional development sessions. In whatever manner it occurs, educators' professional development should always be guided by the goal of expanding their ability to realize their students' potential for learning.

This chapter presents professional development opportunities created by the Teacher Professional Development Program (TPD) at WestEd in collaboration with the New York City Department of Education (NYCDOE) since 2003. The goal has been to develop the expertise of educators in the largest school system in the United States so they can work with adolescent English language learners (ELLs) with high levels of academic engagement, rigor, and depth. This work has involved developing the capacity of instructional support specialists, classroom teachers, and administrators to identify, develop, and enact quality instruction for ELLs. The chapter first presents the conceptual framework that guided the conceptualization, design, enactment, and ongoing refinement of professional development in NYCDOE. It then provides a detailed examination of the application of that framework in the professional development of ELL Instructional Support Specialists, describing their progression from apprenticeship to the WestEd staff, to their appropriation of the process as they led the professional development of teachers of ELLs. The chapter then describes the professional development for teachers, led by WestEd staff and, eventually, by the Instructional Support Specialists. It concludes with a consideration of lessons learned.

A Theoretical Framework for Developing Teacher Expertise

The work involved in building the capacity of NYCDOE's English Language Learner Professional Development Team is multi-layered. It includes the scaling-up and expansion of TPD's *Quality Teaching for English Learners*

(QTEL) professional development program for teachers of all ELLs in English as well as a parallel component addressing the enhancement of teacher expertise to teach rigorous content knowledge in Spanish to Spanish-speaking ELLs. The overall goal of QTEL is to make a significant contribution to the educational success of *all* students in the city by ensuring that Instructional Support Specialists who work with teachers of secondary ELLs have the capacity to scaffold the students' development of conceptual, academic, and linguistic subject matter skills in grades 6–12, when academic subject matter demands become more stringent.

The QTEL professional development model is based on a carefully designed theoretical framework that draws from three main bodies of work: socio-cultural theories of teaching and learning, a sociolinguistic view of second language learning, and a model of the development of teacher expertise (see Figure 10.1). These theories help define how people learn; what language is, how it is learned, and therefore how it should be taught; and how teachers, as adult learners, develop their potential to become accomplished practitioners. These three perspectives are integrated with tools and processes designed to develop the domains of professionalism along which teachers grow: knowledge, vision, motivation, reflection, knowledge of their context, and practice.

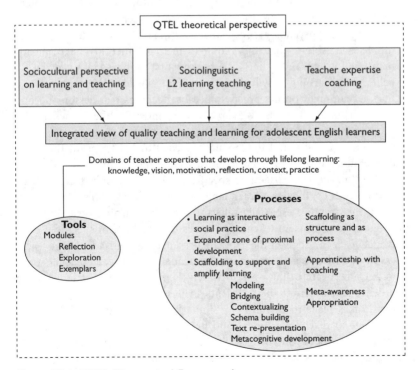

Figure 10.1 QTEL Theoretical Framework.

Socio-Cultural Theory

The socio-cultural theory of learning is based on the work of Lev Vygotsky, a Russian psychologist (1978, 1987), and many educational theorists, researchers, and applied linguists who have continued developing and applying his ideas to their work (e.g., Kozulin, Gindis, Ageyev, & Miller, 2003; Lantolf, 2000; Lantolf & Thorne, 2006; van Lier, 2004). Vygotsky proposed that the basis of learning and development is social interaction. Applied in the QTEL model, this means learners and teachers engage in joint activity that focuses on academic concepts and skills, and provides opportunities for learning through interaction. Learning is viewed as a process of social apprenticeship that takes place beyond learners' current competence, i.e., in their zone of proximal development (ZPD), and helps them appropriate concepts, skills, and language first used in interpersonal encounters. Drawing on this view of learning, the QTEL model is grounded in four basic tenets:

1. *Development follows learning.* We often hear teachers say they cannot teach a specific unit or lesson to their English language learners because they have not yet sufficiently developed their English language ability. These teachers assume that before students can learn concepts and skills, they need to know the related language — in other words, that language and content are two separate entities. This idea, derived from traditional developmental psychology, posits that learning can only be successful after the learner shows that the required mental functions have already matured. Instead, and in line with thinking first proposed by Vygotsky, we believe that learning truly happens only if it is ahead of development, and that development occurs precisely because teachers plan lessons beyond the students' ability to carry them out independently. These teachers also provide students with meaningful practice that enables them to appropriate concepts, skills, and the language needed to use them. In this view, deliberate, well-constructed teaching drives development.

    This means that discipline-specific teachers not only teach subject matter to ELLs; they also teach language or academic skills. Two factors make this premise especially relevant. First, all learning is mediated by language, and thus all teaching involves the teaching of specific uses of language. Second, given the growing presence of English language learners in our schools and their pervasive academic failure, all teachers need to become aware of the ways in which their disciplines use language in order to teach them to their students. Professional development for them, then, takes place in their ZPDs. Similarly, their students will learn the language of disciplinary ideas and processes precisely because they are invited to work beyond their ability, in the ZPD, in supported ways.

2. *Participation in activity is central in the development of knowledge.* Students learn concepts by using them, applying them, comparing them, critiquing

them, etc. Similarly, they learn the language needed to work through new concepts and their verbal communication of them by engaging with others in the use of appropriate language required for the tasks the students perform. Teachers attempting to develop expertise for teaching ELLs also learn through participating in activities designed to use relevant concepts and appropriate language—for example, by analyzing models of lessons designed for students; by practicing, deconstructing, and reflecting on them; and eventually by being asked to create their own lesson plans, teach them, and refine them. By engaging in such activities, they can reflect on and analyze subject matter English, and consider how to construct ways to engage their students in using and practicing key subject matter concepts and processes with others with the goal of eventually appropriating them.

3. *Participation in activity progresses from apprenticeship to appropriation, from the social to the individual plane.* As Vygotsky (1987) explained, "What the child is able to do in collaboration today he will be able to do independently tomorrow" (p. 211). It is essential for ELLs to engage in verbal activity with others, to apprentice into the ways of doing science, mathematics, history, etc., with depth. While ELLs will not be able to produce an accomplished essay after only a few lessons, for example, they can be supported, through carefully designed and enacted teaching, to learn with and from others to develop certain academic practices. Then, they can develop other practices individually, appropriating notions and activities recently introduced to them. Similarly, when teachers are presented with models and helped to understand them in collaboration, they are able to appropriate and successfully apply them given the right support. For example, while a science teacher participating in professional development at first will draw on what she is learning from others to modify her instruction for ELLs and other students who need to develop the scientific uses of English, over time, with practice and support, this teacher will make these practices her own; they will become part of her repertoire.

4. *Learning can be observed as changes in participation over time.* This tenet focuses on the assessment of learning to determine whether it has been successful. To say that a person has learned, one must observe how the person engages in action at different points in time. This difference should be both qualitative and quantitative. At first, an English learner may be minimally participatory in classroom activity, may struggle to understand classroom practices, and observe and imitate what others do. Were we to observe this student a month later, we would expect to see her interacting more and contributing to the task at hand. The appropriation would not be mere repetition of what others said or wrote—although it may be that at earlier stages. Learning and appropriating conceptual understandings and processes manifested through new language entail the production of original conversation and/or writing involving

individual interpretation, evaluation, analysis, synthesis, or reorganization of information. These types of production should increasingly approximate authentic accomplished (expert) performance. Teachers, in a similar fashion, are able to gradually accomplish more over time. Initially they may use some of the professional development lessons as replacement units, but over time, they will produce their own, and even develop innovative practices, following their own understanding of theoretical and practical ideas.

A Sociolinguistic View of Second Language Learning and Teaching

While this chapter focuses primarily on aspects of QTEL that reflect sociocultural theories of learning and teaching, and the development of teacher expertise, the initiative also builds on sociolinguistic notions of language use in social context. The structures and processes designed for instructional support specialists and for teachers are firmly anchored in interactive processes. Sociolinguists view language as a semiotic tool that humans use to communicate with others purposefully and appropriately within specific contexts. What one says and how one says it in a specific situation responds to the intent of the communication and to features of the communicative situation. Successful communication requires that participants in an interaction understand each other's ideas and intentions, respond to them by accepting them, building on what has been stated, or countering arguments in order to accomplish their social purposes. In communication, appropriateness is paramount, not grammatical correctness (Hymes, 1968). While accuracy (correctness) or lexical or grammatical complexity can sometimes be the focus of classroom communication, most often fluency—being able to express and respond to ideas in fluid, although not necessarily correct, ways—is the goal (Ellis, 2005). This sociolinguistic view of language is contrary to how second languages are often taught in schools, where grammar and correctness have been privileged. When teachers give too much emphasis to correctness and not enough attention to the communication and discussion of ideas and arguments, students' sense of themselves as writers (and communicators) can be undermined. The fact that many former ELLs do not seem to trust their own ideas and do not use them in writing when they enter university has been attributed to this tendency in second language teaching (Colombi, 2002).

The Development of Teacher Understanding and Expertise

Socio-cultural theory informs QTEL understandings of how human beings develop their concepts and skills, whether they are students or teachers. To design the *content* of teachers' learning, we adapted Shulman's (Shulman & Shulman, 2004; Shulman & Associates, 1995) model of teacher expertise. This adaptation (Walqui, 1997) (Figure 10.2) depicts two facets of individual teacher understanding and its development:

1. A mapping of the domains that constitute the knowledge, dispositions, emotions, and abilities of accomplished teachers working in specific contexts (the upper part of the diagram).
2. The notion that teacher understanding and expertise develop along a continuum, with certain aspects becoming more salient than others at different times (the timeline at the bottom).

How exactly different domains develop or not over time depends very much on characteristics of the teachers and professional developers and interactions with other educators and their contexts. The more educators work in focused and collegial ways, the more growth we can expect in their professional expertise (Shulman & Associates, 1995; Walqui, 1997; Wei, Darling-Hammond, Andree, Richardson, & Orphanos, 2009).

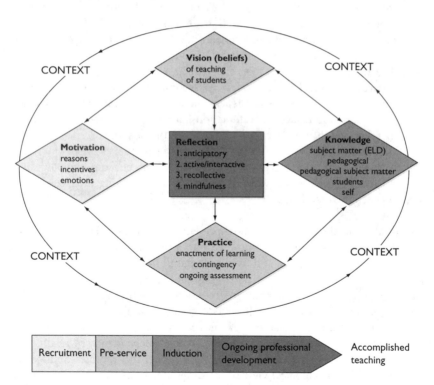

Figure 10.2 Model of Teacher Understanding: Individual Level of Analysis (Shulman & Associates, 1995; adapted by Walqui, 1997).

Throughout their pre-service education and professional lives, teachers develop along six domains:

- *Vision* encompasses teachers' ideologies, objectives, and dreams—all of which impart a sense of direction to their students' learning. Accomplished teachers believe in the educability of every English language learner and seek to ensure equal learning opportunities for all.
- *Knowledge* represents the range of cognitive understandings that inform instruction: general pedagogical knowledge, subject matter knowledge, knowledge of how to teach English as a second language and how to embed that knowledge in the teaching of academic content, pedagogical content knowledge, knowledge of the teaching context and of the students, and teacher self-knowledge.
- *Practice* represents the teachers' skills and strategies for enacting their goals and understandings in their teaching.
- *Motivation* is comprised of the reasons, incentives, and emotions that give energy and meaning to teachers' visions, understandings, and practices.
- *Reflection* in teaching occurs when knowledgeable practitioners try to make sense of their actions in classrooms by engaging in (among other activities) planning, remembering, evaluating, and contemplating—all of which contribute to the understanding of their work in schools.
- The development of teacher expertise is embedded in a *context* that incorporates dimensions of the classroom, school, district, and community, as well as state and federal demands, professional responsibilities, and multi-faceted interactions among all these dimensions. Teachers teach in ever-changing contexts; the demands related to what they need to know and be able to do to educate their students increase exponentially. Consequently, teachers need to be continuously supported to develop new ways of designing and enacting their classes to meet contextual demands.

A caveat about the organizing model presented here is in order. As Shulman and his colleagues (1995) have pointed out, a model (and diagram) such as this one is uni-dimensional and idealized; that is, it fails to represent the considerable conceptual and practical overlap among its components and their dynamic interaction. The domains represented are neither discrete nor neatly separable in categories, nor do they all develop in organized, sequential ways. They constitute an ecological model and coexist in mutually supporting relations; thus they cannot be thought of as existing independently or relating to one another in a linear fashion. The QTEL model incorporates Shulman's domains and this ecological view of the development of teacher expertise; it also aims to provide professional development opportunities that promote the growth of teacher expertise over time.

The Development of Instructional Support Specialists in NYC

As QTEL staff engaged classroom teachers in professional development to support their expertise to work in rigorous ways with ELLs, we[1] also worked on developing the expertise of instructional specialists who support them in classrooms to improve their practice and implement QTEL. The work with instructional leaders developed the capacity of the system to extend the professional development opportunities for teachers and facilitated faithful implementation of a quality program of instruction for ELLs, one that incorporates the socio-cultural approach to learning discussed above. This work involved the professional development of 125 ELL–Instructional Support Specialists (ELL–ISSs) who served as the district's professional development team for the instruction of ELLs.

The work of the Teacher Professional Development Program (TPD) in NYC with ELL–ISSs was based on an apprenticeship model (Lave and Wenger, 1991; Walqui, 2003) of scaffolding academic instruction for teachers of adolescent ELLs (Walqui, 2006). The apprenticeship model develops the skills of the ELL–ISSs through four phases of increasing levels of expertise in the field. The apprenticeship process aims to develop their capacity to support classroom teachers in the enactment of and reflection upon quality lessons that advance students' development of both their acquisition of discipline-specific content and the academic uses of English. Through their participation in the following phases, ELL–ISSs appropriated the tools, resources, language, and understandings to support teachers as they develop their expertise to work with ELLs.

Phase One: Building the Base

This phase involved three sessions of intensive, week-long institutes for 125 NYC professional developers who comprised the ELL–ISSs. The sessions aimed to provide them with a firm base of theoretical understanding and consonant strategies for effectively teaching academic uses of language to ELLs. Each session served a subset of ELL–ISSs for 40 hours of work designed to help them "build the base" of understanding for academically and linguistically demanding work with students. Figure 10.3 shows the apprenticeship relationship of the ELL–ISSs to the WestEd staff in Phase One.

The eight-hour-a-day, five-day institute was designed to support the ELL–ISSs' development in the domains of teacher expertise in Figure 10.2. To build a vision of accomplished teaching with adolescent ELLs and their capabilities, we read, compared, and discussed memoirs, short stories, and essays presenting stories of triumph over intolerance and misunderstanding in language minority settings. We also viewed video exemplars, some presenting accomplished teaching, some based on interviews with writers, teachers, and

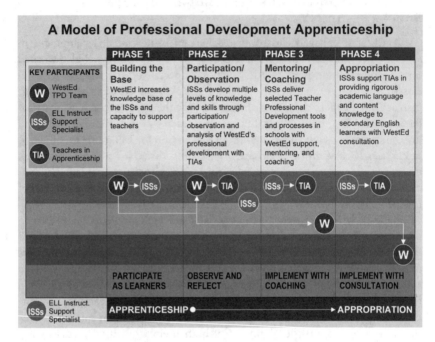

Figure 10.3 WestEd's Apprenticeship Model of Professional Development: Phases 1–4.

students. The ensuing discussions helped us begin to guide and deepen a joint vision of our goal as educators.

To build ELL–ISSs' knowledge, we combined Shulman's model of teacher expertise, socio-cultural theories of learning, and our understanding of second language acquisition. In addition to presenting six types of scaffolding, we proposed conditions that make scaffolded classes successful in second language contexts (Walqui, 2003), including the knowledge and expertise required to work with adolescent ELLs (subject matter knowledge, pedagogical knowledge, knowledge of self, and knowledge of students). To develop these kinds of knowledge, our NYC colleagues read and critiqued professional articles, participated in lessons that modeled well-scaffolded pedagogical practice, designed lessons, and compared their prior understanding of effective pedagogy with ELLs with their emerging notions. The focus was placed on the design and conduct of effective situated practice. The themes and texts used to illustrate and elicit reflection included both texts that were appropriate for ELLs in NYC and those that were appropriate for teachers. About two-thirds of the ideas and materials covered were part of the institutes that ELL–ISSs would eventually run for middle and high school teachers in the city.

In planning ways to enhance ELL–ISSs' motivation, we drew on our understanding that engagement in supported, intellectually rich interaction provides a strong stimulus for educators and binds them together in what over time become communities of practice with shared visions, values, beliefs, practices, and artifacts. During Phase One, our colleagues' motivation was enhanced by discussing important issues and tensions in the profession and collaborating on creating possible lines of action to deal with them. Reading jointly, using the jigsaw approach to discussing readings, and presenting collaborative work to each other generated enthusiasm among ELL–ISSs and helped us build theoretical and practical understanding as well as trust with our colleagues.

We used several approaches to support participant reflection. Sometimes we asked our NYC colleagues to engage in the solution of hypothetical situations they might confront (the "what would you do if?" that characterizes anticipatory reflection); in other instances, we asked them to engage in an activity and then record their interactive reflections as they participated in it. We repeatedly asked them to examine their prior actions to learn for the future (recollective reflection). We were especially concerned that no pedagogical modeling should go unanalyzed in terms of purpose, the kinds of scaffolding provided for a given activity, their impact on students' developing abilities, and alternative pedagogical actions teachers could engage in to substitute for those modeled. For this work we constructed a variety of task analyses, which our colleagues did not initially find easy but whose generative usefulness they came to appreciate over time. A particularly revealing exercise during this phase was the construction by ELL–ISSs of their own models of teacher understanding prior to sharing Shulman's model with them. This activity enabled us to talk about tacit and explicit theories of teaching and learning, and the importance of gaining meta-awareness of their theories of action to then become better supporters of teachers.

The context influenced our work with the ELL–ISSs, as it does in every professional development endeavor. At the macro-level, we planned work to reflect our understanding of the larger sociolinguistic and cultural issues surrounding the education of ELLs and their teachers. At the same time, micro-level events in the NYC context came into play as well. Our NYC colleagues were at the beginning of a school reform initiative that created their positions and instituted a new way of addressing education for all students. Concerns about prior and possible tensions were discussed during the first phase, and we all engaged in thinking through them with a focus on facilitating our work with second language learners.

While evaluations of this first phase were unanimously superlative (Farr, 2006), ELL–ISSs wondered: what will happen when we carry out this professional development with teachers? How will they react? How do we achieve change in their vision of teaching and of their students? How do we get them to make their practice more rigorous? During this first phase, the WestEd staff had been the "more capable peers." They wondered what needed to take place before they were ready to "turn key" (the phrase used in NYC to indicate dissemination) the professional development.

Phase Two: Participant/Observation

Phase Two of the professional development with ELL–ISSs was designed precisely to answer the questions they had at the end of Phase One. We wanted our colleagues to experience the professional development from the perspective of the teachers who participated in it, and to observe and learn as the WestEd team worked to develop teacher expertise.

In Phase Two, ELL–ISSs engaged in participant-observation while TPD staff facilitated professional development with teachers (called *Teachers in Apprenticeship*) from all regions of the city, using the QTEL tools and processes that ELL–ISSs would eventually apply in their work with teachers. We created nested professional development: while teachers went through five days of professional development, two ELL–ISSs were assigned to groups of four. One of them played participant, with limited responsibilities during the morning, while the other observed with a pre-determined focus and took notes verbatim at certain intervals. Prior to the initiation of these series, the WestEd team continued to cultivate the ELL–ISSs' growth by apprenticing them through our Modular Roadmaps (guides developed specifically for the NYCDOE to help users in the selection of activities and tasks appropriate for the specific contexts and needs of NYC teachers).

The TPD team prepared their NYC colleagues for their roles. Observers were asked to focus on how participants interpreted invitations to engage in action. Seated with a group of four teachers, they had to observe and take notes on the following questions: Who understood the invitation? Who did not? What stood in the way of their understanding? Who led the conversations? Did everybody participate in the exchange? What seemed to be some prevalent responses? Where were the outliers? Before our work with teachers, we also discussed with ELL–ISSs presenter notes we had prepared to highlight the purposes and processes of the different activities we would engage in throughout the day. Participant observers had limited and very targeted roles for participation in interactions with teachers. Their roles were to refocus the conversation if it had deviated from intended goals, to ensure that every member of the group contributed, and to ensure that contributions were used in the construction of arguments. They were to participate only by formulating questions when somebody had monopolized the conversation and not let others participate; when one person in the group had no opportunity to express his or her views; when an idea was being discussed time and again, without further development; or when somebody said something that others were not paying attention to. Prior to the professional development session, we practiced how to ask these questions with scenarios that we had constructed based on past professional development experiences in other contexts.

Each day of professional development with teachers was followed by a day with the group of ELL–ISSs involved in the event, unpacking issues that were observed, comparing notes, reading and discussing relevant literature, reinforcing understandings of our model of scaffolding instruction for adolescent ELLs and its application to the context. This type of reflection on how professional development for teachers is enacted and how it is interpreted by them is indispensible for the growth of professional developers. As they later lead in-service sessions, it helps them anticipate and interpret teachers' actions and reactions, and choose appropriately among options that respond effectively to the moment.

Figure 10.3 (Phase 2) illustrates how this second phase begins to shift the relationship between TPD staff and NYC colleagues. While in Phase One there was a friendly asymmetry between "us" and "them," Phase Two redirected that relationship as our NYC colleagues became observers and contributors to the joint understanding of how NYC teachers reacted to QTEL processes and products and how to reinforce their benefits.

Phase Three: Enacting the Professional Development

In Phase Three, TPD staff made sure that our NYC colleagues were ready to present QTEL professional development for five consecutive days, appropriating 80% of the tools and processes (with a daily keynote the primary role for WestEd teammates). Before they were ready to conduct their own QTEL professional development, our NYC colleagues had to meet two prerequisites. First, they had to pass a "written exercise" intended to help them review, synthesize, and apply the knowledge acquired. During our first year of work, in 2004, 20 colleagues volunteered to take the written exercise, and 19 passed it. The exercise consisted of three components: (1) a synthesis of theoretical understandings, (2) reflection and comment on a professional development incident (the context of the in-service and a transcript were provided for study and response), and (3) preparation of a pedagogical sequence for teaching a text from the perspective of how they would use it in their own in-services with teachers. Rubrics for reviewing the exercise were co-developed with a subset of the ELL–ISSs. Second, they had to participate in three or four days of preparation to present the weeklong institute. During the five-day professional development, TPD provided each presenter with a coach who worked with her/him throughout the week, providing support in planning, giving ongoing individual feedback and support, and, if necessary, stepping in when requested during the institute. During the second summer, NYC ran two weeklong institutes with 20 sessions each, all of them coached by TPD colleagues.

These institutes built visions of what was possible with adolescent ELLs, confirmed the thirst teachers had for good professional development, and galvanized the motivation of the participant teachers. With an average of 30 participants per group, we addressed about 600 teachers in a week. All these teachers came together during keynotes once a day, which reinforced the domains of knowledge, motivation, and vision, and began building a community of practitioners that shared the same understanding. Once again, when we observe the "handover" of responsibility from TPD staff to NYC ELL–ISSs and the "take over" of roles by our colleagues, we see the model of apprenticeship unfolding (see Figure 10.3, Phase 3).

Phase Four: Appropriation

During Phase Four, ELL–ISSs designed and provided professional development for teachers (for a minimum of three hours), with TPD staff assuming a consulting role. In this phase, our NYC colleagues videotaped themselves as they led the sessions. Afterwards they selected sections from their videos for further individual reflection and then responded to the following questions:

- Who was my audience?
- What was the goal of the in-service?
- What did I assume these teachers knew, and where did I want them to be by the end of the session?
- What was my plan to get them there?
- What worked according to plan?
- What needed to be changed in action?
- What alternatives did I contemplate? Which did I choose? Why? What would have happened if I had followed "the road not taken?"
- What have I learned for future practice?
- What will I do differently next time?

As mentioned previously, ELL–ISSs could consult with us about their plans, and many did. We offered feedback if requested, but now our relationship was one of peers being asked for advice. The shift in relationships and responsibility was noticeable. Our prominent role at the beginning of the process had diminished, and the symmetry in the relationship had increased. *They* had taken over the responsibility for using QTEL ideas in the creation and development of new professional opportunities for teachers, not part of the tools they had initially been offered. This process of appropriation and reinvention is captured in Figure 10.3 (Phase 4).

After ELL–ISSs successfully completed the four phases, they were certified in *Building the Base* and received all the tools TPD had developed for that intensive five-day professional development. They continue to have them at their disposal to adapt, recreate, and use as needed in their professional lives.

Professional Development of Teachers in NYC

While this chapter has primarily examined the professional development of Instructional Support Specialists (ISSs), the ultimate goal of QTEL was the development of teachers of ELLs in NYCDOE. We worked with ISSs to prepare them to lead professional development for teachers. Prior to our work in New York City, the city's teachers had typically participated in professional development opportunities that were largely atomistic, removed from their everyday practice, of short duration, and lacking in rigor and depth. The generative support needed to enhance their practice and improve instruction for students was absent. Often, teachers attended disjointed professional development sessions that did not build a coherent approach or conceptualization of sustained quality teaching and what constituted this teaching. Nor were the sessions focused on the needs of secondary ELLs.

QTEL's model changed that pattern by engaging teachers in sustained, situated professional development opportunities. These were designed to build a strong theoretical understanding of the socio-cultural context and its impact on learning and how this informs the work to be done with ELLs. For example, one of the first activities used with teachers is a jigsaw reading of memoirs of immigrant experiences to help them explore—through the writers' schooling experiences that led them from initial pride to shame, struggle, and eventual success—and reflect on their own beliefs about the role of schools in the education of ELLs. The majority of American teachers are white and monolingual; in 2001, 76% of practicing teachers in schools highly impacted by the presence of ELLs believed that only one-third or fewer minority students could succeed (MetLife, 2001, p. 10). The QTEL activities challenge teachers' beliefs about what is possible in the education of ELLs. As teachers discuss the memoirs, they develop an understanding of socio-cultural pedagogy and reflect on ways of supporting ELLs' engagement with grade-appropriate, rigorous texts in English. The QTEL professional development model also focuses on ways teachers can support ELLs to develop their full potential through carefully constructed and implemented interactions that are discipline-specific. For example, teachers engage in activities that unpack the linguistic demands of discipline-specific discourse and practice strategies for supporting students' use of it in such processes as mathematical argumentation and proof.

The pedagogical model used with teachers presents six types of scaffolding that guide the engineering of student work. These scaffolding types—modeling, bridging, contextualization, schema building, text re-presentation, metacognitive development (Walqui, 2003) (see Figure 10.1, Processes)—provide support for students to engage in rigorous academic and linguistic engagements in which they could not otherwise participate. The scaffolding model emphasizes the contingent, collaborative nature of support (Bruner, 1983; Vygotsky, 1978). It considers scaffolding as both structure and process, weaving together several levels of pedagogical support, from macro-level planning of curricula over time to micro-level moment-to-moment support, and the contingent modification of support responsive to interactions as they unfold (van Lier, 1996).

During professional development sessions, teachers participate in carefully scaffolded activities that model the kinds of tasks they should plan and enact with their ELLs. Teachers then reflect on them, apply them to new texts, enact them in their classes, and reflect once again on their design and application to understand successes, repair errors, and be ready to adapt them to their own needs. Teachers' engagement in activity is central to the development of their knowledge of how to support students. It facilitates their transition from apprenticeship to appropriation of socio-cultural notions of learning and methods for supporting ELL student growth and development.

The Ever-Changing Context of Education: Lessons Learned

Recently, we have been examining our work from a community level, taking a broader look beyond the individual teacher and ISS to the shared visions, commitments, knowledge, ways of reflecting, and practice that guide the behaviors of a whole group of educators. Working in the largest district in the country on issues related to the education of minorities makes this part of the work difficult but especially necessary. Since the beginning of our work in New York City, the context and structure in which we worked for the first four years has dramatically changed three times: from a centralized Department of Education, to regional offices each with a local superintendent and with resident expertise to help schools in their areas, to the disintegration of regional offices and the "handing over of responsibility" for professional development and financial decisions to school principals, who need to join networks of schools and purchase support (including professional development) through their networks. These major reorganizations of the system impacted the work with ELL–ISSs, whose positions have in fact disappeared.

We have been gratified to observe that the expertise the ELL–ISSs developed has gone with them to their new positions (for example, as principals, assistant principals, and support providers within support networks) and continue to provide ELLs with exemplary educational programs. The task of carrying on the work belongs to the NYC colleagues whose capacity to appropriate the work has been enhanced over time. The comments of Mónica, a certified ELL–ISS who has worked with us from the very beginning of our implementation in NYC, give us hope for the continued impact of the work. She said:

> As I thought about our initial work a couple of years ago, I wrote that vision was the toughest thing to change. Today, however, I think that by

understanding, observing, and deconstructing good practice in our professional development via the video exemplars, we are actually working on the domain of vision and reflection, which are constantly reinforced. Tougher today I see the development of practice. Having to on your own pull ideas together, defend your understandings in the written exercise in Phase Two, and then plan, carry out, video tape yourself, and reflect on your own professional development is difficult. It is hard work. Some of us are more motivated to do it, because we understand its value in appropriating ideas and recreating them in practice, but this is more difficult for other colleagues to understand (is this knowledge?). I also see that the coaching you provided us during Phase Three was essential to guarantee that our practice was the best it could be. I guess all domains support each other.

For the QTEL team the most important lesson learned has been that the work of creating increasingly competent educators to work with academic rigor and depth with ELLs is multifaceted and ideally located at a school site. In this instantiation of professional development, all educators at a site build their expertise to work in developing all students' academic uses of English. Borrowing from our NYC example, this work involves a three-year nested approach in which the school educational leadership—principal, assistant principals, department heads, coaches, and other educators in charge of supporting teachers—first undergoes professional development. Then all teachers engage in professional development—working at times in interdisciplinary teams and most other times in their academic subject matter. A smaller group of teachers in each of the disciplines—those who show the most interest and commitment—are coached and participate in seminars with the expectation that in the second year they will open their classrooms to colleagues, and after three years they will become coaches for their disciplinary peers. A smaller, more select group is prepared to become the professional developers at the end of the project. These colleagues undergo a very similar process to the one the ELL–ISSs followed. We have been testing this model in two high schools in Austin, Texas, with impressive impact on student performance (Gossman, 2008, 2009).

Based on our rich experience in NYC, we recognize that, given the country's current demographics, it is no longer possible to work with only some teachers in a middle or high school to improve the learning of ELLs. All teachers need to be involved. We know that initially not all teachers will be excited by the prospect of engaging in demanding work to strengthen their expertise, but all teachers must be expected to engage in the same work. Those who excel can be the guiding lights at the school and can eventually appropriate the work and continue it beyond the collaboration with external professional developers. We have also learned that it pays to have pedagogical coherence at a school site. If all teachers share the same theoretical background and very similar teaching techniques across subject areas, professional conversations will be facilitated and all students will benefit from the unity of purpose and practices.

Our experiences with QTEL in developing teacher expertise to work with English learners and all other students show that it is possible to engage teachers in the difficult but very rewarding work of becoming increasingly accomplished in the classroom. Substantive change requires ambitious goals, a well-designed plan, the sustained provision of complex and varied levels of support for educators, and theoretical and practical coherence. This effort requires a significant investment of time and money, but it will have sustainable long-term results. The future of our students and communities is at stake.

Note

1. I will use first-person in the discussion of the QTEL activities because I designed and, alongside QTEL teammates, developed and implemented them.

References

Bruner, J. (1983). *Child's talk*. New York, NY: Norton.

Colombi, C. (2002). Academic language development in Latino student writing in Spanish. In C. Colombi & M. Schleppegrell (Eds.), *Developing advanced literacy in first and second language: Meaning with power* (pp. 67–86). Mahwah, NJ: Lawrence Erlbaum.

Ellis, R. (2005). *Instructed second language acquisition: A literature review*. Wellington: New Zealand Ministry of Education.

Farr, B. (2006). *Process evaluation of QTEL implementation in New York City schools*. Paper presented at the Annual Meeting of the American Educational Research Association, San Francisco, CA.

Gossman, G. (2008). *Evaluation of the Quality Teaching for English Learners Program 2007–2008*. Austin, TX: Austin Independent School District, Office of High School Redesign.

Gossman, G. (2009). *Evaluation of the Quality Teaching for English Learners Program 2008–2009*. Austin, TX: Austin Independent School District, Office of High School Redesign.

Hymes, D. (1968). The ethnography of speaking. In J. Fishman (Ed.), *Readings in the sociology of language*. The Hague: Mouton.

Kozulin, A., Gindis, B., Ageyev, V., & Miller, S. (2003). *Vygotsky's educational theory in cultural context*. Cambridge: Cambridge University Press.

Lantolf, J. (2000). *Sociocultural theory and second language learning*. Oxford: Oxford University Press.

Lantolf, J.P., & Thorne, S.L. (2006). *Sociocultural theory and the genesis of second language development*. Oxford: Oxford University Press.

Lave, J., & Wenger, E. (1991). *Situated learning: Legitimate peripheral participation*. Cambridge: Cambridge University Press.

MetLife. (2001). *The MetLife survey of the American teacher 2001: Key elements of quality schools.* Retrieved from www.ced.org/docs/report/report_survey_american_teacher01.pdf.

Shulman, L.S., & Associates. (1995). *Fostering a community of teachers and learners.* Unpublished progress report to the Mellon Foundation.

Shulman, L.S., & Shulman, J. (2004). How and what teachers learn: A shifting perspective. *Journal of Curriculum Studies, 36*(2), 257–271.

van Lier, L. (1996). *Interaction in the language curriculum: Awareness, autonomy, and authenticity.* London: Longman.

van Lier, L. (2004). *The ecology and semiotics of language learning.* Dordrecht: Kluwer Academic.

Vygotsky, L.S. (1978). *Mind in society.* Cambridge, MA: Harvard University Press.

Vygotsky, L.S. (1987). *The collected works of L .S. Vygotsky. Volume 1. Problems of General Psychology,* R.W. Rieber & A.S. Carton (Eds.). New York, NY and London: Plenum Press.

Walqui, A. (1997). *The development of teachers' understanding: Inservice professional growth for teachers of English language learners.* Unpublished doctoral dissertation, Stanford University, Stanford, CA.

Walqui, A. (2003). *Developing the capacity of New York City Department of Education to support teachers of adolescent English Learners.* A proposal presented to the New York City Department of Education.

Walqui, A. (2006). Scaffolding instruction for English learners: A conceptual framework. *International Journal of Bilingual Education and Bilingualism, 9*(2), 159–180.

Wei, R.C., Darling-Hammond, L., Andree, A., Richardson, N., & Orphanos, S. (2009). *Professional learning in the learning profession: A status report on teacher development in the United States and abroad.* Dallas, TX: National Staff Development Council.

Chapter 11

Toward Culturally and Linguistically Responsive Teacher Education

The Impact of a Faculty Learning Community on Two Teacher Educators

Mileidis Gort, Wendy J. Glenn, and John Settlage

Multilingual, multicultural classrooms characterize twenty-first-century America. Continuing and projected growth in linguistic diversity in U.S. classrooms (U.S. Department of Education, 2006) demands that *all* teachers be prepared to work with bilingual students[1] because they are likely to have English language learners (ELLs) in their classrooms at some time (de Oliveira & Athanases, 2007; Meskill, 2005; Villegas et al., 1995). Unfortunately, preparing future educators to teach bilingual learners has not been a priority in teacher education (TE). In most teacher preparation programs, including the one described in this chapter, issues of diversity, linguistic or otherwise, rarely permeate the curriculum (Commins & Miramontes, 2006; Vavrus, 2002). Even when TE programs address diversity, broadly defined, linguistic diversity generally remains ignored (Zeichner, 2003).

Although it is clear that teachers must possess explicit content, pedagogical, and affective knowledge to effectively teach ELLs (de Jong & Harper, 2005; Escamilla, Chavez, & Vigil, 2005; Goodwin, 2002), the challenge of systematically addressing linguistic diversity in mainstream teacher preparation is compounded by the fact that most teacher educators do not possess this knowledge themselves (Costa, McPhail, Smith, & Brisk, 2005; de Oliveira & Athanases, 2007; Meskill, 2005). One way to address this is to engage TE faculty in comprehensive professional development focused on the development of understandings, perspectives, and practices about culturally and linguistically responsive teaching, as well as critical examination and revision of the TE curriculum to make issues of cultural and linguistic diversity central rather than peripheral.

The work presented here represents an initial step in a larger process of TE curriculum reform. We describe a faculty development initiative, including goals, activities, and resulting curricular changes, through the eyes of two focal participants—an English teacher educator and a science teacher educator—responding to the question: "What did participants learn as a result of this professional development experience?"

Theoretical Framework

Our work is informed by work on faculty learning communities (FLCs) as powerful catalysts for initiating, developing, and sustaining faculty involvement in professional development (Cox, 2001, 2004; Decker Lardner, 2003; Hubball & Burt, 2004; Richlin & Cox, 2004; Richlin & Essington, 2004). FLCs are promising contexts for constructing meaningful local knowledge, challenging assumptions, posing problems, studying faculty/student learning and development, and reconstructing curriculum (Cochran-Smith & Lytle, 1999; Cole & Knowles, 2000; Cox, 2004). The learning community model encourages institutional cultural transformation by inviting faculty to cross social, disciplinary, pedagogical, and curricular boundaries (Decker Lardner, 2003; Petrone, 2004). In our work, the FLC provided a context through which to engage in a collaborative and self-reflective process of professional development toward culturally and linguistically responsive teaching.

As teacher educators and researchers, we share Freire's (1970) call for praxis: "reflection and action upon the world in order to transform it" (p. 33). We strive to employ culturally and linguistically responsive pedagogy—instruction that empowers students intellectually, socially, emotionally, and politically, by drawing upon cultural referents in the development of knowledge, skills, and attitudes (Ladson-Billings, 1995), recognizing that students' languages, cultures, and prior experiences must be at the instructional center in order for meaningful learning to occur. Self-reflection is central to our vision and enactment of critically engaged pedagogy. Over time, our work in the collaborative peer environment of the FLC led to shared self-study (Clift, 2004) of the recursive processes of revising and implementing ELL-infused courses based on our developing knowledge and dispositions around culturally and linguistically responsive TE. Within this approach, we blend narrative theory with constructivist learning through collaborative dialogic practice, thus opening spaces for talking and writing in ways that might otherwise be silenced.

Context and Methodology for Faculty Development Initiative

Our study examines the impact of a faculty development initiative focused on culturally and linguistically responsive teacher education on the professional development and practice of two teacher educators at a major research university. Wendy and John (two of the authors of this chapter) were the focal participants of this self-study. Millie (the other author) served as mentor and critical friend (Schuck & Russel, 2005), both challenging and supporting Wendy and John, and encouraging them to rethink and reframe their practice toward culturally and linguistically responsive pedagogy.

Participants

At the time of the study, Wendy, the English educator, was in her fifth year of teaching at the university. A Euro-American, monolingual English speaker, she taught middle and high school students in Arizona for six years prior to completing her Ph.D. and transitioning into post-secondary education. Her teacher preparation program paid little attention to issues of language diversity despite the high prevalence of native Spanish-speakers in the surrounding public schools. John, the science educator, is also a White, monolingual native English speaker. After four years as a high school science teacher, he earned his Ph.D. and has been a science teacher educator since 1992. Millie, the bilingual educator, taught and directed the graduate program in Bilingual/Bicultural Education at the research site for five years. A Spanish–English bilingual and childhood immigrant from Cuba, she taught elementary bilingual learners and supported bilingual teachers in Massachusetts for four years before earning an Ed.D. and joining the teacher education faculty.

Institutional Context

The three-year integrated Bachelor's/Master's teacher preparation program at the institution at which the study took place is housed in a professional School of Education. Students are selectively admitted and enter the program at the start of the junior year. Teacher education candidates parallel the profile of the national teaching force at large—primarily Euro-American, middle class, monolingual English-speaking, and female. During the third year of the program, students enroll in 30 hours of graduate credit, three of which (one course) must be in the area of multicultural education. Students choose from a menu of courses that fall under the general umbrella of "diversity," including language acquisition, foundations of multicultural or bilingual education, and educational linguistics. This is the only required "diversity" course of the program.

Evolution of the Faculty Learning Community with a Focus on Bilingual Learners

To address growing faculty concerns regarding the neglect of multicultural topics and the lack of ELL-focus across the mainstream TE program, a Bilingual Education professor (Millie) established a FLC in the spring of 2006 to support faculty members' attempts to integrate bilingual/multicultural education scholarship and culturally and linguistically responsive pedagogy into their own practice and across the TE program. Participation in the study group was open to all TE faculty.

Over the course of one semester, group members representing English, Science, Math, Social Studies, Bilingual Education, and Multicultural Education gathered on a monthly basis to expand their knowledge about the processes of language acquisition; the role of language in learning and assessment; cultural awareness and sensitivity; and classroom implications in the areas of planning, instruction, and assessment. Two faculty members in Bilingual Education served as mentors and provided participants with various readings and related materials and activities. Sample whole group readings included: "Teaching bilingual students in mainstream classrooms" (Brisk, Dawson, Hartgering, MacDonald, & Zehr, 2002); "Addressing linguistic diversity from the outset" (Commins & Miramontes, 2006); "Our changing classrooms" and "Language acquisition and literature-based instruction" (both in Hadaway, Vardell, & Young, 2001); *What Teachers Need to Know About Language* (Wong Fillmore & Snow, 2003); and other related readings (see Additional Study Group Resources, p. 194).

In preparation for each meeting, group members read and prepared written reflections on the materials provided. During each meeting, group members discussed in whole and small groups their reactions to the readings and worked with mentors to translate concepts, principles, and new under-standings about teaching bilingual learners with the goal of incorporating these concepts, principles, and methods into a revised, ELL-infused syllabus for use the following semester. Representative activities included:

• Reviewing and discussing the stages of second language acquisition and application of this knowledge to sample teacher–student linguistic exchanges in an imagined classroom setting with the goals of (1) identify-ing the stage of second language proficiency represented, and (2) evaluat-ing the teacher's response from a linguistic perspective.

• Evaluating ELL writing samples and discussing classroom teachers' responses to these pieces and the larger issue of ELL assessment in school settings.

• Sharing and discussing state and national policies related to the educa-tion of ELLs and reflecting on how this information might help pre-service teachers recognize the necessity for differentiated instruction for ELLs.

• Reviewing and discussing the Sheltered Instruction Observation Protocol (SIOP) (Echevarria, Vogt, & Short, 2004) and considering how the tool might be used in conjunction with existing lesson plan formats.

• Writing personal journals focused on their experiences throughout the process.

Between monthly whole group meetings, participants met individually with a mentor to receive more personalized support and guidance in the revision of the methods course curriculum. Participants identified or were provided readings related to ELL instruction in their respective content areas (e.g., ELL policy statements generated on behalf of professional organizations, journal

articles describing ELL theories into practice), thus developing richer knowledge and skills on how to incorporate the newly acquired ELL-related
information into their area of specialization.

Some participants implemented the first revised syllabi when they taught
the methods course the following semester. Wendy implemented the syllabus
changes in the subject area methods course required for secondary English
Education students in the fall of their senior year, just prior to student teaching. John implemented the syllabus changes in an elective, graduate-level
course for Science Education students in their third (and final) year of the
program. Throughout the implementation process (including first and subsequent iterations), study group participants and a mentor (Millie) engaged in
electronic discussions surrounding plans, processes, successes, failures, and
emerging and lingering questions.

Data Sources and Analysis

Drawing on sources common to self-study (Bullough & Pinnegar, 2001),
our primary data during the planning stage (while participants were attending the faculty study group meetings) included: (1) notes and reflections
written by each educator during and after faculty study group meetings in
response to readings and conversations with colleagues and group leaders,
and (2) revised syllabi and course materials developed with the support of
mentors. Data sources during the first and second implementation stages
(while educators enacted the revised syllabi in their courses) included: (1)
written journal reflections over the span of the teaching experience; (2)
revised content and teaching materials developed over the duration of the
course, classroom notes, and resulting student work; and (3) electronic mail
and telephone conversations among the methods instructors and their
mentor.

Drawing on the history of narrative that informs self-study, we returned to
the lived experience manifested in our teaching by analyzing the print data
sources within and across each participant. Throughout the process, we
looked for evidence that the developing understandings (i.e., knowledge) and
awareness of ELL issues among participants were reflected in the resulting
practices, curricular choices, professional and personal actions, and beyond.
Wendy and John read and reread their respective data independently and
generated an initial list of categories into which the data naturally fell. Millie
then reviewed the initial categories generated by each participant, suggesting
revisions she thought were needed. All three authors then reviewed and compared the resulting categories and supporting data for each participant to
identify categories that might be combined or eliminated due to lack of data
across participants. As a result of this recursive process, three categories that
were supported by data from both participants remained. The resulting findings, a reflection of individuals' engagement in a process of sense-making, is

personal and candid, capturing fears, frustrations, and other deeply felt emotions, while answering the question: "What did participants learn as a result of this professional development experience?"

Impact of the Faculty Development Initiative

Data analysis uncovered the ways in which the faculty development initiative influenced participants' courses, teaching practices, and developing knowledge about effective ELL education. These "lessons," grounded in narratives resulting from our continuing conversations, model how we addressed the challenges that arose during the processes of course (re)vision and implementation, and reveal the ways in which we continue to grapple with these issues on our collaborative journey toward culturally and linguistically responsive teacher education.

Lesson 1: Conscious Effort is Required to Move Beyond Ignoring, Pretending to Understand, and/or Skirting ELL Issues in "Mainstream" Content Area Methods Courses

In their methods courses prior to participation in the study group, both John and Wendy treated ELL issues as subsumed under working with culturally diverse learners. The semester before John made changes in the science methods course, the first reading he assigned was an essay by Gloria Ladson-Billings describing her school science experiences; the piece also serves as the prologue to a methods textbook he co-authored (Settlage & Southerland, 2007). Briefly, Ladson-Billings describes her struggles in science because her teachers were unable or unwilling to adjust their assignments and expectations to more appropriately respond to her background. Students were asked to respond to the following reflective writing prompt:

> In what ways were diversity issues relevant to your schooling: how were racial, socio-economic, language, and gender differences among the students relevant to your abilities, achievement, and confidence as a science learner? What questions about your science teaching emerged while reading this essay?

Although several aspects of the students' responses were informative regarding their lack of prior experiences with cultural and linguistic diversity, none mentioned the author's ethnicity (which John described for them and which is explicit in the reading) or socio-economic status; only one student referenced non-native English speakers. After students wrote their responses, John and the students considered how individual genetics and parental involvement are not sufficient explanations for the achievement gap, concluding that the quality of teaching the students receive within their science classrooms is very influential. Discussion of language, culture, and students' prior/funds of knowledge in the learning process was absent.

Similarly, Wendy addressed issues of diversity more generally with her students. Essential Questions designed to guide earlier versions of the English methods course focused on the integration and interaction of literature, language, writing, and speaking/thinking in the English curriculum; instructional strategies that optimize student learning, interest, and motivation; the design of activities, assignments, and assessments to meet students' needs and content area objectives; and the development of a reflective stance. Although course objectives claimed to address ways to support the learning needs of all students, ELLs were noted only in passing, primarily in discussions about differentiation. No explicit discussion of strategies necessary to support ELLs and their unique instructional needs was included.

Study group activities and experiences led to a heightened awareness of the lack of specific attention to linguistic diversity in general, and ELLs in particular, in John's and Wendy's methods courses. During a meeting with Millie regarding evaluation of the existing course syllabus, Wendy realized that the young adult texts she selected for the course were written solely by White authors. Wendy tried to justify her choices, arguing that few authors of color publish in the field (a justification she soon learned was completely inaccurate). An early journal reflection highlights Wendy's inner tension in the learning experience:

> I began to wonder. Why had I selected the titles that I did? Why had it not occurred to me to do a simple search to see what diverse titles and authors existed? What titles was I exposed to as part of my own training? The answers resulted in discomfort, anger, and a newfound commitment to change. I selected those titles because they appealed to me as a reader; they reflected my identity as a woman, a white woman, a monolingual white woman with a particular cultural stance. I hadn't thought to examine other titles because I knew what I liked and enjoyed teaching texts I found interesting (despite my insistence that my students select a wide array of texts reflecting the interests, backgrounds, and experiences of their students). The texts assigned during my training reflected the experiences of and were written by white men and women. Even when offered a choice of supplementary novels, the library from which I was invited to select titles lacked color. While it would be easy to blame the institution for my limited education, I wonder why I never thought to push the envelope, to ask the question, "Where are the diverse authors in this collection?"

Wendy's course syllabus was altered significantly as a direct result of the professional development experience. Not only did her revised syllabus include authors of more culturally diverse backgrounds; it also included attention to language. The first revised syllabus included the young adult novel *Tree Girl*

(Mikaelsen, 2004), a fictionalized account of the real experiences of a girl forced to flee her Mayan village and travel to a Mexican refugee camp upon the outbreak of war in Guatemala during the second half of the twentieth century, as well as poems written by Latino writers who reflected upon language and cultural identity in their pieces, including "Learning silence" (Mazziotti Gillan), "Elena" (Mora), and "I Recognize You" (Morales) (all in Santa Ana, 2004). (See Glenn & Gort, 2008, and Gort & Glenn, in press, for a discussion of additional changes in the syllabus, including ELL-focused literature selections and related activities.) These changes reflect how Wendy navigated the selection of materials even when it would have been easier to maintain the status quo. Given the vast array of available literature—and the pressure (perceived or real) for English teachers to be familiar with certain titles—justification to focus on authors whose names and works have already been deemed canonically "worthwhile" might come easily. In the selection of literature for her revised course, however, Wendy included voices representative of a wide array of classroom students as a means to value their lives and languages.

John also expanded the role of ELL issues in his methods course. He added, as a required text, *Making Science Accessible to English Learners: A Guidebook for Teachers* (Carr, Sexton, & Lagunoff, 2006). Revised course objectives included:

1. Compile and justify several techniques that would support English language learners in science.
2. Create, administer, and interpret a science assessment that includes an analysis of language issues, conceptual understanding, and process skills use.
3. Document shifts in personal awareness and appreciation of the influence of student diversity upon instructional decision-making with science teaching and learning.

By explicitly addressing language issues and the ELL population, John created a space in his course to explore the impact of cultural and linguistic diversity in teaching and learning science.

Lesson 2: ELL Infusion Requires a Shift in the Roles of Instructor and Student

ELL infusion compelled instructors to relinquish control of some course components to give voice to those who possessed cultural and linguistic funds of knowledge and were able to speak from experience in ways they themselves could not. Wendy and John realized this was necessary as they considered how to address the complex role of language in learning content in their respective courses. Both wanted to include a language immersion experience for their students—a strategy they learned about in the FLC. Since neither had the bilingual capabilities to individually design and carry out a language immersion experience in which English-speaking students could experience the challenges of learning subject matter while negotiating a new language, John and Wendy enlisted the help of two bilingual students. The ensuing experiences highlighted instructional and contextual factors unique to the two content areas.

John turned to Carolina, a bilingual (Spanish/English) graduate student, to demonstrate a sheltered science lesson (Genesee & Christian, 2008) in Spanish. Carolina had previously enrolled in bilingual education classes with Millie and become knowledgeable about theory and techniques that could be effectively modeled for John's monolingual English-speaking students.

Students were startled when Carolina opened the lesson with a loud "¡Hola!" and began writing on the chalkboard in Spanish. Posted signs around the room announced that English was not permissible. A pre-activity discussion was conducted in Spanish. Printed guides to assist students with the hands-on experiment were in Spanish, and students' answers were to be written in Spanish. Carolina organized students into groups of three and showed them how to use graphing calculators outfitted with distance probes to measure the velocity of moving objects—again, all in Spanish. The next phase of the lesson involved additional physics activities in Spanish with some assistance, namely the use of a word wall and an English–Spanish glossary. These scaffolds proved to be mostly ineffective, though. The glossary came from a language arts textbook that did not include science concepts such as "velocity," "force," or "incline." In addition, the lesson did not restart with the same activity and instead built upon the prior science concepts.

After 20 minutes, Carolina lifted the "no English" ban and held a brief discussion, during which students expressed how the supports were only moderately helpful. Carolina then supplied genuinely useful scaffolds, including a word wall that included all relevant terms to this activity in both Spanish and English. A discussion of cognates around words with similar Spanish and English roots (e.g., "velocity" and "velocidad," "acceleration" and "aceleración") followed. By this point, most of the students were so exhausted that they were unable to uncover the very fundamental science concept that was at the core of this lesson. Thus, even with gradually increased support, students were unable to successfully navigate the twin challenges of learning science while negotiating meaning in an unfamiliar language. The following excerpt from a student's weekly reflection highlights the value of this collaborative approach to ELL infusion:

> I found this experience to be truly enlightening in that it is one thing to read about and speak of the possible difficulties that English language learners may experience in the classroom. It is something of another nature to be an active participant in such a scenario. I experienced the anxieties, frustrations, and failures that many English language learners

encounter daily. Thus, it is essential to acknowledge a child's language development level and prior school experiences so that instruction is appropriately scaffolded and delivered. Moreover, one must remember that language acquisition is a process; student progress will be made steadily if support is provided.

Wendy's adaptation of the language immersion experience emerged during the second ELL-infused course iteration when some students claimed that considerations of cultural and linguistic diversity were unnecessary examples of political correctness. To mediate this tension, Wendy modified a discussion component already in place. Each student in the course was responsible for facilitating a 15-minute class discussion on a text of their choosing. The facilitator was expected to generate quality conversation by posing questions that encouraged higher-level thinking. Wendy borrowed elements from John's *laboratorio de física* language immersion experience and collaborated with Katy, a Euro-American, English–Spanish bilingual student in the course, to plan and conduct a lesson in Spanish.

Katy began her literature discussion in Spanish with no intentional implementation of strategies for ELLs/second language learners. She introduced the focal poem and author ("No es nada de tu cuerpo," by Jaime Sabines) by providing students with a handout that included both the poem and discussion questions in Spanish. She read the poem aloud and allowed students time to read the poem silently and reflect. Katy then invited her peers to join her in a discussion of the poem, in Spanish. After 10 minutes, Wendy posed the following prompt to the class: "In one word, capture and share the emotion you are experiencing right now." Reponses included: "flustered," "lost," "challenged," "struggling," "frustrated," "incompetent," "attentive," "amazed," and "excited." Students then reported what they noticed during the activity. Their comments included:

- The teacher talked more.
- Fewer people participated.
- It is interesting to think about ELLs in this way. In English, I can hazard a guess in response to a question; in Spanish, no way!
- Imagine a kid having to do this every day. In the context, the activity was fun (and temporary). Imagine if you are the only teacher who does this for a kid. What a long day!

Katy continued the discussion around the same poem and question prompts, still in Spanish, but with implementation of key strategies for supporting ELLs (drawn from Lucas and Villegas, 2007). For example, Katy:

1. Provided copies of the poem and questions with English translations of key vocabulary.

2. Had students read the poem aloud line by line (with each student reading a different line in Spanish).
3. Said difficult words in Spanish and English (e.g., "paradox"/"*paradoja*");
4. Encouraged responses in students' first language (in this case, English);
5. Showed a YouTube video featuring photographs of images described in the poem accompanying a reading of the poem by Sabines, the poet.

After 10 minutes, Wendy asked students to think about particular strategies Katy employed that supported their engagement/participation in the language immersion experience. According to her classmates, Katy:

• Spoke slower.
• Used more enhanced body language.
• Provided copies of the poem and questions with English definitions of key words.
• Provided a visual representation that helped transcend the language barrier.
• Smoothly incorporated English translations of key words.

Students' responses suggest an increased awareness of the complex relationship between language and learning and the role the teacher plays in making content (and thus, learning) accessible to students, as well as evidence of empathy toward students who are in the process of learning the language of the classroom. Wendy ended the session discussing the strategies listed in Lucas and Villegas (2007), and comparing them to those noticed during the second (scaffolded) discussion of the poem.

The language immersion experiences generated relevance, empathy, and understanding for pre-service teachers in John's and Wendy's classes. More significantly, the lessons highlighted Wendy's and John's own limitations as instructors. Collaboration with other experts (i.e., Carolina and Katy) who possess appropriate linguistic and cultural funds of knowledge led to an educational experience that John and Wendy themselves could not have provided given their English monolingualism and majority-culture histories and identities.

Lesson 3: FLC Experiences Led to a Revised Definition of Effective Educator

Wendy and John witnessed significant gaps in the preparation of pre-service teachers prior to the ELL study group and course infusion experiences. When students shared their experiences in courses and placements, they expressed troubling perceptions and feelings of incompetence, as well as concerns regarding the practices enacted by their clinical teachers. Their comments included:

- These kids were talking in Spanish. I'm not sure what they were saying, but I know they were talking about me.
- I don't know how I'm going to teach the students in my class who don't speak English. I'm supposed to teach *Macbeth*, but there's no way they'll be able to read it.
- My teacher never calls home because the kids' parents don't speak English.

The ELL study group and course infusion experiences significantly impacted John's and Wendy's perceptions and definitions of effective teacher education, forcing them to address the comments expressed by students despite the difficulties inherent in doing so. Prior to the FLC experience, John, acting in ways that might be described as *uncivil*,[2] urged students to confront the facts of discrimination, the perpetuation of inequities, and the culpability of teachers. Study group experiences helped John understand that pushing students to the fringes of their comfort level is insufficient:

> What I've learned during this study is that violating the pretense of civility is perhaps a necessary strategy in order to advance preservice teachers' regard for culturally and linguistically diverse students.... Others helped me understand that pushing students to the fringes of their comfort level is not sufficient. What must also happen is to provide a space in which contemplation can occur.... As a science methods instructor, I have the responsibility for not only "spreading the social discomfort to everyone" (Mayo, 2002, p. 185) but for creating a climate in which the pauses the incivility creates provide a forum for making decisions about how to act.... Because [the ELL] material is so new to me ... I have been quick to embrace [effective ELL] pedagogical strategies. Since these are also desired by my preservice teachers, we quickly find common ground. Beginning with concrete strategies ... I can begin to invoke new perspectives for teaching science to non-mainstream populations.

The impact of the ELL experience on Wendy's vision of quality education became visible when she considered what it was she expected program graduates to know, believe, and be able to do. While her earlier course emphasized knowledge and pedagogy focused on English content, her developing definition of the effective educator included knowledge and pedagogy focused on ELLs within the English content. Reflecting upon the first revision of the course, Wendy noted:

> After implementation of the first revised syllabus, students were not only better equipped to support ELLs in their future classrooms but demonstrated a genuine and lasting interest in ELLs as a unique population.

Students left the experience poised to serve as both effective teachers willing to continue learning more as well as advocates for students they regularly witnessed being ignored or miseducated in their clinic placements.

In John's and Wendy's revised definitions, effective educators create supportive spaces in which *both* language and culture are explicitly addressed so that culturally and linguistically responsive pedagogical decisions can be made.

Discussion and Implications

Concern over the neglect of multicultural topics and the role of language and culture in teaching and learning led to the creation of a professional development initiative, in the form of a faculty learning community (FLC), with a focus on bilingual learners. Throughout our self-study of the recursive processes of revising and implementing ELL-infused courses, we explored the following question: "What did participants learn in the collaborative journey toward culturally and linguistically responsive teacher education?" Our findings elucidate the various ways in which the faculty development initiative elicited and enriched meaningful opportunities for intellectual and professional growth (Cochran-Smith & Lytle, 1999; Cole & Knowles, 2000; Cox, 2004).

Wendy and John came to the FLC for different reasons, with varying knowledge of and experience in working with diverse learners, and at different stages in their awareness and enactment of culturally responsive pedagogy. Yet both demonstrated a commitment to intellectual and personal development as evidenced by participation in study group discussions, reflective journaling, and efforts toward syllabus revision and implementation. Change resulting from the FLC experience also occurred on a programmatic level, as John's and Wendy's expanded knowledge and awareness extended to their professional work with pre-service teachers. Through ELL-focused class activities, readings, projects, and discussions, John and Wendy helped their students to examine the experiences of bilingual learners in supportive and non-supportive school environments, while, at the same time, inviting them into conversations about the importance of paying attention to students' languages and the cultures in which they are embedded. The most common revisions across the two courses included incorporating ELL-focused discussion and activities across the semester; addressing linguistic issues in particular in contrast to general discussions of diversity; adding readings that attend to topics of content and language learning for bilingual students; and redesigning readings, assignments, and projects to include specific attention to ELLs. Another important common revision included a second language immersion experience in which students faced the challenges of learning subject matter in a new language. Although Wendy and

John continue to adjust ELL course components with each implementation, these changes have become permanent features of their content methods courses.

While each recognizes there is much more to learn, John and Wendy emerged from the FLC experience with richer understandings and a better sense of how to proceed as subject area methods instructors. They acknowledged the inadequate attention they had given to linguistic diversity and ELLs in their methods courses prior to FLC participation. After participating, John and Wendy purposefully created spaces in their respective syllabi and courses to explore the influences of both culture *and* language in teaching and learning, even when it would have been easier to keep the courses as they were—courses that students had rated as exceptional. Infusing ELL issues into the methods courses compelled John and Wendy to make this population a particular and explicit concern.

John and Wendy recognized, too, that they didn't—and couldn't—have all of the answers. Limited by their English monolingualism, they were unable to bring truly authentic experiences with languages other than English into their classrooms. They chose to relinquish some control in their courses by drawing upon the voices and experiences of those who could offer the expertise they lacked—their bilingual/bicultural students. The power of the collaborative language immersion endeavors attests also to the value and necessity of a more culturally and linguistically diverse pre-service population, and the need to recruit a more diverse TE population if real change is to occur in our university classrooms and public schools.

The collaborative professional development and research activities prompted John and Wendy to reconceptualize their views of an effective educator of pre-service teachers. Prior to this work, they believed that holding particular knowledge and exhibiting certain skills about diverse students was sufficient, if not noteworthy (given the neglect of this population in most other courses). It was through scaffolded practices—wherein Millie's expert knowledge, lived experiences, and insistent guidance encouraged revised commitment to ELLs—that the two methods instructors effected tangible changes in their courses. Rather than treating ELL issues within a generalized category of diversity, Wendy and John made linguistic diversity a central and defining theme. No longer do the two methods instructors avoid ELL issues within the content methods course; they have acquiesced to the need to shift their roles and perceptions about being "effective" as teacher educators. Whereas previous versions of their courses allowed Wendy and John to make intermittent gestures toward ELL populations, issues associated with ELLs are now integral to their respective efforts to prepare future teachers. Their actions and the mentorship of a bilingual educator have led to emerging transformations of the focal participants' beliefs and practices toward praxis (Freire, 1970).

Notes

1. The terms "bilingual learners" and "English language learners" are used interchangeably throughout this chapter to refer to students who speak a language other than English at home and are in the process of learning English as an additional language.
2. Civility, and the efforts to conserve that as a cultural norm, effectively preserve the inequities we claim to be of concern. In other words, civility establishes a distance between actors that provides the ambivalence and remoteness that prevents an examination of the hard issues. Violating the pretense of civility ventures into practices that Mayo (2002) advances as incivility:

> By raising hackles, incivility points to the obscured play of power that previously kept hackles down. Done correctly ... incivility entails spreading the social discomfort to everyone.... Rather than mending the distance between social actors, incivility can bring the distance into focus.
>
> (p. 185)

References

Brisk, M.E., Dawson, M., Hartgering, M., MacDonald, E., & Zehr, L. (2002). Teaching bilingual students in mainstream classrooms. In Z.F. Beykont (Ed.), *The power of culture: Teaching across language difference* (pp. 89–120). Cambridge, MA: Harvard Education Publishing Group.

Bullough, R.V., & Pinnegar, S. (2001). Guidelines for quality in autobiographical forms of self-study research. *Educational Researcher, 30*(3), 12–21.

Carr, J., Sexton, U., & Lagunoff, R. (2006). *Making science accessible to English learners: A guidebook for teachers.* San Francisco, CA: WestEd.

Clift, R.T. (2004). Self-study research in the context of teacher education programs. In J.J. Loughran, M.L. Hamilton, V.K. LaBoskey, & T. Russell (Eds.), *International handbook of self-study of teaching and teacher education practices* (pp. 1333–1366). Dordrecht: Kluwer Academic.

Cochran-Smith, M., & Lytle, S. (1999). Relationship of knowledge and practice: Teacher learning in communities. In A. Iran-Nejad & C.D. Pearson (Eds.), *Review of research in education* (Vol. 24). Washington, D.C.: American Educational Research Association.

Cole, A.L., & Knowles, J.G. (2000). *Researching teaching: Exploring teacher development through reflexive inquiry.* Boston, MA: Allyn & Bacon.

Commins, N.L., & Miramontes, O.B. (2006). Addressing linguistic diversity from the outset. *Journal of Teacher Education, 57*(3), 240–246.

Costa, J., McPhail, G., Smith, J., & Brisk, M.E. (2005). Faculty first: The challenge of infusing the teacher education curriculum with scholarship on English language learners. *Journal of Teacher Education, 56*(2), 104–118.

Cox, M.D. (2001). Faculty learning communities: Change agents for transforming institutions into learning organizations. *To Improve the Academy, 19*, 69–93.

Cox, M.D. (2004). Introduction to faculty learning communities. *New Directions for Teaching and Learning, 97*, 5–23.

Decker Lardner, E. (2003). Approaching diversity through learning communities. *Washington Center for Improving the Quality of Undergraduate Education Occasional Paper, 2*, 1–12. Retrieved from www.evergreen.edu/washcenter/resources/upload/Winter2003-Number2.doc.

de Jong, E.J., & Harper, C.A. (2005). Preparing mainstream teachers for English-language learners: Is being a good teacher good enough? *Teacher Education Quarterly, 32*(2), 101–124.

de Oliveira, L., & Athanases, S.Z. (2007). Graduates' reports of advocating for English language learners. *Journal of Teacher Education, 58,* 202–215.

Echevarria, J., Vogt, M., & Short, D.J. (2004). *Making content comprehensible for English learners: The SIOP model* (2nd ed.). Boston, MA: Allyn & Bacon.

Escamilla, K., Chavez, L., & Vigil, P. (2005). Rethinking the "gap": High-stakes testing and Spanish-speaking students in Colorado. *Journal of Teacher Education, 56,* 132–144.

Freire, P. (1970). *The pedagogy of the oppressed.* New York, NY: Seabury Press.

Genesee, F., & Christian, D. (2008). Programs for teaching English language learners. In A. Rosebery & B. Warren (Eds.), *Teaching science to English language learners* (pp. 129–145). Alexandria, VA: National Science Teachers Association.

Glenn, W.J., & Gort, M. (2008). Discomfort, deficiency, dedication: Preservice teachers voice their ELL-related concerns. *English Leadership Quarterly, 30*(3), 9–13.

Goodwin, A.L. (2002). Teacher preparation and the education of immigrant children. *Education and Urban Society, 34,* 156–172.

Gort, M., & Glenn, W.J. (in press). Navigating tensions in the process of change: An English-educator's dilemma management in the revision and implementation of a diversity-infused methods course. *Research in the Teaching of English, 45*(1).

Hadaway, N.L., Vardell, S.M., & Young, T.A. (2001). *Literature-based instruction with English language learners, K-12.* Boston, MA: Allyn & Bacon.

Hubball, H., & Burt, H. (2004). An integrated approach to developing and implementing learning-centered curricula. *The International Journal for Academic Development, 9*(1), 51–65.

Ladson-Billings, G. (1995). Toward a theory of culturally relevant pedagogy. *American Educational Research Journal, 32*(3), 465–491.

Lucas, T., & Villegas, A.M. (2007). *Preparing classroom teachers to teach English language learners.* Paper presented at the annual meeting of the American Educational Research Association, Chicago, IL, April.

Mayo, C. (2002). The binds that tie: Civility and social difference. *Educational Theory, 52*(2), 169–186.

Meskill, C. (2005). Infusing English language learner issues throughout professional educator curricula: The Training All Teachers project. *Teachers College Record, 107*(4), 739–756.

Mikaelsen, B. (2004). *Tree girl.* New York, NY: HarperCollins.

Petrone, M.C. (2004). Supporting diversity with faculty learning communities: Teaching and learning across boundaries. *New Directions for Teaching and Learning, 97,* 111–125.

Richlin, L., & Cox, M.D. (2004). Developing scholarly teaching and the scholarship of teaching and learning through faculty learning communities. *New Directions for Teaching and Learning, 97,* 127–135.

Richlin, L., & Essington, A. (2004). Overview of faculty learning communities. *New Directions for Teaching and Learning, 97,* 25–39.

Sabines, J. (n.d.). No es nada de tu cuerpo. In J. Sabines, *Poemas sueltos.* Retrieved from www.poesi.as/js81060.htm.

Santa Ana, O. (Ed.). (2004). *Tongue-tied: The lives of multilingual children in public education.* Lanham, MD: Rowman & Littlefield.

Schuck, S., & Russel, T. (2005). Self-study, critical friendship, and the complexities of teacher education. *Studying Teacher Education, 1*(2), 107–121.

Settlage, J., & Southerland, S.A. (2007). *Teaching science to every child: Using culture as a starting point.* New York, NY: Routledge.

United States Department of Education. (2006). Minority students increase participation in public education. Retrieved from http://ed.gov/about/reports/annual/2005report/1a/edlite-1a2c-minority.html.

Vavrus, M. (2002). *Transforming the multicultural education of teachers.* New York, NY: Teachers College Press.

Villegas, A.M., Clewell, B.C., Anderson, B.T., Goertz, M.E., Joy, M.F., Bruschi, B.A., et al. (1995). *Teaching for diversity: Models for expanding the supply of minority teachers.* Princeton, NJ: Educational Testing Service.

Wong-Fillmore, L., & Snow, C. (2003). *What teachers need to know about language.* Washington, D.C.: Center for Applied Linguistics. Retrieved from http://faculty.tamucommerce.edu/jthompson/Resources/FillmoreSnow2000.pdf.

Zeichner, K.M. (2003). The adequacies and inadequacies of three current strategies to recruit, prepare, and retain the best teachers for all students. *Teachers College Record, 105,* 490–519.

Additional Study Group Resources

Horan, D.A. (2006). *Supporting English language learners in mainstream classrooms.* Chestnut Hill, MA: Boston College Lynch School of Education—Title III Project ALL, Office of Professional Practice and Induction. Retrieved from www.bc.edu/schools/lsoe/title-iii/meta-elements/pdf/BCTitleIIIbooklet2006.pdf.

Morahan, M. (2003). *Bilingual students in the secondary classroom: A reference for practicum students at Boston College Lynch School of Education.* Chestnut Hill, MA: Boston College Lynch School of Education—Title III Project ALL, Office of Professional Practicum Experiences. Retrieved from www.bc.edu/schools/lsoe/title-iii/meta-elements/pdf/fall03sec.pdf.

Ramírez, A.G. (1995). Concepts of language proficiency. In A.G. Ramírez, *Creating contexts for second language acquisition: Theory and methods* (pp. 36–57). White Plains, NY: Longman.

Reed, B., & Railsback, J. (2003). *Strategies and resources for mainstream teachers of English language learners.* Northwest Regional Educational Laboratory. Retrieved from www.nwrel.org/request/2003may/ell.pdf.

Chapter 12

Toward Program-Wide Coherence in Preparing Teachers to Teach and Advocate for English Language Learners

Steven Z. Athanases and
Luciana C. de Oliveira

Coherent, program-wide preparation of teachers to work with English language learners (ELLs) is a critical area of need. Despite research on diverse second language teaching and learning issues, little research has been reported on teacher education for ELLs (Hollins & Guzman, 2005; Lucas & Grinberg, 2008). Even in preparing teachers for diverse and underserved populations, attention to ELLs has been scant (Zeichner, 2005). This chapter addresses this need, examining how one program sought to prepare all teachers to meet the needs of ELLs through a program-wide approach with conscious attention to content, processes, and context. Drawing on research on teacher education program coherence, we map a framework that guided data analysis in this case study and that serves as a heuristic for other programs to use in developing, documenting, and studying program-wide attention to teaching ELLs.

Theoretical Framework

Teacher Preparation for English Language Learners

Although the number of ELLs in the U.S. has grown dramatically in recent years (Kindler, 2002), little is known about the kind of preparation teachers of ELLs need or receive, particularly in pre-service programs (Gándara, Maxwell-Jolly, & Driscoll, 2005; Goodwin, 2002; Lucas & Grinberg, 2008; Merino, 1999). Yet teachers in mainstream classes increasingly work with ELLs and are responsible for meeting their content and language needs (August & Hakuta, 1997). Challenges for teachers of ELLs include communication with parents, teachers' limited knowledge of home and community issues, lack of sufficient time to teach English and school subjects, and varied academic and linguistic needs of ELLs (Gándara et al., 2005). Others include the need to effectively link academic language with content (Schleppegrell, 2004); assessments that conflate content knowledge and language proficiency (Abedi, 2007); limited instructional materials; and the need to diversify instruction amid pressures related to standards, content coverage, and standardized tests (de Oliveira & Athanases, 2007).

Many challenges can be addressed in teacher education. Future teachers can examine language and content needs of ELLs (August & Hakuta, 1997; Villegas et al., 1995) by studying ELLs' learning patterns. Teachers can move beyond "good teaching" strategies for native English speakers (Harper & de Jong, 2004) to develop pedagogical content knowledge regarding linguistic diversity (Adger, Snow, & Christian, 2002; August & Hakuta, 1997), through learning best practices for ELLs (see Samway & McKeon, 2007; Téllez & Waxman, 2006; Verplaetse & Migliacci, 2008). However, in large-scale studies, teachers report inadequate preparation to teach ELLs (Darling-Hammond, Chung, & Frelow, 2002; Gándara et al., 2005). According to one survey study, fewer than 13% of U.S. teachers received preparation or development in teaching ELLs, but 41% had taught these students (NCES, 2002).

Various factors prevent programs from adequately tackling this great need. Few faculty and supervisors have knowledge and expertise to address ELL issues in courses or fieldwork. Some programs struggle to identify schools with adequate numbers of ELLs to provide future teachers with substantial exposure to them. Further, the field suffers from a slim research base that has not informed educators about which disciplinary and pedagogical bases best prepare teachers for such work in which kinds of communities (Merino, 1999). A growing literature reports change efforts by individual faculty (e.g., Costa, McPhail, Smith, & Brisk, 2005) and modification of program structures or processes to prepare teachers to teach ELLs. Still, these initiatives seldom develop coherent, program-wide attention to ELLs (Lucas & Grinberg, 2008).

Challenges and Promise of Building Coherent Programs for Learning to Teach ELLs

Challenges of developing and studying program-wide attention to ELLs relate, in part, to challenges of developing coherent programs in teacher preparation in general—that is, programs with clear links between vision, coursework, and clinical field experiences (Grossman, Hammerness, McDonald, & Ronfeldt, 2008). Programs frequently evidence fragmentation among courses, curricula, and activities (Villegas & Lucas, 2002; Zeichner, 1993). The existence, conception, and development of program coherence rarely have been documented and studied (Darling-Hammond et al., 2005; Goodlad, 1990; Hammerness, 2006; McDonald, 2005). The work requires understanding of how different visions of teaching and learning undergird programs and the extent to which programs provide "explicit articulation of the vision of teaching that the preparation aims for" (Zeichner & Conklin, 2005, p. 702). One recent study of a five-year program effort to strengthen coherence found faculty developed a vision grounded in teaching principles that graduates applied to varying degrees in practice (Hammerness, 2006). In preparing teachers for diversity, "what we need to know is the meaning that these teacher preparation programs make of difference, diversity, and social justice" (Ladson-Billings, 1999,

p. 241). A mission that prioritizes diversifying faculty and student populations and supports policies and practices related to equity and cultural and linguistic responsiveness in instruction and curriculum may also be necessary (Villegas & Lucas, 2002). Examination of the clinical experience, and students' perception of it, are essential, especially as it links with program vision and coursework experiences (Grossman et al., 2008).

Ongoing dialogue and debate can enable faculty to develop program vision and coherence. From his own and others' research, Howey (1996) outlined areas for dialogue: (a) a defensible conceptual framework, (b) themes that provide continuity and coherence for what it means to learn to teach, and (c) socialization and educational experiences that allow themes to be manifest. Howey found widespread problems in developing agreement about a conceptual framework and student goals thematically linked across courses and related activities. However, in case studies of six exemplary programs, Howey and Zimpher (1989) found that frameworks articulated shared ideas about schooling and teaching, and that programs included focused experimental models fostering faculty collaboration, investment, and ownership. Villegas and Lucas (2002) describe how one institution used a range of structures to reach agreement about infusing culturally responsive teaching principles into a curriculum. These included a Center of Pedagogy, a leadership program, summer institutes for professional development of multiple partners involved in teacher education, inquiry projects, and ongoing conversations.

Fostering dialogue and collaboration can be challenging. The question of who comprises teacher education faculty and should therefore help develop curriculum can be an obstacle to progress (Cochran-Smith, 2003). This is particularly true when faculty hold diverse disciplinary affiliations, as well as roles and responsibilities, in K-12 and higher education. Other problems include lack of institutional support (Lanier & Little, 1986); lack of time and research resources at institutions where innovations likely have occurred (Zeichner & Hoeft, 1996); and few longitudinal models of teacher education research (Wilson, Floden, & Ferrini-Mundy, 2002).

Further, research on teacher education tends to feature the impact of structural characteristics rather than of program substance (Zeichner & Conklin, 2005), including content and pedagogy. Little research has examined such concerns in the context of teaching diverse learners or promoting social justice (Wilson et al., 2002). However, recent work has documented successes and challenges of program coherence in culturally competent teaching (Ladson-Billings, 2001; Villegas & Lucas, 2002); learning to teach for social justice (Darling-Hammond, French, & Garcia-Lopez, 2002; McDonald, 2005; Quartz & the TEP Research Group, 2003); and learning to advocate for equity in classrooms and schools (Athanases & Martin, 2006). Even when programs address diversity, however, language issues often get swamped by broader diversity concerns (Lucas & Grinberg, 2008; Zeichner, 2003). Given minimal attention to developing and studying program coherence in teacher education, it is no surprise that little work has documented such coherence in preparing teachers to teach ELLs. The present study addresses this issue, describing and analyzing ways one institution addressed this goal program-wide.

Designing Teacher Education Programs: A Framework to Infuse Attention to Teaching ELLs

In teacher education research, programs must be "studied in a way that acknowledges their complexity and their ties to the settings in which they are located and the people who inhabit them" (Zeichner & Conklin, 2005, p. 699). To capture such complexities, we drew on programs research, especially Darling-Hammond et al. (2005), to map a framework to examine program-wide attention to preparing teachers to teach and advocate for ELLs. The framework organized data collection for a case study we report, and it can serve as a planning tool for programs seeking to develop attention to teaching ELLs. The framework (Table 12.1) includes three program domains. "Content" refers to what is taught about ELLs and how it is embedded in a defensible conceptual framework and themes that provide continuity. Learning "processes" allow themes to be enacted through tools of practice. Examining process adds analytic depth to studies of programs that typically are more complex and contradictory than is generally described in the literature (Kennedy, 1998; Zeichner & Conklin, 2005). "Context" refers to all those who prepare teachers, highlighting a community that may share and develop practices, dispositions, and a growing base of knowledge for teaching ELLs. As Table 12.1 shows, each domain includes guiding questions shaped by teacher education programs research. The table also identifies, per domain, program planning and data gathering points for studying a program's attention to teaching ELLs.

Method

Researchers need to document not just the probable (what likely will occur) but also the possible—what *can* be done, and how it is organized, developed, and pursued (Shulman, 1983). This argues for studying a teacher education program whose graduates feel well prepared to meet ELLs' needs. The present study fulfills this purpose, also referencing previous program research. The central research question was: how did one teacher education program infuse attention to teaching English language learners in the content, processes, and context of its work?

Context for the Study

The program is part of a California university that, at the time of the research, credentialed between 105 and 125 teachers per year in a post-baccalaureate

Table 12.1 A Framework for Planning, Documenting, and Evaluating Program-Wide Attention to Teaching English Language Learners (ELLs)

Program Planning & Documenting Considerations	Support for Learning to Teach ELLs by Program Domain		
	Content	*Processes*	*Context*
Focus	Program content related to teaching ELLs and how it is organized and infused in the program	Activities in coursework, field placements, and records or simulations of practice that develop knowledge, skills, and dispositions for teaching ELLs	Activities shaped by various players that support learning to teach ELLs
Guiding questions	• Is there a conceptual framework, a set of themes, or other form of cognitive map of ways in which understandings of work with ELLs cohere? • Are language-oriented courses required or offered as electives? • Is course content on teaching ELLs infused throughout program & courses?	• How does the program enable the framework/content of teaching ELLs to be manifest, developed, enacted, internalized? • How does the program develop teachers' readiness to teach ELLs through coursework opportunities, fieldwork experiences, and non-fieldwork learning from practice (e.g., observations, simulations, presentations)?	• In what ways and to what extent does the program foster development of a community of practitioners across various constituent groups who share skills, knowledge, and dispositions for teaching ELLs?
Relevant program planning and data gathering points	• Conceptual framework and themes • Language-oriented courses • Infusion of ELL content program-wide	• Coursework opportunities, materials, and tools • Fieldwork experiences	Constituent groups and their participation in preparing teachers to teach ELLs: • Teacher educators • Pre-service teacher cohorts • K-12 teachers and schools • Families and communities

program. (Certification is awarded only after completion of a Bachelor's degree in California.) Faculty included research professors, clinical faculty who served as lead supervisors of student teaching, and K-12 adjuncts. Student teachers were placed for an academic year in diverse, generally high-need urban and rural schools with an average of 60% of students on free/reduced lunch. Urban sites tended to be poor, often with populations at nearly one-third African American, one-third Latina/o (mostly Mexican American), one-third Asian of varied ethnicity, and small numbers of White students; rural schools included many Latina/o children of migrant farm workers. Schools had high numbers of ELLs with a staggering array of first languages— the dominant first language being Spanish, with other key languages including Vietnamese, Hmong, Russian/Ukrainian, and Lao. Program graduates tended to work in high-need schools and continued teaching in them at an unusually high rate (Merino et al., 2001). In line with other U.S. efforts to recruit new teachers of color (e.g., Bennett, 2002), this program developed outreach on campus and beyond; generated small financial support for selected students; and developed with a nearby state university an alternative certification route through summer and evening courses for working professionals. Through these efforts, the program increased the number of students of color from none to an average of 27% in four years (Merino & Holmes, 2002). Responding to an option of the California Commission on Teacher Credentialing (CCTC) to develop an experimental model, the program director, a Chicana researcher on ELL learning issues, worked with faculty to propose a five-year experimental program on teaching culturally and linguistically diverse youth. Once the proposal was approved, the faculty finalized the program, including guiding principles, planned practices, and a self-study. We highlight these efforts in the Results section (pp. 202–210).

Participants

Participants included 17 faculty and supervisors (three research, 12 clinical, and two adjunct personnel) who prepared teachers in multiple subjects and secondary subjects (English, science, math, and agriculture). Over 300 credential students in a five-year period completed surveys and provided work samples, and 38 later participated in focus groups representing graduates in grade levels and subject areas taught, race/ethnicity, and teaching context. Most had taught from one to three years and worked primarily in lower income urban and rural communities, with culturally diverse students and high numbers of ELLs. Over one-third of focus group participants were teachers of color, mostly Mexican American (eight), with some African American (three) and Asian American (three). This chapter's first author was recruited to conduct focus groups of graduates because of his knowledge of teacher education and experience with discussion facilitation, but also because he was a new research faculty member and therefore a stranger to program graduates, a fact that might increase focus group participants' candor. The second author, a non-native English speaking graduate student at the same institution at the time of the study, was recruited to collaborate in data analysis because of her expertise in language education, K-12 second language development issues, and adult education. Together we mined program data for analyses that inform this chapter.

Data Sources

Data included program/institutional documents; faculty syllabi, lessons, portfolios, questionnaires, interviews, and transcribed meeting discussions; preservice teachers' work samples (80) and exit surveys (300+); and graduates' reflections on preparation gathered in surveys and focus groups. Surveys asked respondents to describe their school sites, communities, students' ethnicity and SES, and current or most recent teaching assignment, and to rate program elements and their impact on learning to teach and advocate for diverse youth. Five three-hour focus groups of 5–10 currently teaching graduates were conducted, focused on program elements of greatest impact and ways schools supported and constrained teachers' goals and work. (See Athanases & Martin, 2006, for detailed focus group prompts, procedures, and foci.)

Data Analysis

To answer our research question about how the program infused attention to content for learning to teach ELLs, we examined documents, syllabi, questionnaires, interviews, and other participant data. Following Howey (1996) and Darling-Hammond et al. (2005), we considered guiding questions (Table 12.1) related to: conceptual framework and themes for teaching ELLs; language-oriented courses; and infusion of ELL content program-wide. Analyses of process and learning context used data from documents, faculty, and graduates on coursework opportunities, fieldwork experiences, and the developing community of practitioners for work with ELLs.

Quantitative and qualitative datasets were coded and tabulated, and charts and data displays (Miles & Huberman, 1994) mapped response categories by participant group. We examined charts and displays for similarities and differences across groups, and analyzed documents to cross-reference responses by participants, illuminate program features, and frame interviews and focus group discussions as we analyzed data. We coded teacher educator data for themes and ways they were addressed in teaching and supervision. We analyzed how these themes related to those identified by graduates. For focus group data, we examined 300 transcript pages, yielding a corpus of teacher narratives we parsed for structural elements, following Polkinghorne (1988), and content. (For detailed analyses and results, see Athanases & de Oliveira,

2008.) Results solidified after we considered analyses from datasets in relationship to each other; this triangulation strengthened clarity of findings and conclusions.

Results

Results align with the three Framework domains (Table 12.1) to answer our broad research question: how did one teacher education program infuse attention to teaching English language learners in the content, process, and context of its work?

Content for Teaching ELLs

Conceptual Framework and Themes for Teaching ELLs

The program had a conceptual framework featuring teaching of ELLs, also referred to as linguistic minority (LM) students. The experimental program proposal and final report to the CCTC noted the program "is designed to prepare teachers to work effectively with students developing proficiency in English, and to gain knowledge of culture and cultural diversity." The framework consisted of four roles for teacher educators and future teachers, one foregrounded: "First and foremost, we undertake to help candidates and educators become *Advocates for Educational Equity* in addressing inequities of schooling and society, especially in communities that are culturally, linguistically and socio-economically diverse." Three other roles were identified in support of advocacy: reflective practitioner, collaborative professional, and researcher on practice. Of note is that linguistic diversity in the populations graduates would serve was explicitly highlighted in document language for three of the four roles. Because of the centrality of the advocate role as evidenced in program documents and practices, we highlight it, reporting only briefly on the other roles as support for the primary role of advocate.

Advocacy for equity guided program philosophy, and faculty strongly emphasized helping candidates develop as advocates. The program framework clarified that the knowledge base for teaching ELLs includes not only effective pedagogy but knowledge of ELLs as learners and knowledge of the contexts within which the work occurs. This includes understanding social and political contexts within which ELLs come to school and are taught, and the policies surrounding such work. This framework suggests that effective teaching of ELLs often necessitates assuming the role of advocate for ELLs in and beyond the classroom. Documents identified a need to address inequities of schooling and society, especially in culturally and linguistically diverse communities. In questionnaire responses and faculty meeting discussions, faculty reported goals of developing the advocate role throughout courses and assignments, teaching and modeling it, and articulating it to K-12 cooperating teachers for program clarity. Such efforts were evidenced in faculty self-inquiry and program-wide inquiry in the form of data collection and analysis. In writing about the role of advocate during a faculty meeting, one teacher educator reported that his concept of advocacy includes:

> Providing student teachers with the theoretical understanding of learning and language acquisition so that they can construct appropriate learning experiences. In addition, once equipped, these novice teachers can advocate for linguistic minority students by participating in school-based decisions which influence students' opportunities to learn.

We found consistency in faculty conceptions of the advocate role, in particular. In questionnaires, discussions, and lesson materials, multiple faculty members highlighted ELLs, expressing the central tenet that new teachers need to learn to set the bar high for all students in content learning and to develop stronger pedagogical content knowledge (Grossman, 1990; Shulman, 1987) for a repertoire of strategies to differentiate instruction, particularly for ELLs. In support of this role, several faculty also reported that they promoted reflection and encouraged checking biases about expectations for ELLs. They noted the process requires time, self-examination, and skills.

Documents that articulated program goals noted that candidates also need to learn how to effect change in the teaching of ELLs through site leadership and involvement with reform. Faculty echoed this, noting the need for knowledge of context in teaching ELLs. Foundations courses introduced context issues through *Savage Inequalities* (Kozol, 1991) and other readings, and several faculty highlighted socioeconomic disparity in their teaching. Syllabi for three instructors' sections of Cultural Diversity and Education used *Affirming Diversity* (Nieto, 2008), which treats linguistic diversity in the context of institutional structures, and course readers, all addressing the larger social context of inequity and the need to respond to it. Several educators noted their attention to exploring how textbooks, curriculum, and school supplies vary greatly from district to district due to economic disparities, particularly relevant to ELLs. Other national and state level issues included knowledge of how allowing ELLs to use their first language in classroom meaning-making was both research-sound and potentially contested by policy and some community members, particularly before and after the vote on Proposition 227, the English Only Initiative that became law in California. Several faculty argued that new teachers need an ethnographic stance, researching demographics, languages spoken, degree of parent facility with English, and parent comfort with the school site.

Faculty reported challenges in developing this framework of roles with students. Because of an evolving focus on advocacy and reflectively defining it at meetings and retreats, the concept was slippery at times. How would one know it when seeing it? How was it taught? Working from agreed-upon, sharply delineated conceptions might have focused efforts more readily. On the other hand, enabling conceptions to evolve allowed grounded theory to develop. Kay, a multiple-subjects instructor/supervisor, captured the tension. She called for clarity:

> I hadn't talked about it enough, nor had the handbook addressed it much except to lay out the role(s), so I think that's something our program needs to do more effectively, and that's to showcase the roles, which is to bring them to everybody's awareness.

A moment later, however, Kay noted: "Perhaps the question is how much do you want to define [the roles] and how much should the teachers play a part in defining them?"

In fact, new teachers did define the roles for themselves through program activities, as we found in analyzing retrospective focus groups—evidence that they internalized a portion of the program's conceptual framework. Regarding the role of advocacy, graduates' narratives of enacted advocacy, reported as grounded in the program, shared four cross-cutting themes: a goal of equitable access to resources and support; convictions about working for equity; interceding on behalf of students in need; and engaging co-advocates (Athanases & de Oliveira, 2008). ELL needs especially prompted advocacy in and beyond classrooms, including instructional tailoring, out-of-class tutorials, hunts for better texts and tests, a library field trip, creation of a culture/computer club, heightened parent contacts, and launching of a bilingual parent group (de Oliveira & Athanases, 2007). That teachers defined the advocate role after program completion may indicate value in wrestling with it continually rather than having it pre-defined. One teacher thought she came to the program an already-formed advocate: "But this program proved me wrong. Discussions and reflections helped me to personally define the term and work towards becoming an advocate, and I hope to continue my development in this area throughout my career."

Language-Oriented Courses

Several required or elective program courses explicitly focused on teaching ELLs. In focus groups, graduates noted that gaining foundational knowledge of language and its development was a key element of feeling well prepared to teach ELLs (Athanases & Martin, 2006). One teacher noted how she uses the "powerhouse of information" from the course *Language Development in the Chicano Child* that was "heavy on linguistics and theory." This course featured diversity among language minority populations, and language acquisition among bilinguals. English language arts teachers valued the academic rigor of their required linguistics course *Teaching English as a Second Language*. One teacher reported she could review a student's paper and identify an ELL's first language by grammar error patterns. A science teacher said what she learned about ESL in program coursework she now could apply to science learning, noting she would have liked even more linguistics preparation to help her evaluate students' written and oral work.

Infusion of ELL Content Program-Wide

Analyses of documents, syllabi and assignments, student work, faculty portfolios, and meeting field notes found the program infused attention to cultural and linguistic diversity and equity beyond language-specific coursework (Athanases & Martin, 2001). Issues of language development and diversity were embedded throughout curricula, evidenced in at least nine program courses. Foundations courses for undergraduates and credential students laid the groundwork, addressing relevant concerns in at least one-third of session topics. Syllabi for undergraduate fieldwork courses in tutoring K-12 children in local schools included work with ELLs. Teacher supervision seminars included attention to the interactive influences of diversity in language, culture, ethnicity, and socioeconomics. ELL topics were found in the syllabi of different multiple-subjects instructors who, over the course of several years, taught language arts methods. One instructor, for example, integrated ELL issues, including second language acquisition theory and stages, ESL/second language instruction methodology, assessing ELLs, and dialect variations, supported by *The More-Than-Just-Surviving Handbook: ESL for Every Classroom Teacher* (Law & Eckes, 2000).

Processes for Learning to Teach and Advocate for ELLs

The second Framework domain (Table 12.1) is Learning Processes. In this section, we discuss activities for learning to teach ELLs through coursework and fieldwork experiences.

Coursework

A striking array of assignments, materials, and activities identified in the data served to develop readiness to teach ELLs. Faculty and graduates noted instruction in addressing language needs of ELLs linked with subject matter learning as key. Five of six multiple subjects instructors documented lessons relevant to ELLs focused on learning to construct group activities, demonstrations and modeling, applied practice, diagrams, visual cues, dramatic readings, pictures on overheads, hands-on learning, and activity based instruction. Illustrations of how to assess and support ELLs' learning included charts and other visual representations. Student teachers created multimedia projects to assist ELLs with concepts from literary works, incorporating pictures, simple graphics, and sounds to convey information in multimodal formats. One instructor noted a need to link language support with content by demonstrating "geometry in Spanish, science experiments in Italian" in her lesson activities. An agricultural education instructor used Kozol's text and ideas, requiring student teachers to examine lessons for ways they may disadvantage children of migrant workers who, unlike farmers' children, may lack extended access to farm animals for class projects. Math methods instructors required lesson plans with ELL considerations, and guests demonstrated ways to teach language issues in math and to understand semantics, syntax, and vocabulary in math texts. In secondary science methods, teachers included in lesson plans ways they addressed language demands for ELLs, created lessons three times a year on "common topics explicitly serving needs of ELLs," and created and discussed concept maps about teaching science to ELLs.

These efforts by teacher educators appear to have had an impact on graduates' practice. New teachers reported providing language support for ELLs with visuals, maps, media, drama, and multiple modes of explanation; scaffolding complex reading and writing tasks; and tailoring lessons with differentiated support—tracing these to teacher preparation. Course projects recalled as particularly effective included analyzing a case study student developing English usage (using work samples, observations, and interviews) and designing an instructional intervention to strengthen learning of an ELL in class. A community study assignment, cited as one of great impact, was designed to help candidates learn about cultural and linguistic diversity and richness in communities their schools served. The assignment also challenged candidates to explore their own perceptions of advocacy through reflective exercises. Another key activity was an inquiry project often featuring teaching and learning of one or more ELLs.

As already noted, reflection played a role in developing readiness to teach ELLs. Course activities included journals to support reflection on "diverse learners and learning styles and cultural differences;" analysis of an ESL lesson; in-class quick-writes on concepts including "educational equity" and "language proficiency." Noting an increase in positive student perceptions in their reflections on diversity in classes, a faculty member explained: "We redesigned our lesson plan format to include a section in which students must write what they will do to accommodate the needs of ELLs." To illustrate one way to promote reflection on context related to ELLs, one instructor wrote of modeling how to advocate beyond the classroom for ELLs in opposing a problematic policy. She noted of the California English-Only Initiative:

> I felt I needed to be active in working for a NO vote. I shared with students dates, etc. of various events so they could attend. At a benefit rally, 11 out of my 12 students attended, plus others.... They were able to meet and watch other activists in practice. I believe this cohort is still active in their advocacy.

Several graduates reported the power of this activity in teaching them a need to act on behalf of ELLs in a policy climate not always aligned with research on language development and learning. Surveys indicated new teachers felt well prepared to teach ELLs by meeting their language needs across grade levels and subject areas and to assume the role of advocate for equity for ELLs in classrooms and schools (Athanases & Martin, 2001; Merino et al., 2001). These results frequently were linked to course assignments.

Fieldwork Experiences

Student teaching placements mediate coursework and campus-based program experiences (McDonald, 2005). The program we examined developed readiness for teaching ELLs through several means related to fieldwork. Most placements included ELLs, and graduates reported that long-term school-based apprenticeships aided efforts when supervisors probed on equity in conferences and seminars and when schools included faculty role models as advocates for equity for ELLs and other students (Athanases & Martin, 2006). Graduates identified how several teacher educators (on campus and in supervision conferences) fostered passion for teaching and advocating for ELLs and modeled relevant strategies. Teacher educators described ways they stressed a need to attend to ELLs. One described challenging a student teacher about passing over an ELL during oral report time; the boy later got to read his report in Spanish.

Context: Community of Practitioners Developing Teaching for ELLs

The third Framework domain (Table 12.1) is context. Here we discuss constituent groups and how they participated in building a community of practice related to learning to teach ELLs.

Teacher Educators

The teacher educators, particularly clinical faculty who taught courses and served as lead supervisors for student teaching, played an ongoing active role in preparing teachers to teach ELLs and in reflecting on and inquiring into their own teaching and supervising practice. Without faculty buy-in and development, frameworks remain documents without processes to make themes take hold in new teacher practices. For example, during one year of the five-year experimental program, an hour at one faculty meeting per month fostered development and evaluation of framework roles and their relevance to teaching ELLs. Faculty wrote about, discussed, and illustrated with lessons and artifacts how they sought to help future teachers develop an understanding of and commitment to the roles. Quarterly retreats included consideration of program development and documentation. Faculty held a two-and-a-half-day retreat to reflect on and write about teaching and action research related to teaching ELLs and developing program roles. Fieldnotes identified signs of deep commitment among faculty to preparing all teachers to work effectively with ELLs and to promoting the framework. The program's associate director credited the director with having the vision and persistence to keep ELLs and advocacy for equity in program focus.

As further evidence of faculty participation in preparing teachers to teach ELLs, several faculty presented papers on this work at professional meetings. One studied 12 pre-service science teachers' different experiences in classes with or without LM students (Pomeroy, 1999). He concluded that placement with LM students had a great impact on lesson adaptations but that program efforts to equip teachers with teaching skills for LM students is necessary regardless of placement with LM students. Another faculty member researched ways new teachers integrated literature response and academic language pedagogy for ELLs (Holmes, 2006). These are among ways faculty modeled themes of advocating for equity and reflecting on and inquiring into one's practice—in this case, related to their own practice of preparing teachers to teach ELLs.

Pre-Service Teacher Cohorts

Peers serve as resources for learning to teach and advocate for equity for ELLs (see Sakash & Rodriguez-Brown, this volume). Several graduates pointed to the influence of the diverse group of students in the program in shaping their perspectives on race, culture, and language issues. Several also indicated that strong interactions and collaborative learning with fellow students played a major role in their preparation to teach and advocate for diverse youth. These reports support Goodlad's (1990) finding that more salient than institution or program size in preparing teachers effectively may be the degree to which programs organize short-term small group activities and cohort structures that support development of learning communities. Cohort arrangements promoted a learning communities structure that supported pre-service teachers' learning to teach ELLs in several program venues. Merino and Ambrose (2008), for example, showed through a case study of a beginning teacher how a teacher learning community in this program was critical to one new teacher's successful inquiry process into the learning of an ELL. Faculty mentors and first-year teacher peers (completing a Master's degree tied to their credential) provided input and helped shape this new teacher's study of an ELL.

K-12 Teachers and Schools

K-12 teachers and schools played key roles in supporting program goals of teaching and advocating for ELLs. For example, one faculty member reported on his "science methods road show" in which student teachers visited classrooms of science teachers who demonstrated instructional methods, with specific attention to working with culturally and linguistically diverse youth. Also, faculty followed several graduates who had demonstrated success in working with ELLs and facilitated their moving into the role of cooperating teacher, a role that enabled them to guide and model effective teaching practices for ELLs. Bilingual teachers especially reported appreciation for school-based models and mentors who could help them navigate instructional landmines of an English-only climate. In particular, they needed help understanding how to discuss their philosophies and practices with colleagues. A course assignment involving surveying colleagues on school policies and climate related to support for ELLs helped educate new teachers about ELL needs and available resources. Graduates reported in focus groups that they learned to engage co-advocates in their schools—teachers, counselors, and administrators who could assist them in determining ways to meet the needs of ELLs.

Teachers spoke of confidence and spirited renewal when they worked in the company of colleagues and/or administrators equally committed to equity, and in settings where others shared conviction and commitment to make changes to serve ELLs and others with needs not being met. However, such alignment was inconsistent, and often these new teachers attempted to enact the role of advocate for equity for ELLs but acknowledged the position as lone wolf, risking confrontations with other educators (Athanases & de Oliveira, 2007). One problem may relate to program articulation. As noted, Kay, a multiple-subjects instructor, spoke of the need to more explicitly articulate to K-12 colleagues the roles the program sought to develop in future teachers. The challenge relates to cooperating teachers' conceptions of their role because, as Kay notes, they "see themselves as giving the feedback on discrete lessons but not necessarily perceiving themselves as having an instrumental role in the development of the teacher." Kay suggested faculty could strengthen the communication so this kind of collaborative effort might increase.

Families and Communities

The program espoused tapping families and communities as partners in teaching ELLs. One graduate reported how she had learned in the program to design and study an intervention for struggling ELLs and to tap families as partners in strengthening children's literacy development. For a community project assignment, students got involved in ELLs' communities by interviewing a parent or other local adults. One instructor described this assignment as key for students: "They begin to value what the parents have to say ... they start to recognize that the parents know things. What a revelation." Goal statements written three times per year by 50 multiple subjects students from two cohort years showed that, after five weeks of intense program activity, 30% identified goals that focused less on classroom routines and management and more on ways to use language, culture, parents, and community as resources to strengthen learning. By spring, students in these cohorts reported success in accomplishing some goals but were split overall on engaging parents. Successes included pulling in parent helpers to class and exploring in a spring research topic multiple ways to link parents with classrooms.

Lack of success in work with parents was tied to school-site modeling: "This wasn't really a goal of my master teacher, so it was difficult for me to learn effective ways to bring (in) parents, although I do know that I want to do this." Graduates' reports of successes traced acts of engaging parents in the program, including outreach to parents and building structures to support parent involvement in children's education. Several graduates reported that to tap parents as partners often required serving as language interpreters and cultural ambassadors for them. One reported how she extended her role of advocate to parents in creating a bilingual parents' association so these parents might begin to feel ownership of the school and of their children's education. As the program director noted, the program needed to extend these kinds of activities to deepen its commitment to engage parents and communities as partners in the education of ELLs.

Conclusions and Lessons Learned

There is a dearth of research literature on program-wide attention to preparing teachers to teach ELLs. Also, there are challenges and institutional impediments to developing program-wide attention to any substantive concerns in preparing teachers. Nonetheless, the case study we have reported in this chapter documents how one program infused attention program-wide to learning to teach ELLs, and how its graduates perceived that work in preparing them to teach ELLs. The case instantiates the possible, analyzing what can be done to build coherence in programs to prepare teachers to work with ELLs. It shows that attention across three domains—content, processes, and context—is possible, maybe necessary, to focus on ELLs program-wide. The case provides evidence of the importance of faculty development and ongoing commitment with various constituencies to develop explicit attention to ELLs programmatically.

Our study and the literature we reviewed suggest that developing a shared program vision and conceptual framework that grounds efforts to build a coherent program to prepare teachers of ELLs is essential. However, our study suggests that, while articulation of such a vision anchors the work, an openness to new iterations of the concepts enables participants, especially pre-service teachers, to develop their understandings over time. Similarly, Villegas and Lucas (2002) found the need for flexibility in vision work so all participants could challenge and help shape program principles and participate in their own professional development in order to model the principles.

Like the exemplary programs Howey and Zimpher (1989) studied, the program we examined used (a) a conceptual framework that articulated shared ideas about schooling and teaching (in this case, focused on ELLs) and (b) an experimental model that fostered faculty collaboration, investment, and ownership—in this case, through ongoing reflection, dialogue, and inquiry supported by faculty meetings and retreats. Program-wide attention to ELLs (according to our framework and our study) coheres when program content is reinforced throughout documents, dialogue, and coursework; when coursework and field placement processes enact the program vision; and when the larger context of multiple parties share in the vision and process of learning to teach ELLs effectively. This final piece is particularly challenging to realize. It may require (a) stronger links than typically occur between campus faculty and supervisors and their K-12 partners, and (b) cooperating teachers who are carefully selected by the program for their alignment with program vision (Grossman et al., 2008). In preparing teachers to teach ELLs, this requires identifying K-12 teachers who have adequate numbers of ELLs in class for pre-service teachers to teach and who are aligned with conceptions of teaching ELLs grounded in research-informed pedagogy and best practices for ELLs. Pre-service teachers need such extended experiences of practice teaching with ELLs to apply relevant coursework strategies and to feel qualified to teach ELLs (Gándara et al., 2005; McDonald, 2005; Merino, 1999).

This may be a tall order. It suggests that a program developing a coherent model for preparing teachers to teach ELLs needs to consider careful attention to the context within which such work will occur. This includes the sociopolitical context as illustrated in our study. It also includes the local context. As Grossman et al. (2008) note, students are more likely to evaluate program experiences as coherent when faculty and school-based supervisors have aligned vision and practices. This alignment can develop through the kinds of structures, summer institutes, and other professional development opportunities Villegas and Lucas (2002) described. However it occurs, program alignment across constituent groups can help develop the community of practitioners who begin to share vision and practice for the important work of teaching and advocating for ELLs in classrooms and beyond.

Authors' Note

We acknowledge members of the teacher education faculty of the program studied, for their development and inquiry efforts. We also thank Kathleen J. Martin, Kameelah Elarms, and Vanessa Ayala-Pech for assistance with program documentation and assessment.

References

Abedi, J. (2007). High-stakes tests, English language learners, and linguistic modification. *Sunshine State TESOL Quarterly, 6*(1), 1–20.

Adger, C.T., Snow, C.E., & Christian, D. (Eds.). (2002). *What teachers need to know about language.* Washington, D.C.: Center for Applied Linguistics.

Athanases, S.Z., & de Oliveira, L.C. (2007). Conviction, confrontation, and risk in new teachers' advocating for equity. *Teaching Education, 18*(2), 123–136.

Athanases, S.Z., & de Oliveira, L.C. (2008). Advocacy for equity in classrooms and beyond: New teachers' challenges and responses. *Teachers College Record, 110*(1), 64–104.

Athanases, S.Z., & Martin, K.J. (2001). *Fostering advocacy for all learners in a teacher education program.* Paper presented at the American Educational Research Association Annual Meeting, Seattle, April.

Athanases, S.Z., & Martin, K.J. (2006). Teaching and learning advocacy for educational equity in a teacher credential program. *Teaching and Teacher Education, 22*(6), 627–646.

August, D., & Hakuta, K. (Eds.). (1997). *Improving schooling for language-minority children: A research agenda.* Washington, D.C.: National Academy Press.

Bennett, C.I. (2002). Enhancing ethnic diversity at a Big Ten university through Project TEAM: A case study in teacher education. *Educational Researcher, 31*(2), 21–29.

Cochran-Smith, M. (2003). Learning and unlearning: The education of teacher educators. *Teaching and Teacher Education, 19,* 5–28.

Costa, J., McPhail, G., Smith, J., & Brisk, M.E. (2005). Faculty first: The challenge of infusing the teacher education curriculum with scholarship on English language learners. *Journal of Teacher Education, 56*(2), 104–118.

Darling-Hammond, L., Chung, R., & Frelow, F. (2002). Variation in teacher preparation: How well do different pathways prepare teachers to teach? *Journal of Teacher Education, 53*(4), 286–302.

Darling-Hammond, L., French, J., & Garcia-Lopez, S.P. (Eds.). (2002). *Learning to teach for social justice.* New York, NY: Teachers College Press.

Darling-Hammond, L., Hammerness, K., with Grossman, P., Rust, F., & Shulman, L. (2005). The design of teacher education programs. In L. Darling-Hammond & J. Bransford (Eds.), *Preparing teachers for a changing world: What teachers should learn and be able to do* (pp. 390–441). San Francisco, CA: Jossey-Bass.

de Oliveira, L.C., & Athanases, S.Z. (2007). Graduates' reports of advocating for English language learners. *Journal of Teacher Education, 58*(3), 202–215.

Gándara, P.C., Maxwell-Jolly, J., & Driscoll, A. (2005). *Listening to teachers of English language learners: A survey of California teachers' challenges, experiences, and professional development needs.* Santa Cruz, CA: Center for the Future of Teaching and Learning.

Goodlad, J.I. (1990). *Teachers for our nation's schools.* San Francisco, CA: Jossey-Bass.

Goodwin, A.L. (2002). Teacher preparation and the education of immigrant children. *Education and Urban Society, 34*(2), 156–172.

Grossman, P.L. (1990). *The making of a teacher: Teacher knowledge and teacher education.* New York, NY: Teachers College Press.

Grossman, P., Hammerness, K.M., McDonald, M., & Ronfeldt, M. (2008). Constructing coherence: Structural predictors of perceptions of coherence in NYC teacher education programs. *Journal of Teacher Education, 59*(4), 273–287.

Hammerness, K. (2006). From coherence in theory to coherence in practice. *Teachers College Record, 108*(7), 1241–1265.

Harper, C.A., & de Jong, E.J. (2004). Misconceptions about teaching English-language learners. *Journal of Adolescent & Adult Literacy, 48*(2), 152–162.

Hollins, E., & Guzman, M.T. (2005). Research on preparing teachers for diverse populations. In M. Cochran-Smith & K.M. Zeichner (Eds.), *Studying teacher education: The report of the AERA panel on research and teacher education* (pp. 477–548). Mahwah, NJ: Lawrence Erlbaum.

Holmes, P. (2006). *Academic literacy in the literature classroom: Investigating instructional decisions of new teachers of English learners.* Unpublished doctoral dissertation. Davis, CA: University of California, Davis.

Howey, K. (1996). Designing coherent and effective teacher education programs. In J. Sikula, T.J. Buttery, & E. Guyton (Eds.), *Handbook of research on teacher education* (2nd ed., pp. 143–170). New York, NY: Simon & Shuster Macmillan.

Howey, K.R., & Zimpher, N.L. (1989). *Profiles of preservice teacher education: Inquiry into the nature of programs.* Albany, NY: State University of New York Press.

Kennedy, M.M. (1998). *Learning to teach writing: Does teacher education make a difference?* New York, NY: Teachers College Press.

Kindler, A.L. (2002). *Survey of the states' limited English proficient students and available educational programs and services: 2000–2001 summary report.* Washington, D.C.: National Clearinghouse for English Language Acquisition.

Kozol, J. (1991). *Savage inequalities: Children in America's schools.* New York, NY: Crown.

Ladson-Billings, G.J. (1999). Preparing teachers for diverse student populations: A critical race theory perspective. In A. Iran-Nejad & P.D. Pearson (Eds.), *Review of research in education, 24* (pp. 211–247). Washington, D.C.: AERA.

Ladson-Billings, G. (2001). *Crossing over to Canaan: The journey of new teachers in diverse classrooms.* San Francisco, CA: Jossey-Bass.

Lanier, J., & Little, J.W. (1986). Research on teacher education. In M. Wittrock (Ed.), *Handbook of research on teaching* (3rd ed., pp. 527–568). New York, NY: Macmillan.

Law, B., & Eckes, M. (2000). *The more-than-just-surviving handbook: ESL for every classroom teacher* (2nd ed.). Winnipeg: Peguis Publishers.

Lucas, T., & Grinberg, J. (2008). Responding to the linguistic reality of the mainstream classroom: Preparing classroom teachers to teach English language learners. In M. Cochran-Smith, S. Feiman-Nemser, & J. McIntyre (Eds.), *Handbook of research on teacher education: Enduring issues in changing contexts* (pp. 606–636). Mahwah, NJ: Lawrence Erlbaum.

McDonald, M.A. (2005). The integration of social justice in teacher education: Dimensions of prospective teachers' opportunities to learn. *Journal of Teacher Education, 56*(5), 418–435.

Merino, B.J. (1999). Preparing secondary teachers to teach a second language: The case of the United States with a focus on California. In C.J. Faltis & P.M. Wolfe (Eds.), *So much to say: Adolescents, bilingualism and ESL in the secondary school* (pp. 225–254). New York, NY: Teachers College Press.

Merino, B.J., & Ambrose, R.C. (2008). Beginning teachers' inquiry in linguistically diverse classrooms: Exploring the power of small learning communities. In C. Craig & L. Deretchin (Eds.), *Teacher education yearbook XVII: Teacher learning in small group settings* (pp. 242–260). Lanham, MD: Rowman & Littlefield.

Merino, B.J., & Holmes, P.V. (2002). *Preparing teachers as advocates for educational equity through teacher research*. Paper presented at the American Educational Research Association Annual Meeting, New Orleans, April.

Merino, B.J., Martin, K.J., & Pryor, K., in collaboration with Goldman, B., Murai, H., & Teacher Education Work Group. (2001). *Graduates' perspectives on the role of their teacher education program in facilitating their growth as advocates for equity in learning: Survey results relating the experimental model to the standards*. Report to the California Commission on Teacher Credentialing.

Miles, M.B., & Huberman, A.M. (1994). *Qualitative data analysis: An expanded sourcebook* (2nd ed.). Thousand Oaks, CA: Sage Publications.

National Center for Education Statistics. (2002). *1999–2000 schools and staffing survey: Overview of the data for public, private, public charter and bureau of Indian affairs elementary and secondary schools*. Washington, D.C.: U.S. Department of Education, Office of Educational Research and Improvement.

Nieto, S. (2008). *Affirming diversity: The sociopolitical context of multicultural education* (5th ed.). New York, NY: Allyn & Bacon.

Polkinghorne, D.E. (1988). *Narrative knowing and the human sciences*. Albany, NY: State University of New York Press.

Pomeroy, J.R. (1999). *The use of lesson adaptation strategies by preservice teachers in classrooms with and without language minority students*. Paper presented at the International Conference on Teacher Research. Magog, Canada.

Quartz, K.H., & TEP Research Group. (2003). "Too angry to leave": Supporting new teachers' commitment to transform urban schools. *Journal of Teacher Education, 54*(2), 99–111.

Samway, K., & McKeon, D. (2007). *Myths and realities: Best practices for language minority students* (2nd ed.). Portsmouth, NH: Heinemann.

Schleppegrell, M. (2004). *The language of schooling: A functional linguistics perspective*. Mahwah, NJ: Lawrence Erlbaum.

Shulman, L.S. (1983). Autonomy and obligation: The remote control of teaching. In L.S. Shulman & G. Sykes (Eds.), *Handbook of teaching and policy* (pp. 484–504). New York, NY: Longman.

Shulman, L.S. (1987). Knowledge and teaching foundations of the new reform. *Harvard Education Review, 57*(1), 1–22.

Téllez, K., & Waxman, H.C. (2006). A meta-synthesis of qualitative research on effective teaching practices for English language learners. In J.M. Morris & L. Ortega (Eds.), *Synthesizing research on language learning and teaching* (pp. 245–277). Amsterdam: Johns Benjamin.

Verplaetse, L.S., & Migliacci, N. (Eds.). (2008). *Inclusive pedagogy for English language learners: A handbook of research-informed practices*. New York, NY: Lawrence Erlbaum.

Villegas, A.M., & Lucas, T. (2002). *Educating culturally responsive teachers: A coherent approach*. Albany, NY: SUNY Press.

Villegas, A.M., Clewell, B., Anderson, M., Goertz, M., Joy, F., Bruschi, B., & Irvine, J. (1995). *Teaching for diversity: Models for expanding the supply of minority teachers*. Princeton, NJ: Educational Testing Service.

Wilson, S.M., Floden, R.E., & Ferrini-Mundy, J. (2002). Teacher preparation research: An insider's view from the outside. *Journal of Teacher Education, 53*(3), 190–204.

Zeichner, K. (1993). Traditions of practice in North American teacher education. *Teaching and Teacher Education, 9*(1), 1–13.

Zeichner, K.M. (2003). The adequacies and inadequacies of three current strategies to recruit, prepare, and retain the best teachers for all students. *Teachers College Record, 105*(3), 490–519.

Zeichner, K.M. (2005). A research agenda for teacher education. In M. Cochran-Smith & K.M. Zeichner (Eds.), *Studying teacher education: Report of the AERA panel on research and teacher education* (pp. 737–759). Mahwah, NJ: Lawrence Erlbaum.

Zeichner, K.M., & Conklin, H.G. (2005). Teacher education programs. In M. Cochran-Smith & K.M. Zeichner (Eds.), *Studying teacher education: Report of the AERA panel on research and teacher education* (pp. 645–735). Mahwah, NJ: Lawrence Erlbaum.

Zeichner, K., & Hoeft, K. (1996). Teacher socialization for cultural diversity. In J. Sikula, T. Buttery, & E. Guyton (Eds.), *Handbook of research on teacher education* (2nd ed., pp. 525–547). New York, NY: Macmillan.

Chapter 13

Toward the Transformation of Teacher Education to Prepare All Teachers for Linguistically Diverse Classrooms

Tamara Lucas

There is no doubt that young people learning English as a second (or third) language constitute a growing proportion of the K-12 student population in the United States. If they are to have access to a quality education—fulfilling the laudable promise of public education in the U.S.— teachers must be prepared to teach English language learners (ELLs) just as they are prepared to teach other students. The authors in this book have argued for the transformation of teacher education and professional development to ensure that all teachers develop expertise for teaching ELLs. Using multiple lenses, they have examined different facets of the changes needed, highlighting the complexity of the undertaking and, at the same time, offering inspiration to others engaged in the process. They have examined the demographic and policy contexts for preparing teachers of ELLs; articulated principles and conceptual frameworks that can inform the content and processes of teacher preparation; explored teachers' perceptions of what is involved in teaching ELLs; and presented examples of innovative approaches for developing the needed expertise.

Some salient themes cut across multiple chapters. Each of these themes suggests actions that could or should be taken by teacher educators. One theme is that demographic changes, federal and state education policies, and prevailing political views in recent years have led to an unmistakable trend toward greater inclusion of ELLs in mainstream classrooms. As discussed in most of the chapters in the book, inclusion is, in fact, the powerful engine driving the urgency for all teachers to develop the orientations, knowledge, and skills of linguistically responsive teachers. As with so many other educational trends that take on a life of their own, the wisdom of this one—that is, the wholesale inclusion of ELLs in mainstream classes—is questionable. Thoughtful and reasoned analysis is needed to develop meaningful criteria for determining which ELL students will benefit from inclusion and which should not yet be placed in mainstream classes. Educators in K-12 schools and higher education institutions should engage in such analysis. In the meantime, increasing numbers of classroom teachers will be expected to educate ELLs, and teacher educators must take responsibility for preparing them to do so.

Another pervasive theme is that to teach ELLs well, teachers must have special expertise that goes beyond good teaching of students for whom English is the home language—expertise that, with a few exceptions, has not been included in the preparation of mainstream teachers. This theme is threaded throughout the book, but is especially salient in the sections on Conceptual and Contextual Foundations, and Curriculum Content. The introductory chapter (Lucas, Chapter 1) makes the case that special expertise is essential for teaching ELLs because of the inextricable connections among language, learning, and schooling. The nature of the growing immigrant and ELL population, the challenge of identifying ELLs in schools, the relatively low academic achievement levels of these students (Valdés & Castellón, Chapter 2), and, as discussed above, the increasing inclusion of ELLs in mainstream classes as a result of education policy and the national political climate (Villegas & Lucas, Chapter 3) also support the need for special expertise for teaching ELLs. Frameworks that summarize the essential knowledge, skills, and orientations (or dispositions) constituting such expertise are presented in Chapters 4 and 5 (Lucas & Villegas; de Jong & Harper). One particular type of linguistic knowledge needed by teachers of ELLs is examined in depth in Chapters 6 and 7 (Gebhard and her colleagues; Brisk & Zisselsberger).

A related theme is that the preparation of teachers for ELLs must address the complexities of the process, going beyond the superficial and oversimplified approaches now common. This point is most explicitly made by de Jong and Harper (Chapter 5), who report on mainstream teachers' perceptions that the expertise for teaching ELLs consists almost exclusively of cultural awareness and specific instructional strategies for increasing the comprehensibility of content. They make a forceful argument that teacher educators must engage teachers in examining the underlying reasons for making instructional modifications, in exploring the factors to consider in making instructional decisions for ELLs, and in developing skills for analyzing language. Other chapters also highlight the necessity to prepare teachers in more specialized and sophisticated ways for teaching ELLs. Chapters 6 and 7 (Gebhard et al.; Brisk & Zisselsberger) show how two institutions are helping teachers develop linguistic understandings and skills for promoting students' academic language abilities. Chapter 8 (Walker & Stone) highlights efforts at one institution to help teachers understand the content-specific nature of academic English and develop skills for integrating content and language learning. Chapter 11 (Gort, Glenn, & Settlage) shows how English and Science methods instructors revised their courses to engage students in more sophisticated learning about fostering ELLs' access to these two content areas after they had participated in a professional learning community focused on the education of ELLs.

The fourth theme, explicitly discussed by Gort, Glenn, and Settlage (Chapter 11) and Walqui (Chapter 10) and implied by all the chapters in the book, is that one of the priorities for transforming the preparation of teachers for teaching ELLs must be to support teacher educators in building their own knowledge of linguistically responsive teaching. Aware of the growing number of ELLs in mainstream classes, teacher educators increasingly recognize they need opportunities to develop their own expertise so they can better prepare teachers for linguistic diversity. Those working within each context must decide what approach to faculty development is most practical and promising—for example, engaging teacher educators in ongoing professional learning communities led by colleagues with the relevant knowledge and expertise (Gort et al.), offering professional development opportunities led by colleagues or by experts from outside the local setting (Walqui), systematically preparing local educators to become leaders in the professional development of their colleagues (Walqui), or encouraging faculty with expertise to team-teach with or to coach colleagues. Another strategy for higher education institutions is to hire new faculty members with expertise in ELL education for positions in mainstream teacher education programs, where they can bring their knowledge to curriculum redesign as well as to their own courses and their work with colleagues (Sakash & Rodriguez-Brown, Chapter 9). Whatever approach is taken, K-12 teachers cannot be well prepared to teach ELLs in their classes if their own teachers (that is, teacher educators) do not possess the knowledge, skills, and commitment for preparing them.

Another salient theme is that collaboration across multiple institutional and professional boundaries is essential for transforming the preparation of teachers for teaching ELLs. Responsibility and expertise for preparing teachers is shared by many individuals and entities, including faculty in different academic departments in higher education institutions, faculty and administrators in K-12 schools, and individuals and organizations leading professional development efforts. While collaboration among these groups is part of any well-designed teacher preparation program, it is especially important in preparing teachers of ELLs. Because the education of ELLs has been perceived as something special, not part of the routine responsibilities of mainstream teachers, the preparation of teachers for teaching ELLs has been seen as the responsibility of specialist ESL or bilingual teacher educators, not those in mainstream programs. Several chapters in the sections on Program Design and Coherence illustrate ways collaboration enhances the resources and potential within particular contexts to foster the orientations, knowledge, and skills for teaching ELLs. These chapters show the benefits and promise of collaborations involving higher education faculty in different departments and different roles (Gort, Glenn, & Settlage, Chapter 11; Sakash & Rodriguez-Brown, Chapter 9); higher education and K-12 faculty (Athanases & de Oliveira, Chapter 12); pre-service teachers in mainstream and bilingual or ESL programs (Sakash & Rodriguez-Brown); mainstream and bilingual or ESL practicing teachers (Sakash & Rodriguez-Brown; Walker & Stone, Chapter 8); external professional development providers and school- or district-based staff preparing to become leaders of professional development

(Walqui, Chapter 10); and even pre-service teachers and higher education faculty members (Gort, Glenn, & Settlage).

The sixth common theme—highlighted in several chapters in Part II of the book—is that the preparation of teachers of ELLs must be closely tied to the realities of schools and classrooms. Presentations of abstract, decontextualized content and skills are unlikely to lead to meaningful learning for teachers, who need opportunities to connect what they are learning about teaching to its application in the classroom. Again, while this is an essential element of all well-designed teacher preparation programs, it is especially important for teachers of ELLs because many future teachers have had no substantial contact with ELLs before completing their teacher preparation programs, and many practicing teachers have had minimal opportunity to learn about ways to support ELLs' learning. Because of this lack of prior experience, teachers are especially unprepared to envision ways to apply what they learn about teaching ELLs. Several chapters in this book illustrate ways teacher educators can situate teacher learning within the authentic work of teachers—for example, arranging for pre-service teachers to tutor ELLs in the schools (Walker & Stone, Chapter 8); having in-service teachers bring their own students' work to courses and seminars for discussion (Gebhard et al., Chapter 6; Sakash & Rodriguez-Brown, Chapter 9); engaging teachers in inquiry projects in their own schools (Brisk & Zisselsberger, Chapter 7; Gebhard et al.; Sakash & Rodriguez-Brown); planning professional development that relates directly to required curriculum and textbooks (Brisk & Zisselsberger; Gebhard et al.); working directly with teachers in the classroom as mentors and coaches (Brisk & Zisselsberger; Walqui, Chapter 10); and engaging district instructional support staff and school leadership as well as teachers in coherent professional development related to the education of ELLs (Walqui).

The final cross-cutting theme is that there is no one "best practice" or approach for preparing teachers to teach ELLs. The chapters in Part II describe a variety of efforts to prepare both in-service and pre-service teachers, as well as teacher educators and school district instructional support staff. In each context, decisions were made about the most appropriate and practical approach for the particular place and time, taking into account factors such as the immediate needs of future and practicing teachers and teacher educators; human resources (including the knowledge, skills, and priorities of teacher educators vis-à-vis ELL education); other resources (including financial ones); and the nature and size of the teacher population and the ELL population in the K-12 schools. Based on these factors, some initiatives are more fully developed and far-reaching than others. All of them, however, have laid a foundation for continued progress toward ensuring that teachers of ELLs in local schools develop expertise for teaching them well.

Recommendations for practice are implied in the themes discussed above. Drawing on and extending the lessons learned from the individual chapters, I offer some additional recommendations for both practice and research. First, to successfully infuse attention to teaching ELLs into a teacher education program, teacher educators should take the time to step back from the immediate need to which they may be responding and consider how best to build a coherent program, taking into account the community and professional context, program vision and guiding principles, curriculum content, and program processes and structures (see Lucas, Chapter 1; Athaneses & de Oliveira, Chapter 12). While this can slow down progress at first, the ultimate outcome is likely to be more successful in terms of support for the program, program longevity, and the quality of teacher and student learning. A second, and related, recommendation is that pre-service and in-service teacher preparation efforts should be conceived as part of one continuum of teacher development rather than as separate endeavors. Thoughtful planning regarding the appropriate content and processes for pre-service preparation, induction, and professional development will foster coherence within and across teacher preparation initiatives and provide much-needed guidance for everyone involved in teacher preparation about how to organize and focus teacher learning at different stages in teachers' careers (see Villegas & Lucas, Chapter 3).

Recommendations for research are relatively obvious: we need more research on almost every aspect of the preparation of mainstream teachers for teaching ELLs. The only area for which a substantial body of work already exists is the content of the curriculum—that is, the knowledge, skills, and dispositions needed by teachers of ELLs. We need systematic study of what is now being done to prepare classroom teachers to teach ELLs. Nationally, how many institutions of higher education, school districts, private organizations, and other entities are taking steps to prepare pre-service and in-service teachers for ELLs? What are the characteristics of such efforts—curriculum content, program design, coherence, staffing? How do these characteristics and strategies vary by institutional context? What are the characteristics of teacher educators in these programs? Beyond descriptive studies, we need to understand the implications and impacts of the various efforts to prepare classroom teachers to teach ELLs. What are pre-service and practicing teachers learning from these initiatives? Is there evidence that they are successfully educating ELLs? What are the connections among the characteristics of teacher educators, what they teach, how they teach, and how successful they are? Research in all these areas would make major contributions by informing the work of those already struggling to find ways to prepare all classroom teachers to teach ELLs well and those who will do so in the future.

The authors in this book are teacher educators; we have, in a way, written this book for ourselves. We intend it as a resource for teacher educators like us who are working within their own contexts as well as at state and national levels to improve the preparation of mainstream teachers for teaching ELLs. It is with these unknown colleagues in mind that we have included details about the design and implementation of the initiatives described so others can use our experiences in their own work. We hope the book contributes to the professional conversation about why all teachers—not just specialists in English as a Second Language and bilingual education—need to develop particular types of expertise to teach ELLs, what that expertise entails, and how to foster its development in future and practicing teachers.

The challenges involved in transforming teacher education in the ways suggested in this book should not be minimized or underestimated. The task is complex, requiring work and commitment by many people over a number of years. No one person within a particular context or setting can be responsible for the entire project. Individuals must identify the particular efforts to which they will give their attention, along with like-minded colleagues, at the same time being mindful of other facets of the project to transform teacher preparation. As the chapters in this book have shown, there are many opportunities for action—to influence policy at national, state, and local levels; to reorganize the teacher education curriculum in one institution or one state; to create in-service and pre-service programs separate from the regular curriculum, perhaps through grants; to work with a small group of pre-service or in-service teachers in developing the orientations, knowledge, and skills for teaching ELLs; and to advocate for ELLs in communities and beyond. I hope this book offers some cogent ideas and inspiration for those seeking to ensure that sometime in the future it will be reasonable to assume that all classroom teachers have had the opportunity to develop the expertise for teaching English language learners.

About the Authors

Steven Z. Athanases, Professor of Education at the University of California, Davis, conducts research and teaches about diversity and equity in English teaching and in teacher education and development. He received the 2006 Association of Teacher Educators Distinguished Research Award. His recent research examines the potential of pre-service teacher inquiry to develop teachers' ability to meet the needs of culturally and linguistically diverse youth in high-need urban and rural schools.

María Estela Brisk is a Professor of Education and chair of the Teacher Education, Special Education and Curriculum and Instruction Department at the Lynch School of Education, Boston College. Her research and teacher preparation interests include bilingual education, bilingual language and literacy acquisition, methods of teaching literacy, preparation of mainstream teachers to work with bilingual learners, and teaching writing. Dr. Brisk is the author of several books.

Juan Pablo Jiménez Caicedo is a doctoral candidate in Language, Literacy & Culture in the School of Education at the University of Massachusetts, Amherst. His research interests include second language acquisition and the academic literacy development of English language learners in K-12 contexts, socio-cultural theories of learning, Systemic Functional Linguistics, and the professional development of language educators.

Martha Castellón is a doctoral candidate in Educational Linguistics at Stanford University. She has been an elementary classroom teacher, research associate, and co-creator of professional development materials for teachers and administrators who work with English learners. Her dissertation research examines the "metaphorical distances" that secondary English learners must travel in order to succeed in mainstream classrooms.

Ester J. de Jong is an Associate Professor in ESL/Bilingual Education at the University of Florida. A native of the Netherlands, she was Assistant Director for Bilingual Education for the Framingham Public Schools in Massachusetts, working closely with teachers in two-way immersion, general bilingual education, and English as a Second Language programs. Her work has focused on teacher preparation for linguistic diversity, additive bilingual programs for all children, and language policy and its impact on teachers and teacher practice.

Luciana C. de Oliveira is Assistant Professor of Literacy & Language Education at Purdue University. Her research focuses on issues related to teaching English language learners (ELLs) at the K-12 level, including the role of language in learning the content areas and teacher preparation for ELLs. She has held several leadership positions in TESOL and California TESOL (CATESOL) and was the President of Indiana TESOL (INTESOL) in 2009. Her recent research focuses on a knowledge base for teaching ELLs at the elementary level.

Meg Gebhard is an Associate Professor in the School of Education at the University of Massachusetts, Amherst, where she is the Chair of the Language, Literacy, and Culture Concentration. Her publications focus on understanding L2 academic literacies, teachers' professional development, and the discourses of educational reform in the United States. She serves on the editorial board for *TESOL Quarterly* and *Language Arts*.

Wendy J. Glenn is an Associate Professor in English Education at the University of Connecticut. She received the 2009 University Teaching Fellow award and was named a Fulbright Scholar to Norway in 2009–2010. As a scholar, Wendy explores questions related to young adult literature, writing, and culturally responsive pedagogies.

Mileidis Gort, Assistant Professor of Literacy and Bilingual Education at the University of Miami, conducts research on the early bilingual and biliteracy development of English- and Spanish-speakers in dual language programs, educational policies affecting bilingual learners, and faculty-initiated curricular reform efforts toward culturally and linguistically responsive teacher education. From 2007 to 2009, Dr. Gort served as co-editor for the *Journal of Literacy Research*.

Candace A. Harper, Associate Professor in ESL/Bilingual Education at the University of Florida, has been an ESL/EFL teacher and teacher educator in the U.S., Australia, Bosnia, and France. Her research examines the nature and development of ESL teacher expertise, the preparation of general educators to work effectively with ELLs, and the school-based collaboration of ESL specialists, reading teachers, and other educators working toward ELLs' language and content learning goals.

Tamara Lucas, Editor, is a Professor of Educational Foundations and Associate Dean in the College of Education and Human Services at Montclair State University. Her research explores the education of culturally and linguistically diverse students and the preparation of their teachers. Earlier in her career, she taught ESL, directed a federally funded resource center for bilingual education in California, and conducted research on urban teacher education programs, bilingual teacher leadership development, and secondary schooling for linguistic minority students.

Amy Piedra is a fourth-grade teacher employed by Springfield Public Schools in Springfield, Massachusetts. She has taught English language learners in urban elementary schools for over 10 years. She earned a Master's degree in Education through the ACCELA Alliance at the University of Massachusetts, Amherst. She is interested in Puerto Rican children's literature and teaching writing.

Flora Rodriguez-Brown is a Professor in Curriculum and Instruction, and in the Literacy, Language and Culture Program at the University of Illinois at Chicago, where she has coordinated the programs to prepare teachers of second language learners since 1982. Her research interests are in literacy and second language learning, learning at home, socio-cultural issues in literacy learning, and the home–school connection.

Karen Sakash is a Clinical Professor Emerita in the College of Education at the University of Illinois at Chicago, where she coordinated the graduate elementary education program from 2002 to 2008 and was a bilingual teacher educator in the Department of Curriculum and Instruction from 1991 to 2008. She currently directs a Title III National Professional Development Program grant focused on preparing secondary teachers of ELLs.

John Settlage is an Associate Professor at the University of Connecticut with previous stints at the University of Utah and Cleveland State University. His research focuses on issues of access related to science learning and these efforts inform his courses in science education at the undergraduate and graduate levels. He co-authored a book (with Sherry Southerland) entitled *Teaching Science to Every Child: Using Culture as a Starting Point*, published by Routledge.

Karla Stone is a Title III Professional Development Specialist with the Robbinsdale Area School District in Minnesota. She works closely with practicing teachers, helping them identify the academic language needs of English language learners across the content areas. She is also an adjunct instructor in and coordinator of the University of Minnesota's DirecTrack to Teaching program. Her dissertation explored the sense-making processes of high school English language learners with statewide accountability testing in Minnesota.

Guadalupe Valdés is the Bonnie Katz Tenenbaum Professor of Education at Stanford University. She specializes in language pedagogy and applied linguistics. Much of her work has focused on the English–Spanish bilingualism of Latinos in the United States and on discovering and describing how two languages are developed, used, and maintained by individuals who become bilingual in immigrant communities.

Ana María Villegas is Professor in the Curriculum and Teaching Department at Montclair State University. Previously, she was Senior Research Scientist in the Education Policy Research Division at the Educational Testing Service. She received the Margaret B. Lindsay Award for Distinguished Research in Teacher Education from the American Association of Colleges for Teacher Education in 2004. Her research and publications focus on culturally responsive teaching and teacher education, and increasing the diversity of the teaching force.

Constance L. Walker is a faculty member in Second Languages and Cultures Education at the University of Minnesota, where she is involved in the preparation of teachers for second language contexts. Her research examines the experiences of teachers who work with culturally and linguistically diverse populations, and school policy and practice related to second language learners. Walker is directing the TEAM UP Project, a Title III teacher development project focusing on collaborative processes for serving students learning English as a second language.

Aída Walqui directs the Teacher Professional Development Program at WestEd, which consists of the Quality Teaching for English Learners (QTEL) and the Strategic Literacy Initiative. Under her leadership, QTEL, funded by IES, has designed and implemented tools and processes to promote the academic success of English learners and their teachers. Walqui's primary area of interest and research is teacher expertise in multilingual contexts and how to promote its growth across the continuum of teacher professional development.

Jerri Willett is Professor in Language, Literacy and Culture and Chair of the Teacher Education and Curriculum Studies Department at the University of Massachusetts. She has taught English literature, drama, and ESL at all levels—from preschool children to adults—in the U.S., Hong Kong, Britain, Mexico, and Colombia. Her interests are in practices and policies that support the academic language development of English language learners, and the development of teachers' understanding of language from critical and system-functional perspectives.

Margarita Zisselsberger is a doctoral candidate at the Lynch School of Education at Boston College. Her research interests include the interrelationship of language and learning, and more specifically the writing development of culturally and linguistically diverse (CLD) learners. Her current research examines how classroom contexts play a critical role for CLD students' writing development.

Index

Abedi, J. 27–8, 195
academic achievement 20, 27–8, 39, 127, 136, 217; gap 20, 27–30, 128, 183
academic content learning 3, 28, 39, 55, 61–2, 65–7, 75, 88, 129, 131, 166, 203
academic language 86, 93–4, 112, 131, 195, 208, 217; proficiency 45, 57, 63, 76
academic literacy 92–3, 107
academic performance 20, 27, 29, 84, 115, 117, 175; gap 20, 27–30, 128, 183, 188
academic writing 61, 93–4, 96–9, 101–2, 105–6, 111–12, 114–21, 124, 133, 153, 163
ACCELA Alliance 91–8, 101–2, 107–9
accreditation requirements 41–8, 49n1
action plans 137–8
action research 68, 87, 92, 129, 146, 191, 198, 207–8
advising 64, 145–6, 149, 156, 172
advocacy 7, 9, 11, 30–1, 47, 57, 60, 65, 84, 86–7, 147, 190, 197–8, 201–11, 221
American Association of Colleges for Teacher Education 21, 45
Antunez, B. 73, 143
apprenticeship 160–3, 167–8, 170, 172, 174, 207
Asian population 31, 32n5, 200
Asian students 26–8
at-risk students 30
Athanases, S.Z. 7–9, 11–12, 60, 178, 195, 197, 201, 204–5, 207, 209, 218
August, D. 6, 28, 91, 195–6
Austin, T. 10, 92, 109, 175

Bakhtin, M. 98
Bartolomé, L. 7, 59, 86
Bernhardt, E.B. 73, 111
bilingual education 38, 67, 77, 111, 130, 145–6, 156–7, 180, 186, 221; faculty 156, 180–1
Bilingual Education Act 38–9
bilingual learners 88, 111–12, 115, 123, 178, 180–1, 190
bilingual teacher(s) 73, 88, 143–5, 147–50, 153, 156–7, 180, 209; education programs 130, 144–5, 147, 149–50, 155
bilingualism 38, 45, 64, 73, 75, 146
Birman, B.F. 129
Bode, P. 94, 108
Brisk, M. 3, 5–8, 10, 45, 61–2, 74, 76, 87, 108, 178, 181, 196, 217, 219
Butt, D. 113–14, 123

Capps, R. 22, 27, 36–7
case study 91–2, 94–7, 108, 130, 132–5, 195, 198, 206, 208, 210
certification see teacher certification
children's literature 101–2, 107–8, 114, 130, 184–5, 187
Christian, D. 58, 186, 196
Christie, F. 93, 114
Clewell, B.C. 24, 149
Cochran-Smith, M. 56, 73, 129, 179, 190, 197
cohorts 78, 107, 128, 130, 132–3, 135, 137, 149, 199, 208, 210
collaboration 9–10, 64, 68, 92, 96, 109, 114, 118, 128–9, 135–40, 143–5, 147–53, 155–7, 160, 163, 169, 173, 175, 179, 183, 186–8, 190–1, 197, 201–2, 208–9, 211, 218
Commins, N. 178, 181
comprehensible input 19, 57, 63, 65, 75, 76–80, 82–3, 84, 86
conceptual framework 8, 11–12, 56, 65,

67–8, 101, 123, 130, 160–1, 197–9,
    201–4, 210–11, 216
Conklin, H.G. 196–8
Consentino de Cohen, C. 24
content area teachers 45, 91, 117, 124,
    130–1, 135, 182, 184
content-based language instruction 74,
    91, 93, 96, 131, 133
context 5, 7–8, 12, 20, 35, 47, 58–9, 65, 74,
    76–7, 80–3, 85, 87, 95, 101, 112–13, 115,
    118, 125, 135, 139, 144, 153, 156, 161,
    168, 170–1, 179–80, 186–7, 195, 198–9,
    201–2, 206–7, 211, 217–21; classroom
    10, 20, 55, 67, 79, 84, 97, 111, 138;
    cultural 123; education 174; policy 36,
    48, 216; political 13, 35, 37, 47;
    situational 112, 135; social 93–4, 106,
    164, 203; sociocultural 173;
    sociopolitical 7, 59, 86, 211; teaching 42,
    129, 131, 137, 140, 165–6, 169, 197, 200,
    203
conversation 63, 163, 170, 187;
    instructional 42, 64; professional 138,
    143–4, 147, 176, 182, 183, 190, 197, 221
conversational language proficiency 57, 63
Cope, B. 93, 114
courses 62, 68, 130, 132–3, 145–6, 148–9,
    153, 180, 183–5, 188, 190–1, 196–7, 199,
    200–3, 207, 218–19; ACCELA 92, 96, 98,
    101–2; adding 8–9, 11; focus 140, 155–6;
    graduate 137; language-oriented 128,
    143, 204–5; modifying 8–9, 157;
    required 45–7, 59, 77, 131, 144, 152;
    revision 179, 181–2, 189–90, 217
Crawford, J. 37–9, 47, 59
critical literacy 108
Crowell, C.G. 144
culturally and linguistically responsive
    teacher education 179, 183, 190
culturally diverse learners 81, 127, 183,
    190, 197, 206
culturally responsive pedagogy 179, 180,
    190
culturally responsive teaching 4, 13, 56,
    68, 73, 86, 178, 179, 197
Cummins, J. 40, 61–4, 73, 86
curriculum 41, 60, 75–7, 86–8, 91, 97,
    106–8, 124, 131, 136–7, 148, 153,
    178–9, 181, 184, 197, 203, 219–20;
    access 29, 31, 39, 47, 74; content 4,
    6–10, 12–13, 39–40, 47, 138, 217, 220;
    design 42, 147, 149, 218; differentiated

155; framework 11, 92, 96; planning
    137; revision 67–8, 92, 178, 190

Darling-Hammond, L. 9–11, 29, 36–7,
    41, 48, 109, 128–9, 140, 165, 196–8,
    201
de Jong, E. 4, 6–7, 40, 46, 74–5, 85–7,
    111, 139, 178, 196, 217
de Oliveira, L.C. 7–9, 11–12, 60, 178, 195,
    201, 204, 209, 218, 220
demographic(s) 4, 20, 29, 47, 73, 131,
    136, 175, 203, 216; changing 22, 28, 74,
    88, 91, 95, 127; context 13, 35;
    landscape 36–7; trend 3
Derewianka, B. 94
Desimone, L. 129
Dewsbury, A. 114
Driscoll, A. 40, 73, 195
DuFour, R. 129, 136
Dyson, A. 94

Eaker, R. 129
Echevarria, J. 8, 65–6, 129, 181
Edstam, T. 138
educational equity 7, 40, 60, 75, 197, 202,
    204–9
English Language learners 3–8, 13,
    18–20, 22, 24–31, 35–43, 48, 55, 57–67,
    73–7, 85–7, 91–7, 103, 106–8, 111–12,
    114, 124–5, 127–40, 143–9, 160,
    178–82, 200, 216–17; identification
    24–5, 76; teacher education 4, 11–12,
    56, 151–7, 160–4, 167–72, 175, 195,
    198–9, 202; teaching 9–10, 35, 44–7,
    49, 68–9, 78–80, 82–4, 88, 139–40, 146,
    148, 150, 152, 156, 162, 169, 173–4,
    178, 183–91, 195–6, 198, 201–11, 216,
    218–21
English only movement 37, 91–2, 96, 108,
    206, 209
equity, educational see educational equity
ESL 40, 45, 55, 62, 67, 73, 75–9, 81, 92,
    105, 115, 128, 148, 152–3, 166, 205–6;
    certification 77, 144–6, 152, 157n1;
    program 39, 87, 147, 157; teacher 6,
    10, 59, 61, 74, 84–6, 88, 96, 130, 134,
    136–8, 143–6, 149–51, 155–6, 204,
    218
external funding see grant funding
faculty 9–12, 178–9; development 147,
    183, 190, 210, 218; learning
    community 180, 185, 188–91

family 3, 18–19, 25, 31, 57–9, 61–2, 64,
84, 102, 105–7, 120, 137, 147, 155; and
community 79, 81, 199, 209–10;
literacy 146
Feiman-Nemser, S. 49
Ferrini-Mundy, J. 197
fieldwork 8–9, 11, 196, 199, 201, 205, 207;
experience 42, 45, 68, 77, 143, 147, 155,
211
Fishman, B.J. 139
Fix, M. 27, 36–7, 128
Floden, R.E. 197
fluency 26, 38, 57, 63, 85, 164
foreign born 20–2, 29, 127
Fortune, T.W. 9, 133
Freire, P. 179, 191
Fry, R. 24, 27
funds of knowledge 76, 184–5, 188

Gallagher, L.P. 139
Gándara, P. 40, 73, 195–6, 211
Garcia, E.E. 197
Garet, M.S. 129, 139
Gass, S.M. 63
Gay, G. 7, 56, 73, 86
Gebhard, M. 5, 7, 10–11, 61–2, 87, 92, 96,
107–9, 123, 217, 219
Gee, J. 94
Genesee, F. 186
genre 93–4, 96–7, 101–2, 106–8, 112–19,
123–4
genre-based pedagogy 93–4, 97, 101,
106–7, 114, 168, 202, 208, 211
Gersten, R. 85
Gibbons, P. 8, 61, 63, 65–7, 76, 87, 108,
129
Gollnick, D. 49
González, J.M. 9–10, 62, 76, 140
Goodlad, J.I. 196, 208
Goodwin, A.L. 178, 195
grant funding 137, 155–6
Griego-Jones, T. 143
Grossman, P. 11, 196–7, 203, 211
Guzman, M.T. 195

Hadaway, N. 9, 181
Hakuta, K. 6, 28, 195–6
Halliday, M.A.K. 5, 91, 93, 112–14
Hammerness, K. 11–12, 36, 196
Harman, R. 107, 123
Harper, C. 4, 6–7, 40–1, 46, 74–5, 85–7,
111, 139, 178, 196, 217

Hasan, R. 114
high stakes testing 91–2, 108
Highly Qualified Teachers 40, 42–3
Hillocks Jr., G. 114
Hispanic/Latino population 20–3, 146,
155, 185
Hispanic/Latino students 24, 26–7,
29–30, 95, 150, 153–4
Hmong population 18, 26, 31, 127, 133,
200
Hoeft, K. 197
Hollins, E.R. 195
Hornberger, N. 35–40
Howey, K.R. 197, 201, 211
Hyland, K. 94

Iams, M. 59, 86, 128
immigrant 21–2, 36–8, 55, 95, 127–8,
130, 144, 173, 180, 217; origin 29–31,
173; population 28, 217; students 24,
39, 112, 144
Improving America's Schools Act, 1994
39, 129, 136
inclusion (of English language learners)
7, 35, 38–41, 47–8, 74–5, 138, 216–17
inequity 30, 39, 59, 203
infusion 68, 87, 185–6, 188–9, 199, 201,
205
institutionalization 149
instruction 4, 6, 10–11, 13n1, 19, 41,
45–7, 58, 62, 67, 73–5, 88, 91–3, 96, 99,
101, 107–8, 111, 114–15, 118–21,
124–5, 132, 137, 144–5, 147, 152,
157n1, 163, 166, 179, 181, 197, 203
instructional approach 8, 39–40, 55–6,
59, 82
instructional changes 84–6, 138
instructional expertise 8, 76, 146, 148,
160–1, 164, 167, 173, 205, 219
instructional gap 143, 148
instructional needs 136, 150, 186, 195
instructional practice 60, 97, 107, 116,
120, 131, 139, 153, 209
instructional repertoire 3, 163, 203
instructional scaffolding 8, 57, 63, 65–6,
171, 187
instructional strategies 40, 78–9, 85, 123,
131, 184–5, 204, 206, 217
interaction 80, 83, 135, 151, 164, 166,
169, 184; classroom 8, 63–4, 99, 102–3;
social 5, 57–8, 151, 162; student 31, 61,

86, 153, 208; teacher 30, 93, 98, 137, 150, 157, 165, 170, 173–4

K-12 schools 12, 30, 36, 73, 87, 91, 93, 96, 115, 118, 127–8, 145, 147, 149–50, 153–4, 157, 197, 199, 200–2, 205, 208–9, 211, 216, 218–19
Kalantzis, M. 93, 114
Kamberelis, G. 102
KewalRamani, A. 24, 26, 28
Knapp, P. 94
Knight, S.L. 139
Krashen, S. 63, 65, 88

Ladson-Billings, G. 7, 56, 179, 183, 196–7
Lange, D. 140
language and identity 56–9, 86, 93–4, 101, 185
language and schooling 4–5, 10, 12, 35, 61, 65, 74, 76–7, 125, 133, 173, 183, 202, 217
language arts 124, 186, 205; curriculum 107, 124; English 77, 85, 92, 96–7, 124, 130, 204
language background 26, 57–8, 61–2, 65, 76, 79, 84–6, 132–4
language demands of classroom tasks 57, 62, 76, 80–1, 83, 87, 112, 115, 140, 206
language development 78, 82–3, 86, 93, 101, 131, 187, 204–5, 207; English 39, 60, 62, 84; second 73, 80, 85, 87, 201
language immersion experience 185–8, 190–1
language oral 61–2, 64, 66, 67, 75, 82, 85, 94, 97, 99–100, 102, 106, 108 113, 121, 205, 207
language oriented coursework 7, 199, 201, 204–5
language proficiency 6, 13n1, 25–8, 31, 38–40, 45, 48, 55, 57, 60–4, 73, 76–9, 80–3, 96, 120, 131, 146, 148, 150, 181, 195, 202, 206
language sociopolitical dimension 7, 57, 59–60, 86, 211
Latino students see Hispanic/Latino students
learning process 6–7, 29, 62, 64, 128, 184, 188, 192, 205, 211
Lemke, J. 93
licensure 45, 139; programs 130–1; requirements 9, 11, 35, 39–41, 45–8, 49n1, 76–7, 146, 150–1

Lieberman, A. 124
limited English proficient/proficiency 13, 21, 24–7, 32n.3, 37, 39, 111, 115, 127
linguistic accuracy 59, 75, 112, 123, 164
linguistic diversity 3, 6, 44–6, 48, 87–8, 178, 181, 183–5, 187, 191, 196, 202–3, 205–6, 218; value for 7, 57, 59–60, 65
linguistic isolation 21, 24, 32n1, 32n2, 144
linguistically responsive teachers/ teaching 48, 55–7, 59–65, 67–9, 178–80, 183, 190, 216, 218
literacy 31, 45–6, 58, 60–1, 64, 75–7, 79–80, 83–4, 87, 91, 107–8, 111, 117, 123, 125, 137, 156, 209; coach 115
Lucas, T. 3–4, 6–8, 11, 40, 48, 55–6, 59–62, 65, 67–8, 74, 130, 187–8, 195–7, 210–11, 217, 220

McDonald, M. 11, 196–7, 207, 211
McTighe, J. 101
mainstream teachers 48, 74, 76–7, 85–6, 115, 136–7, 143–4, 148, 150, 152, 155–7, 218; candidates 9, 11–12, 41–3, 45–6, 59, 62, 68, 77–9, 82, 84, 87, 143–7, 149–51, 155, 157; preparation 6, 36, 46, 88, 149, 178, 217, 220
Martin, J. 93, 114, 120–1, 123
Martin, K.J. 197, 201, 204–5, 207
Maxwell-Jolly, J. 40, 73, 195
Mellgren, M. 140
Menken, K. 73, 143
Merino, B.J. 195–6, 200, 207–8, 211
metalanguage 62, 114, 144, 181
migrant 19, 200, 206
Migration Policy 20–1
Miramontes, O. 178, 181
multicultural education 59, 86, 108, 143, 180; teacher courses 59, 143, 146
multiculturalism 43, 146
multicultural literature 97, 101, 107, 108, 109
Murray, J. 27

narrative 93–7, 98–102, 105–8, 113–14, 118–21, 122, 179, 182–3, 201, 204
National Assessment of Educational Progress 27–8, 32n4
National Center for Education Statistics 55, 196
National Clearinghouse for English Language Acquisition 25–6, 111, 127

National Council for the Accreditation of Teacher Education 41–4, 46, 48, 49n1
New London Group 93
Nieto, S. 10, 58–60, 73, 76, 92, 94, 108–9, 203
No Child Left Behind Act of 2001 25, 38–9, 47, 74, 91–2, 111

partnership university-school/district 91–2, 108n1, 114, 146, 151
Passel, J.S. 27
Penfield, J. 3, 143
Penuel, W.R. 139
Pew Hispanic Center 22
policies, teacher education 4, 30, 35–7, 41–2, 45–9, 76–7, 91–2, 147, 152, 216
political context 7, 13, 29, 35–8, 43, 47, 59, 92–4, 202, 211, 216–17
Porter, A.C. 129
practitioner research see teacher research
practitioners 43, 161, 166, 172, 199, 201–2; community of 207–11
praxis 179, 191
professional associations 44–6, 48
professional development 8–11, 45–6, 49, 68, 73, 76–7, 91–2, 108–9, 112, 115–18, 123, 128–9, 136–40, 149, 152–3, 160–75, 178–9, 183–4, 190–1, 197, 211, 216, 218–20
program coherence 6, 11–13, 36, 48, 125, 175–6, 195–8, 210
program design 8–9, 92, 153
Puerto Rican 22–3, 108; students 95–6, 101

Quartz, K.H. 197

Ranney, S. 9, 133
Reeves, J.R. 59
reflection 132–3, 137–8, 140, 161, 166–9, 171–2, 175, 179, 181–2, 184, 186, 201, 203–4, 206, 211
register 111–13; oral 106; written 108 see also systemic functional linguistics
responsive teaching 4, 7, 48, 54, 56–7, 59–65, 67–9, 73, 86, 178–80, 183, 190, 197, 216, 218
Rodriguez-Brown, F.V. 10, 47, 59, 143–4, 146, 149, 152, 208, 218–19
Ruiz-de-Velasco, J. 128

Sakash, K. 10, 59, 143–4, 148–50, 208, 218–19

scaffolding, instructional 8, 57, 63, 65–7, 78, 80, 83, 85–7, 101, 161, 167–9, 171, 173, 206
Schleppegrell, M. 5–7, 64–5, 94, 96, 108, 111–12, 114, 123, 195
school reform 108, 146, 155, 169
science education 30, 44, 77, 82, 93, 128, 130, 132–5, 139, 163, 182–3, 185–6, 205–6, 208–9, 217
second language learning 7, 45, 57, 59, 61–5, 73, 75–81, 83–8, 111–12, 124–5, 128, 131–2, 138, 143, 146, 156, 161, 164, 168–9, 181, 187, 190, 205
Seger, W. 107, 123
self-study 43, 179, 182, 190, 200
Shafer, J. 10, 59, 86, 128
Shannon, S.M. 152
sheltered instruction 8, 181, 186
Shin, D.S. 21, 107–8
Short, D. 8, 26–7, 65, 86, 129, 181
Shulman, L. 137, 165–6, 168–9, 198, 203
Snow, C.E. 6, 9, 57, 62–3, 75, 85, 111, 181, 196
social justice 87, 92, 196–7
sociocultural theory 56, 59, 65, 86, 92–3, 113, 160–4, 167–9, 173–4
sociolinguistic consciousness 56–7, 59
sociolinguistics 161, 164, 169
standardized tests 27, 39–40, 88, 195
standards 11–12, 37–8, 41–2, 44–6, 48, 74, 88, 92, 97, 107, 108, 111, 146, 149, 195
standards-based instruction 108
Stone, K. 9–11, 62–3, 138, 217–19
systemic functional linguistics 7, 91–3, 99, 102, 108, 115, 117, 120, 123–5; field, mode, tenor 113–15; pedagogy 93–5, 97, 101, 106–7, 114; register 105, 107, 111–13

teacher 128–9; expert 136, 140, 151, 157, 188, 191, 218; certification 9, 11, 35, 37, 41, 45, 47–8, 55, 73, 77, 145–6, 155, 157, 200; development 10, 44–6, 49, 62, 73, 76, 91–2, 108–9, 112, 115, 118, 123, 128–32, 135–7, 139–40, 153, 160–5, 166–7, 169–75, 178–9, 183–4, 190–1, 196–7, 209, 211, 216, 218–20; learning 92, 139, 208, 219–20; novice 134, 147, 203; performance 42, 164; preparation 3, 6, 9, 11–12, 30, 37–8, 40–5, 47, 49, 56, 68, 73–4, 76–7, 87–8, 130–2, 143–5,

149–50, 157, 178, 180, 195–6, 206, 216, 218–21; reflection 166–9, 171–2, 175, 179, 181–2, 184, 186, 201, 203–4, 206, 211; research 8, 40, 43, 68, 87, 91–2, 96–7, 107–9, 117, 120, 146, 149, 156, 162, 179, 191, 195–202, 207–8, 210, 219–20

teacher education 6, 28–9, 36, 41–5, 48–9, 55–6, 62, 67, 73, 77, 107, 130–1, 144, 146, 148–50, 178–80, 183, 189–90, 195–8, 200, 216–20; curriculum 46–7, 62, 68, 140, 221; expertise 4, 7–13, 37, 40, 47, 56, 74, 145, 147, 156–7, 160–8, 170, 175–6; in-service 91–2, 107, 128, 135–6, 138–40, 148–9, 156, 171–2, 221; knowledge base for 46, 75, 78–9, 84–5, 202; post baccalaureate 130, 198–200; preservice 10–12, 46–7, 49, 68, 73–4, 78–9, 84, 87, 127, 129–35, 143–5, 147, 155, 157, 166, 181, 188–91, 195, 199, 201, 208, 210–11, 218–20; state requirements 35, 39–41, 45–8, 49n1, 76–7, 131, 146, 150

Teacher Education Accreditation Council (TEAC) 41, 43–4

Tedick, D.J. 140

Téllez, K. 130, 196

test bias 28, 203

text analysis 62, 78, 84, 93, 97–8, 101–2, 107–8, 116–17, 121, 123, 201, 205

text organization 66, 94, 113–15, 117, 124, 134, 164

textbook mandates 27, 96–7, 101–2

Thompson, G. 113

Title III 39, 128–9, 136, 156

Title VII 39

transitioning 144–5, 152–3, 156, 180

Trumbull, B. 5, 64

tutoring 131–5, 139, 205

U.S. Census Bureau 21–3, 25–6, 32n1

Valdes, G. 3, 6, 9, 55, 57–8, 60–1, 65, 217

Vardell, S. 181

Verplaetse, L. 8, 61–2, 64–5, 67, 196

Villegas, A.M. 3, 6–7, 11, 48, 56, 59–61, 68, 74, 130, 149, 178, 187–8, 196–7, 210–11, 217, 220

Vygotsky, L. 4, 65, 93, 162–3, 173

Wagner, S. 144, 149, 151–2

Walker, A. 59

Walker, C.L. 9–11, 62–3, 86, 128, 133, 135, 138, 140, 217–19

Walqui, A. 6, 8, 10–11, 63–5, 144, 165, 167–8, 173, 217–19

Watkins, M. 94

Waxman, H.C. 130, 196

Whitmore, K.F. 144

Wiggins, G. 101

Willett, J. 5, 10, 61, 87, 92, 96, 109

Wilson, S.M. 197

Wiseman, D.L. 139

Wong-Fillmore, L. 6, 9, 62–3

writing instruction 8, 82, 85, 93–4, 99, 101–2, 104–8, 111–12, 114–21, 123–5, 150–1, 153, 183–4

Yamaguchi, R. 139

Yoon, K.S. 129

Young, T. 181

Zeichner, K. 3–4, 55, 130, 178, 195–8

Zimpher, N.L. 197, 211

zone of proximal development 65, 161–2